SAP® Business ONE Implementation

Set up and run an ERP for small-to-midsize companies
with the SAP Business ONE application

Wolfgang Niefert

BIRMINGHAM - MUMBAI

SAP® Business ONE Implementation

First published: May 2009

Production Reference: 1220509

Published by Packt Publishing Ltd.
32 Lincoln Road
Olton
Birmingham, B27 6PA, UK.

ISBN 978-1-847196-38-5

http:// www.packtpub.com

Cover Image by Wolfgang Niefert (wniefert@niefert.com)

Credits

Author
Wolfgang Niefert

Reviewer
Adrijan Tkalec
Søren Holm Poulsen
Dr. Pradeep Tapadiya

Acquisition Editor
David Barnes

Development Editor
Swapna Verlekar

Technical Editor
Dhiraj Bellani

Copy Editor
Sneha Kulkarni

Indexer
Rekha Nair

Editorial Team Leader
Abhijeet Deobhakta

Project Team Leader
Lata Basantani

Project Coordinator
Rajashree Hamine

Proofreader
Joel T. Johnson

Production Coordinator
Adline Swetha Jesuthas
Aparna Bhagat

Cover Work
Adline Swetha Jesuthas

About the author

Wolfgang Niefert studied Wirtschafts-Informatik at the European Business School in Oestrich-Winkel, Germany. The international management program focused on Business Management, Information Systems, and Economics. He has more than fifteen years of experience with international SAP implementations. With a certification for the SAP Production Planning PP module with the SAP academy in London, he is able to relate larger SAP solutions to SAP Business ONE. Wolfgang has worked in Germany, Switzerland, UK, USA, Poland, Russia, and Saudi Arabia.

A certification for the Aris Toolset by IDS Scheer in Switzerland completes his system-independent perspective on processes and modern business engineering. In Europe, his work with NIEFERT GmbH has lead to multiple project solutions, including quality control systems with SAP integration. These systems are live today with 24x7 worldwide operation. As part of high-availablity projects, he acquired certifications in Hewlett-Packard Cluster Design. Wolfgang provided training for cluster systems with Oracle Failsafe in Europe and the USA.

Wolfgang is the managing director of NIEFERT Certified Solutions (NCS, LLC) in San Diego, CA.

NCS LLC is an SAP Channel Partner and recognized SSP (Software Solutions Partner) for SAP.

He designed the N2ONE Portal solution which integrates with SAP Business ONE in real time. NCS LLC is also a Microsoft Certified Solution Partner and publishes the Momentum Reporter for Excel. This solution allows the visual design of database queries and retrieves query results directly in Excel.

As a true renaissance consultant with a broad knowledge and skillset in multiple fields, Wolfgang provides a 360-perspective on modern business solutions. Orchestrating project areas, and translating visions into realities, is his core competency. Keeping complex tasks simple and down-to-earth can be a challenge. However, Wolfgang's key philosophy is that only simplicity holds the power for growth. A solution that starts out simple has a chance to be simple in the end.

In his spare time, Wolfgang has established a recognized portfolio of Black and White Large Format landscape and portrait photography.

I want to personally thank my dad, Kurt Niefert, who provided guidance and business insight throughout my career. A special thanks goes to my wife, Rami, who manages time like no other. Her uplifting personality makes my every day. A great thanks to Skyler and Chiara for their amazing friendship and fresh outlook on life. Finally, a big kiss goes to my mother in Germany for her true love. The last thank you goes to my family and Nasser. You will not be forgotten.

About the reviewers

Adrijan Tkalec has more than ten years of experience in the software development industry. He maintains a network of international consultants who work on highly innovative software development projects. Namely, a dynamic document management solution and an industry-independant forms generator have gained international attention.

He personally manages complex data migration projects for SAP Business ONE and other related ERP solutions. The migration of data for financial systems requires the understanding of underlying business logic and financial valuation methods. Adrijan is an expert who seamlessly bridges the gap for financial consulting expertise and the technical data layer. Thereby, potentially complex projects appear simple when working with such an expert.

Adrijan is currently employed with the leading software company that provides services for **lease- and financing-related industries**. They are covering 75% of the lease market in Eastern Europe. He has been involved with management consulting and corporate finance consulting. This included the industry-specific process documentation for customers in the financial services business.

When time allows, Adrijan is an active photographer. His panoramic images capture local landscapes that exceed your vision.

Søren Holm Poulsen has a long and documented track record of a superb ability to understand process and convey highly technical information to customers and partners . Lately, this has been within the ERP market. The focus of his work has been to find the optimal solution to the present and future needs of the customer from a customer value perspective.

His educational background is a marketing degree from Aarhus Business School (Best in Denmark), and most recently as a certified SAP Business One Implementation consultant.

Throughout his career , Søren Holm Poulsen has had a strong international focus and speaks four languages.

His public resume can be found on http:// www.linkedin.com.

In the future, Søren Holm Poulsen would be interested in facilitating ERP companies (VAR's and ISV's) to expand and grow their business in a leadership role as an employee, consultant, or partner.

Finally, Søren Holm Poulsen greatly appreciates the opportunity to work with Wolfgang Niefert on this interesting project.

Dr. Pradeep Tapadiya has twenty years of experience developing commercial software applications. He was the chief architect of HP OpenVIew ManageX, an award-winning software application. Dr. Tapadiya has authored two books: NET Programming and COM+ Programming. He is also a contributing editor for technical articles. In 2009, he was selected as "Pros to Know" by Supply Chain Magazine. Dr. Tapadiya holds a doctoral degree in Computer Science from Texas A&M.

Table of Contents

Preface

Simplicity is a key success factor in today's complex business world. The new SAP Solution, called **SAP Business ONE**, promises a simple, yet powerful feature set for fast-growing companies. In this book, you will find the answers to help you separate the marketing promise from the real-world features.

What this book covers

Section 1 – SAP Express Implementation

The first section is focused on quickly getting SAP Business ONE up and running. You will learn about the essential configuration steps that you need to undergo. We will leave nothing behind and you will see all the steps. Upon completion, you will be equipped with the required skills and tools to tackle the SAP system without fear. Section 1 - SAP Express Implementation comprises three chapters:

1. Getting Ready to Implement SAP Business ONE – In this chapter, you will learn how SAP can help you improve your business. This chapter also covers the most common terminology related to SAP and the Business ONE solution.

2. SAP Business ONE Express Implementation Walk-through – This is hands-on to the max. You will start configuring a new SAP system.

3. Reporting and Analysis: Getting Ready for Growth – With a running SAP system, we can now retrieve information. You will see that the system is used as an **information collection skeleton.**

Using a step-by-step implementation approach, we will configure a simple system, and then expand the configuration to match state-of-the-art business methodologies.

The **Lemonade Stand** case study showcases the key value an integrated system like SAP Business ONE can provide, even at a very simple business level. We will collect data as the **Lemonade Stand** operates, and view dashboard reports to better understand the business. Even experienced users may find the tips and tricks in this section beneficial.

Section 2 – Implementing SAP Business ONE in your own Company

The second part of the book will take a different approach and show you what an implementation looks like if you first undergo a thorough analysis to identify potential improvements in the way you run your business. The second section naturally is a bit longer. I have adopted the concept to introduce a specific functionality organized in sections. For example, I will talk about sales, inventory, and service in separate chapters. Each chapter will also include a proven add-on that enhances the standard functionality. This way, you will see that SAP Business ONE is a **business engine**. This engine can be used by industry experts to plug in their industry-specific know-how seamlessly.

Learning by example is a good way to understand new concepts and technologies. Therefore, we will be implementing a complete SAP Business system, including add-ons, as part of the case study. The case study starts out in section one with an ad hoc implementation of a Lemonade Stand. In the second section, we will professionally expand this idea and develop a beverage distribution center with outsourced production. This will include advanced inventory optimization. The workflow will be optimized using existing functionality, and proven add-ons that significantly improve the standard features.

Finally, we will connect SAP to the Web and introduce the N2ONE Portal solution. This solution presents SAP features in a web interface with real-time integration. The book will be completed with the chapter focusing on growth. I will introduce a franchise architecture for SAP Business ONE. This architecture will be applied to the case study to help you learn how to get started with this concept. Each chapter has a section that assists you with applying knowledge for your own project. Ideally, you will be in business with the completion of this book.

What you need for this book

- A piece of paper and a pencil

- A business idea and vision to confront the difficult while it is still easy

- A lack of patience for islands of data

- SAP Business ONE installation or trial system – You can request a demo at `http:// www.expanding-your-view.com`

- A trial for add-ons is available at `http:// www.expanding-your-view.com` upon request

Who this book is for

This book is written for technically savvy business owners, entrepreneurs, and departmental managers. Making decisions with the **right** information is a competitive success factor. SAP Business ONE can be seen as the **business engine** that helps drive your business towards success. In today's economic climate, the implementation of guerrilla-style business units, based on SAP Business ONE, is crucial. The information in this book can be used for new implementations and also existing systems that need improvement. If you have SQL skills, you can leverage your knowledge and connect to SAP tools and features that are built on queries. If you are a departmental sales manager, you can benefit from the advanced sales stages and workflow concept in this book. The seasoned inventory and warehouse manager can immediately utilize the inventory optimization and warehouse management concepts. Your web technicians will benefit from the e-commerce information and will see how your web strategy can be aligned with SAP Business ONE. As a business owner, your key players from sales to fulfillment can gain back control and you can grow your business to the next level using modern franchising concepts.

Conventions

In this book, you will find a number of styles of text that distinguish between different kinds of information. Here are some examples of these styles, and an explanation of their meaning.

New terms and **important words** are shown in bold. Words that you see on the screen, in menus or dialog boxes for example, appear in our text like this: "clicking the **Next** button moves you to the next screen".

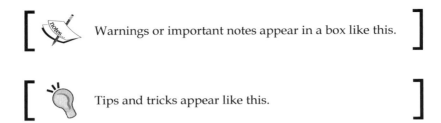

Warnings or important notes appear in a box like this.

Tips and tricks appear like this.

Reader feedback

Feedback from our readers is always welcome. Let us know what you think about this book—what you liked or may have disliked. Reader feedback is important for us to develop titles that you really get the most out of.

To send us general feedback, simply drop an email to feedback@packtpub.com, and mention the book title in the subject of your message.

If there is a book that you need and would like to see us publish, please send us a note in the **SUGGEST A TITLE** form on http://www.packtpub.com or email suggest@packtpub.com.

If there is a topic that you have expertise in and you are interested in either writing or contributing to a book, see our author guide on http://www.packtpub.com/authors.

Customer support

Now that you are the proud owner of a Packt book, we have a number of things to help you to get the most from your purchase.

Downloading the example code for the book

Visit http://www.packtpub.com/files/code/6385_Code.zip to directly download the example code.

Errata

Although we have taken every care to ensure the accuracy of our contents, mistakes do happen. If you find a mistake in one of our books—maybe a mistake in text or code—we would be grateful if you would report this to us. By doing so, you can save other readers from frustration, and help us to improve subsequent versions of this book. If you find any errata, please report them by visiting http://www.packtpub.com/support, selecting your book, clicking on the **let us know** link, and entering the details of your errata. Once your errata are verified, your submission will be accepted and the errata added to any list of existing errata. Any existing errata can be viewed by selecting your title from http://www.packtpub.com/support.

Piracy

Piracy of copyright material on the Internet is an ongoing problem across all media. At Packt, we take the protection of our copyright and licenses very seriously. If you come across any illegal copies of our works in any form on the Internet, please provide us with the location address or website name immediately so that we can pursue a remedy.

Please contact us at copyright@packtpub.com with a link to the suspected pirated material.

We appreciate your help in protecting our authors, and our ability to bring you valuable content.

Questions

You can contact us at questions@packtpub.com if you are having a problem with any aspect of the book, and we will do our best to address it.

1

Getting Ready to Implement SAP Business ONE

"That stinks!" I said after I picked up the dirty sock. "No," was the reply "it is the smell of victory." You see, it depends on how you look at things. What appeared to be a dirty sock was indeed a valuable sports artifact worth a lot of money.

"What does this have to do with the SAP Business ONE application?", you may ask. Well, SAP Business ONE helps you separate the unnecessary clutter from the success drivers of your business. The solution does this with real-time data for all departments. In case you thought that the sock example is a bit far-fetched, I would like to counter this and explain that there is a theory in quantum physics called the Observer Effect. It essentially states that an act of observation changes the phenomenon being observed. In our example, only a closer observation revealed the object's true value. The same thing goes for a business. It is only with the right data that you can observe and make decisions that leads your business in a successful direction. I will provide a list of examples where additional information can change your view on things and impact your decisions. I am not talking about the big picture here, but rather a detailed level where you can easily lose sight, though you shouldn't.

Have you noticed that there are managers who can pretty much run any kind of business and make it a success? How do they do it? Is there a specific way that we can follow to run our business? You may say that it takes a **great idea**. That's true. However, what about **timing** and operating the business? One thing is for certain, it is not enough to only have a great idea. You must also be able to develop it from the start to the end.

What do successful business owners have in common? Do they all use SAP Business ONE? No, but they are able to establish metrics and measure performance, which allows them to make the right decisions. This is where SAP Business ONE comes into play. It is designed to help you collect the right information and run reports in real-time. **In this book, I will introduce SAP Business ONE and show you how observing your business data in real time can lead to a multitude of subtle changes that will make the difference between failure and success.**

At this point, all you need is a business idea, this book, and SAP Business ONE. This book is for any technically savvy entrepreneur with a vision to make his or her business a success. These entrepreneurs understand that technology can be used as an enablement platform for a business venture. In order to make this venture a success, the technology used must be challenged every day.

Setting the stage for the book—how does your business "tick"

This chapter introduces the core idea of looking at SAP Business ONE as a **business engine**. This business engine is designed to help you collect information about your business, where having the information versus not having the information can make the difference between success and failure. Let's say that a multitude of decisions are made on a daily basis, which can benefit from better information. Look at your own business, for example. I am certain that you have a system that manages your finances and is potentially a lead management solution. Maybe you also have some production that is industry-specific and handled by an industry solution. In this simple example, there are already many potential areas for improvement.

To make the point, I will ask you some questions about your business. You may call this the **Observer Effect in Business**. The questions range from sales to inventory and service. Basically, I am focusing on the entire **value chain**. This is a key idea in an integrated software package such as SAP. The added value of having an integrated process versus disparate systems that require synchronization.

Sales leads and follow-up

Do you have a sales process, and is it organized in stages?

Can you run a report and get information about the stages, and thereby forecast the expected sales?

What happens if one of your best sales people leaves? Can you continue the sales and manage the customers?

Are you using Act!, **salesforce.com**, Microsoft CRM, and need to synchronize with your finance back-end?

Delivery

Can you provide tracking information for customers?

Do customers need to call you to get tracking information, or do they get an updated email once the order leaves your warehouse?

Will you get a notification about a successful delivery that can be opened from the sales order?

Inventory

Do you have excess inventory?

Do you also run into situations where there is not enough inventory for an important order?

Do you manage inventory shortages by **overstocking**?

Are you using an Excel spreadsheet to manage your inventory reorder times and quantities?

Warehouse

Do you have a method to verify the deliveries before they leave and enter the warehouse?

Do you know the cost of any mistakes?

Service and support

Can you relate a large sales opportunity to incoming service calls? For example, can you manage a service call for a customer with large proposals on the table differently than for a customer who has not ordered in a long time and is behind in payments?

Can customers check the tracking numbers via a web portal?

Can customers review past orders and re-order easily?

Is it possible to place service calls via the Web?

Are sales people aware of the current sales calls for large opportunities?

Manufacturing

Can you easily replace a component in a BOM (**Bill of Material**) with a new one?

Can you trace any item from the sales to the initial purchase of parts, assembly, and delivery?

E-commerce

Does your e-commerce provider charge an extra fee for taking credit card orders?

Do you have to synchronize your web orders with your accounting system?

Can you track customer activities on the Web?

Can you send customized newsletters to customers based on their buying behavior?

Do you receive an alert once a new web order is placed?

Do you have newsletter tracking information for customers that you can evaluate during the sales process?

Can you contact customers based on their newsletter reading activity and past purchase history?

Is your web intelligence integrated with your customer management system? For example, it would be good if a customer calls and you could see his or her open quotes, open service calls, newsletter activity, and order history.

How long does it take you to start a web site with e-commerce? Just think about it for a second. This should be an automated process. You should be able to have dozens of sites up and running, send out newsletters, track feedback, and measure success. In a later chapter, I will introduce you to the concept that is based on the SAP Business ONE Engine.

Industry

Are you using form fields in your system for different purposes because it does not provide the right naming based on your industry?

Are you using an industry solution for one part of your business and have a standard finance package that does not quite integrate?

ROI and budget for your own system

All of the above questions address common business issues, which result in additional time and money spent. Essentially, by automating the processes and providing the right information where it is needed, you can save money and make better decisions. Therefore, for your own business, you can ask yourself the questions above and assign a monetary value to each one. The monetary value is either a plain number, or a calculation based on the time you spent to get the information. For example, if you indeed manage your inventory re-order quantities in an Excel spreadsheet, imagine this could be done automatically without your manual intervention. Once you add up all the numbers, you have your budget for a potential new system that overcomes these issues.

What this chapter will cover

During the course of this chapter, I will cover the following areas and lay the groundwork for the hands-on chapters that are to follow. However, what would all the hands-on exercises be worth if you can't apply them to your own business? That's why I have taken a dual approach to cover this. I will introduce a toolbox that will help you identify the main areas of your business, which may benefit from an integrated system. Then, a case study is used to explain the new features with an example.

- Toolbox for your business – Wouldn't it be nice if you had a toolbox that could help you improve your business? I will introduce you to a simple concept that will help you create your own toolbox. It's simple, and it works.

- The case study – What's the simplest entrepreneur-style business out there? It's the **Lemonade Stand**. Even kids can run it. What if we take it to the next level? In this section, I will explain what your business has in common with the **Lemonade Stand**.

- Start with a piece of paper – We will never lose touch with the real world. That's why you will be included in all the chapters as we move along. In this section, you will use the toolset to identify issues with your own business.

- SAP Business ONE, a business engine – Now you know the issues of your own business and you have a toolset. At this point, SAP Business ONE is introduced as a **business engine**. What does this mean? Read on and you will see why SAP Business ONE is different.

- Introducing key terms – Before we continue, some commonly used terms will be introduced. For example, **real-time** and **profitable growth** will be explained

- SAP Business ONE 100-word definition - This will summarize the SAP product message with the official SAP definition for their product.
- Why projects fail – Did you know that in soccer you need to practice with your left foot if you want to improve your right foot? Let's find out why projects fail and hope we will learn something about doing them the right way.

Toolbox for your business

Maybe you have a toolbox in your garage which is filled with many different tools. You never use most of them. However, once you need a tool, you are likely to find the right one in there. In order to establish a toolbox for your business, we first need to identify the required tasks that need to be completed. Based on the tasks at hand, the tools will be designed. Basically, we will follow this sequence:

1. Identify the problem areas – Asking the right questions
2. Solutions for problem areas – Paper and pencil
3. Proven examples – Case study
4. Fix It – Project plan and tips

Based on the previously mentioned **observer effect**, I would like to call this concept the **Business Observer Toolbox for Operational Xcellence** — in short, **BOTOX**. Many successful businesses are already using it. However, nobody will admit to it.

Identify the problem areas—asking the right questions

Before we can fix a problem, we first need to identify it. It sounds obvious. However, it's easier said than done if it's your own business. You may be tangled up in a series of competing interests that need to be balanced. Or, maybe you are just blind. Asking the right questions is the key element to bring problem areas to light. Therefore, the first element in our BOTOX system is a set of questions. Please review the questions I asked in the beginning of the chapter. They are focused on identifying a potential **disconnect**. As you go through the questions, make a note every time you have to access more than one system. Be aware of the repetitive steps and synchronizations that you need. You need to be demanding! Demand a solution that can do it all in a simple workflow.

Solutions for problem areas—paper and pencil

Based on the questions asked, you may find surprising answers that will reveal the problem areas. How do you think these problems can be solved? As a business owner, you are the **expert**. Write down your ideas. The second element in our toolbox is a piece of paper and a pencil. Your goal should be a simple, integrated solution. That's why you should document all the different systems you are using. Make a circle for each system and create an arrow connecting it to the next system. For example, create a circle for your web site, CRM, finance system, email, newsletters, and so on. I will help you a bit more later in this chapter.

Proven examples—case study

Using the example provided in this book, you can select proven techniques and workflows that will help you achieve end-to-end processes. End-to-end essentially means that all the information is integrated and transparent. The case study serves as a platform to present how you use the tools and techniques introduced in each chapter. Therefore, an important aspect of our toolbox is a structured set of examples. Alongside the case study, I will also provide some tips and tricks which you can use for your own project.

Fix It—project plan and tips

The final elements in our toolbox will help you translate the concepts and ideas into action. Namely, a template-style project plan is used as a step-by-step instrument to move forward with the implementation. As the implementation is organized into **sections** that represent common departments, the project plan is also structured into sections. Therefore, you can take the parts you need for your own project.

The case study—why your company is like the "Lemonade Stand"

The purpose of the case study is to provide an easy-to-understand example for the new techniques that are presented in each chapter. In order to challenge the **simple** aspect of SAP Business ONE, which is advertised as **simple yet powerful**, I choose what is commonly known as **The Lemonade Stand** as our case study. During the course of the case study implementation, this simple example reveals surprising challenges that are similar to those that most small- and mid-sized businesses are facing on a daily basis. Basically, your business may have surprising parallels with **The Lemonade Stand**.

Here are the main characteristics of the Lemonade Stand that may also be a driving factor for your business:

- Ad-hoc operation – The Lemonade Stand is characterized by its ad-hoc concept, where the key players gather some money and invest in the basic ingredients to sell the product for immediate profit.

- Local coverage – The ad-hoc concept is further enhanced with the local coverage, where a good location for sales is selected based on local expertise.

- Growth is virtually impossible – The concept does not allow for growth. The Lemonade Stand makes a profit, but has no growth plan. Basically, it incorporates the challenge to run it professionally, because it seems advantageous to run it on a **let's-get-things-done** basis, while any professional approach appears to be nothing more than a burden.

- Short-term focus – The concept is based on a short-term focus only. There is no long-term growth plan.

If you think about it, many of the above factors can be found with small- and mid-sized businesses. After all, you need to make money and cannot focus on long-term strategies.

It is interesting to note that in today's economy, short-term profitability and seasonal flexibility are important success factors. However, short-term profits need to be made not only today, but also in a year, and maybe in five years.

Therefore, we will use the case study to overcome these issues. We will essentially implement the SAP Business ONE system for the Lemonade Stand and wrap the entire thing into a long-term strategy.

Start with a piece of paper

At this point, I would like to engage you a bit. As you know, the case study serves as an example for the information that is presented in each chapter. Therefore, we can take the characteristics of the Lemonade Stand listed above and see if you can find them in your business. Take a piece of paper and a pencil to write down the different departments you have in your business. For example, write down **Sales** and make a circle around it. Start with **Sales** on the top left of your paper and arrive at **Purchasing** at the bottom left. You can use arrows to connect the circles. For example, from Sales to Inventory, Delivery and Purchasing. On the right side of the paper, write down the main functions that each circle performs. For example, next to Sales write down what needs to get done in your business as a part of the sales process. You may have a list such as the following: sales stages, forecast, pipeline, inventory check, proposal, order entry, and so on.

The idea is to establish a circular flow-type representation of your business where one department provides information to the next department.

Now that you have the main components of your business written down, you can identify where the actual data is stored. For example, is all of the data in one system with access for the department that needs the data? You potentially have multiple systems that need to interact and synchronize data. Those will be the aspects that we will target as they hold the greatest potential for improvement.

SAP Business ONE—a business engine

At this point, you may argue that there was sufficient reason to establish specialized systems for a dedicated purpose. Indeed, this approach is called the **best-of-breed** implementation. However, it is the very reason for the **disconnected** enterprise. In this book, SAP Business ONE will be used to overcome this challenge by means of industry-specific add-ons that are fully integrated with the software. Essentially, SAP Business ONE is a business engine which provides the most common business management and financial features. This engine can be transformed to seamlessly represent industry-specific requirements.

Introducing key terms and concepts

In this section, I will introduce the key terms and concepts related to the SAP world. The following areas will be covered in the process:

- Real time and islands of data
- Positioning SAP Business ONE against other SAP products
- Profitable growth
- Establishing metrics
- Prototyping
- The virtual enterprise
- SAP 100-word definition

Real-time information instead of islands of data

The SAP Business ONE system provides better information in real time. Therefore, it helps to minimize the risk involved with the daily decisions the entrepreneur or business owner has to make.

Many business owners have taken a **don't-fix-it-if-it-is-not-broken** approach and stay put with their solutions that are already in place. The solutions are most often a combination of a small accounting package and some home-grown software to fix a business need. As their business evolves, new solutions are added, which will lead to a **patch-worked** solution. In order to make the right decisions, usually Excel reports are created to analyze data for reporting. You may also consider license requirements, different platforms, and programming languages that ultimately lead to a scattered environment with a high cost.

In this environment, manual steps are often required to synchronize data. Extra effort is needed to prepare the reports and they are never 100% accurate. **This is not exactly a 360-degree view of a business. However, a complete view of the key performance indicators of a business is precisely what is required to make the best decisions.**

The **patchwork** approach of managing a small business facilitates the status quo environment. However, in today's business world, change is a permanent factor. The scenario mentioned above most commonly leads to **islands of data** and inadvertently tends to **paralyze** the business as key information is not obtained. This happens because the existing system produces not enough or too much information in multiple locations.

The aforementioned scenario, which is described as islands of data, also surfaces in the best-of-breed approach. The best-of-breed, also known as the best-in-class approach, is a valid strategy for larger companies where software solutions are selected on a departmental level in order to meet the needs of every individual in a department.

The departmental level that contributes to the value chain of a business is described as an enterprise resource. Traditionally, enterprise resources were highly specialized and disparate systems. Companies were faced with systems that could not easily communicate. It was virtually impossible to obtain real-time reports because the information was hard to integrate and analyze. On the one hand, the systems produced a massive amount of information, and on the other hand, the information could not be used as it was impossible to integrate the data with the other information sources.

SAP is founded with the vision to overcome the disparate islands of data, and therefore, enable the analysis of the **right** information. This vision has lead to the early development of the SAP R/2 and R/3 systems. The R/2 System was mainframe-based. With the continuing trend towards client-server architecture, the R/3 Solution was developed by SAP. The R/3 System established the term **ERP (Enterprise Resource Planning)**. With this approach, real-time reporting became a reality and enabled the companies which were formerly **paralyzed** with their status quo system to grow their businesses.

Positioning SAP Business ONE against mySAP—All-In-One and Business ByDesign

The foundation of this concept is that though each department has unique requirements which need to be met. There are also similarities that are industry independent. The R/3 system provided workflows and business processes for the most common industries.

During implementation, the relevant processes are selected, activated, and then adjusted for the business. Today, those available processes can be selected via interactive solution maps.

At present, the R/3 System is called mySAP ERP. A new, enhanced functionality is added by SAP to the mySAP solution. Traditionally, the R/3 System required massive consulting power to implement. In order to meet the requirements of companies with an industry focus, SAP established the SAP All-In-One Solution. This is a template-based version of the standard SAP R/3 System. The all-in-one templates are usually represented by SAP Partners who have a key expertise in a specific industry.

SAP Business ONE takes those concepts and applies them in a compact package. Therefore, **if your company is using multiple systems and struggles with Excel reports and manual data synchronization, then SAP Business ONE is the ideal solution to integrate all those disparate** *islands of data* **into one system with** *real-time* **data.**

Consequently, what was once available only for large enterprises is now at the fingertips of small- and mid-sized businesses.

However, it is important to note that the SAP Business ONE System, unlike the SAP All-In-One Solution, is not based on the R/3 system. The SAP Business ONE Solution is a new development that does not use any code base from R/3. Previously, SAP was mostly able to service large corporations. In order to move to a smaller business, the template version of R/3, called All-In-One, was established. However, since All-In-One is actually using the same code base, it requires significant resources to implement and manage.

The SAP Business ONE Solution is positioned at the other end of the scale for small- to mid-sized businesses. This leaves a gap, which is filled by SAP, with another solution called **Business ByDesign**. Business ByDesign is a solution that can be accessed via a browser and is used as a service.

Therefore, the SAP Solution scale starts with SAP Business ONE to SAP ByDesign, continues to SAP All-In-ONE, and ends with SAP mySAP. However, there are overlapping areas and the selection of the right package must be based on individual requirements.

Real-world note

I recently talked to a family owned furniture business and they explained that they **tried** to grow their business. The business owners intended to manufacture a custom furniture set and distribute it via wholesalers. However, they ran into some problems and were not able to cope up with the results. They learned their lesson and now are happy to be back where they were before. Consequently, they established the notion that they do not want to grow anymore as it imposes a big risk on their business and family.

The frustrated owner explained that they had the following key problems:

In order to meet the projected demand, they kept a large inventory of their products. They also hired an additional sales person to manage the new sales activity. The previously working systems suddenly slowed down and caused major hiccups during operation. They were not able to provide an accurate delivery status for customers. Their inventory was too high on the one hand, and too low for urgent deliveries for important wholesale customers. Then, the sales person left and all their contacts and communication was lost too.

An important law of nature is that you either **grow or die**, and this furniture business certainly tried to grow. However, they almost ruined their business over it. Their system was designed for status quo and could not handle growth. Their entire operation ended in chaos due to the addition of a bit of change.

This example showcases the importance of an integrated approach with a system that is ready to grow from the outset. **The only foundation for growth is to keep it simple and leave room for expansion.**

Business hell versus profitable growth

Ultimately, a business owner who seeks to grow his or her business may realize that the current system which appeared to be working was actually not working. Without the right information, growing a business is like trying to grow for the hell of it. Mostly, people get what they ask for. Therefore, if you grow your business for the hell of it, you may end up getting **business hell**. The key is to accomplish **profitable growth**.

If you believe your business is any different, then consider the following list of islands of data:

- QuickBooks accounting system
- ACT! CRM system
- Excel reports
- Access inventory database
- Web presentation with newsletter subscription
- Web e-commerce store with online orders
- Outlook emails
- Office documents on the server

Please evaluate the following screenshot that shows a fairly standard situation with too many **Islands of Data**:

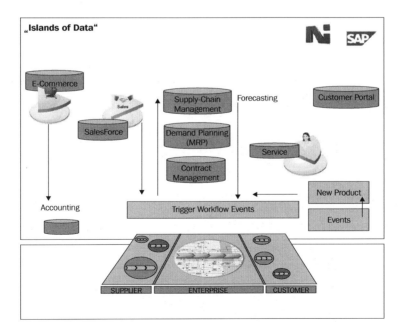

Now, please review the most obvious communication channels and workflow situations:

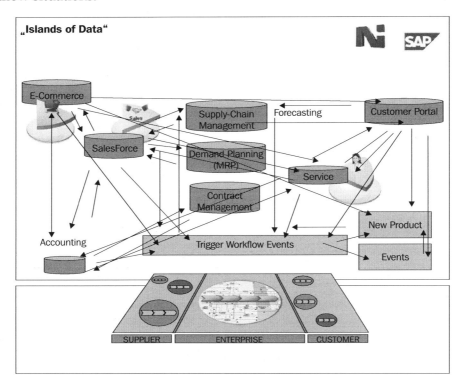

It is obvious that there is no room to grow.

SAP Business ONE is a single package that can cover all of the **Islands of Data** above and integrate them into one data source for real-time reporting. In the chapters to come, we will showcase how SAP Business ONE is simple. In addition, as outlined above, complexity may surface even in a simple environment if the dots are not connected in the right way.

Consequently, the key is not to grow your business because it may grow into a business hell. It is rather a **profitable growth**. What is **profitable growth** and how can we get there?

What is profitable growth

Analyzing past and present data based on a real-time integrated system, such as SAP Business ONE, provides the starting point for profitable growth. SAP Business ONE provides elaborate reporting and analysis functionality to satisfy the changing information needs of the business.

It sounds very straightforward. However, it is the key problem in today's business solutions. In order to get the right reports, the system must be designed to automatically gather the relevant data that will be used for reports.

When designing an integrated system, it is crucial to plan ahead. The most critical step to get started is knowing the design of the Chart of Accounts. It provides the foundation for all of the transactions that will be managed later in the system. Each transaction generates financial data, which flows into the previously designed chart of accounts.

The **CoA** (Chart of Accounts) design is often overlooked. However, it may also lead to **overdesign** once attention is given to its design. It is considered a good practice to follow a simple design. In addition, it is worth noting that the CoA is strictly meant for financial data compliance. Therefore, the data collected here is the basis for tax filing. However, an integrated ERP system should also provide an information system for internal controlling.

Consequently, we utilize the CoA that follows a simple design and also implements a controlling system that will collect data for reporting. It is the controlling system that will provide information for all departments on a daily basis.

ERP systems are only as good as the data entered into them. Therefore, the initial design and setup to create the framework that will hold the data is important. The collected data will be in all the right places for further analysis and decision making. SAP Business ONE will provide all of the reporting data in real time.

What is real time

The term *real time* is used in different areas of Information Technology. In production environments, real time describes a guaranteed response time within a given time frame. In the ERP world, real time means that there is no synchronization or separate programming required to obtain all of the information. Every report in the system has access to all the information immediately.

Establish metrics—the cost of no investment

Once the information skeleton with the CoA and controlling is implemented, the business is ready for growth. At this point, it will be possible to continuously collect data and make all the right adjustments.

It will be the end of **growing for the hell of it**, and the starting point of **profitable growth**. It is important to quantify each potential problem area, and therefore, document the monetary improvement as that is the ultimate goal to streamline the business operation in the most efficient way.

The following are some example questions that can be answered with the collected information:

- How much inventory waste do we have?
- How many returns do we have? What is the cost of each return?
- How is picking managed? Is the picking route automated?
- What happens if my key sales person leaves? Do we have all the contacts' information and notes?
- Do we have a sales methodology? Do we have a sales pipeline?
- Can we plan for material requirements based on received orders?
- Do we consider common lead times for ordering important parts, or do we just keep excess stock?
- How many service calls do we get from customers?
- Who are the most profitable customers?
- Does our e-commerce store integrate with our inventory?
- Do we have an automated self-service portal to take care of common customer questions?

The list above is also a reference to sample questions for businesses that are **too busy** for an integrated system. It clearly shows the potential **cost of no investment**. It may be worthwhile to calculate the **cost of no decision** in case you are on the verge of deciding on a new system. The purpose of a new SAP system is to save costs, which will enable a profitable growth.

By assigning a monetary value to each non-efficient process, the business owner will be able to justify the relevant improvements.

With the right reporting data, this **change management** is a part of the system operation. **What is called** *total quality management* **in larger companies is a consequential side effect of an integrated system.**

Designing "metrics" for your own business

The following items summarize the process you can use to design metrics for your own business:

- Design Financial Skeleton – This is the CoA design which will hold all of the financial information based on the transactions performed in the system.
- Design Controlling Data Skeleton – This is the **Data Collection Framework** you establish on the actual SAP forms. It is used to collect the information you need for making informed decisions for your business.

Therefore, before we apply this knowledge to our case study in the next chapters, you may want to review your own system and see if you have a CoA and a separate Controlling system that allows collecting data as the system is used.

What is prototyping

Prototyping is the iterative process of designing a system based on user feedback. In software development, there are similar flavors for this to address the specific user type. These flavors are called **rapid prototyping** and **extreme programming**. Extreme programming uses an iterative design approach to gradually add one feature at a time to the initial prototype, and attempts to minimize **irreducible complexity**.

In the SAP Business ONE project environment, a combined approach has proved to be successful. It has proved important to get users up and running as soon as possible. Therefore, the SAP Implementation guide covers the essential steps to get the system up and running quickly. Users go through this wizard-style interview process and provide the configuration parameters. The system is then ready to be adjusted in the **prototyping mode. Therefore, a project starts with a quintessential analysis based on a questionnaire and is followed by a Prototyping phase.**

This goes in line with other IT-related project management methodologies. For example, in software development projects, the so-called **waterfall** model historically gathered a complete set of requirements for a software project. Once complete, the software development process would start. This led to the same problem as described above for the SAP projects. In order to follow this analogy, we may consider the latest software development principles as a guide to where the SAP project management may go.

Extreme programming is a practice to create immediate results for the end user and add features as the user actually works with the quickly assembled solution.

The virtual enterprise

Another dominant trend is described as **virtualization** and **service orientation**. The enterprise of the future is a **virtual enterprise**. How does SAP address this trend? The virtual enterprise is characterized by disparate entities that work independently, but exchange information to produce integrated services and products. SAP has developed the Enterprise Service Architecture (**ESA**). This architecture provides a platform for independent systems to produce and consume services on a single integration platform.

Therefore, the future system will allow large-scale SAP systems to be integrated with services produced by other vendors. In turn, this will extend the integrated business workflows further into specialized solutions that address industry-specific requirements.

Interestingly, the foundation of the ERP system was to overcome disparate, specialized solutions and integrate them into a single system. Today, again the market requirements force businesses to consider specialized solutions for a specific need. However, with the knowledge acquired in previous iterations of this process, the platform for integration is already established as the ESA.

In order to adapt this to the small business owner, we are using the **template** concept for SAP Business ONE in this book. This way, the entrepreneur will have the toolset to cope with changing market needs and set the foundation for growth.

SAP 100-word definition of SAP Business ONE

100-word business positioning statement:

Designed exclusively for small businesses, SAP Business One is a single, affordable business management solution that integrates the entire business across financials, sales, customers, and operations. Combining with additional industry-specific capabilities, SAP Business One can adapt to your unique and fast-changing business needs. With SAP Business One, small businesses can streamline operations, act on instant and complete information, and accelerate profitable growth.

SAP® Business One is delivered by experienced local resellers and is trusted by thousands of small businesses around the world.

Why projects fail?

Now, a final word about why projects fail which may help to understand the possible factors that may lead to a failing project. With this knowledge, potential issues can be addressed in the early phases of an implementation project.

The key problem with ERP implementation projects is to manage the right expectations. Since the SAP Business ONE system has a complete feature set for all of the departments in a company, it is easy to underestimate the required service for an implementation. Therefore, a proper project plan should include a set of specifically defined services and the configuration. However, a proper project specification should also define what is specifically not included.

It is vital that the ROI for a planned project has a monetary value associated with each section of the implementation. It is also vital that each section of the project implementation is measured against a timeline, available resources, and a budget.

This leads to the ultimate problem area in each project—the budget. For obvious reasons, the budget must be right. Therefore, the implementation partner and the customer must complete their due diligence to make sure that a project is not underestimated. **The infamous** *fixed priced proposal* **with rather undefined specifications is almost guaranteed to lead to problems down the road.**

Finally, a key success factor for a successful project is to have the support of C level and all the departments that are involved or affected by the implementation.

Summary

In this chapter, I introduced you to a toolbox designed to help you identify the common issues related to business management. Once the issues are identified, you can select the tools to resolve them. The toolbox provides you with the right tools to address common SAP Implementation challenges.

You learned why the simple **Lemonade Stand** case study is of great relevance for your business. Finally, the introduction of the most common terms found in the SAP project world has prepared you for your own project and enabled you to talk the SAP language.

2

SAP Business ONE Express Implementation Walk-through

In this chapter, we will perform an **express implementation** of the SAP Business ONE application. The main purpose of this task is to help you understand the potential scope of such a project. For example, let's compare some plain facts between SAP mySAP ERP and SAP Business ONE. If you receive the installation package for SAP mySAP ERP, you will get at least one large box full of DVDs and installation instructions. With SAP Business ONE, you will get one CD and all the software with the most basic add-ons is included. Later, you may get an additional Crystal Reports™ CD. However, it is no match to SAP mySAP ERP when it comes to the number of installation CDs. Customers often mention hearing that SAP is only for large companies. But when it comes to the number of CDs and DVDs included in the installation packages, SAP Business ONE really is for small companies. Therefore, in this chapter, we will evaluate what's in the package.

The **express configuration** will walk through all of the installation steps required to get the system up and running for the **Lemonade Stand Inc**. case study.

Though the installation is simple, it can always be more efficient, right? I will take this opportunity to predict the futuristic way for implementing ERP systems such as SAP Business ONE. You may apply the knowledge about the essential configuration steps for your own project in order to scale the resources properly. In addition, you may plan ahead and get ready for the **future way**.

There are many ways to get the system up and running. We will perform an **ad hoc** implementation that requires no analysis or preparation. It's time now to get going!

Configuring a new SAP Business ONE company Lemonade Stand Inc.

In this section, you will see the technical requirements for the basic SAP Business ONE installation. In addition, you will briefly see the available options if you want to configure a system quickly.

Prerequisites for the case study

The prerequisites are pretty straightforward without any unusual surprises, as long as you have a common Windows system. Certainly, you need to check the current requirements to comply with the requirements related to specific Windows and SQL Server versions.

For the case study in this book, you will use a Windows Server 2003 Standard Edition operating system with a Microsoft SQL Server 2005 Standard Edition. Here is the complete list of requirements:

- Microsoft Windows Server 2003 Standard Edition
- Microsoft SQL Server 2005 Standard Edition
- Microsoft IIS configuration as part of Windows 2003 Standard Edition
- Microsoft Office 2003 to show SAP XL Reporter Integration
- SAP Business ONE installation CD with server and client components
- SAP Business Objects Crystal Reports CD for SAP Business ONE

Options to configure a system quickly

There are different approaches when it comes to implementing a system. You can install the system and configure the software based only on the essential steps that you will see here. You may also opt to use the implementation of the new system to introduce changes to the way you operate your company. In this case, you may first perform a thorough analysis before you translate those settings into the actual SAP Business ONE configuration parameters. The latter approach will help you streamline your operations and improve the way you collect data for reporting.

The options you have are as follows:

- Configure the system ad hoc
- Use a template database
- Perform a thorough analysis

The ad hoc prototyping method

This approach can be used if your company has very basic requirements and your processes match the available features. When combined with prototyping, this approach can actually result in efficient solutions because you configure the system as you walk through the processes. This usually means the actual forms are opened in SAP Business ONE and data is entered. This is done while the Admin Section is open in another window to allow the settings that drive the front-end forms. For example, we will see how the **sales opportunities** work in SAP. The usage of this module requires the definition of **sales stages**. Therefore, we will implement the sales stages in the Admin Section and then immediately use them.

This approach must be supported by a thorough analysis if the relevant processes are very detailed and a visual walk-through will not cover it sufficiently.

Use a template database

Many companies have similar requirements. Therefore, specific settings and adjustments in the SAP forms and reports can be saved as a template. In our **Lemonade Stand** case study, we can save the configuration of the actual system and use it later as a starting point for new locations that run independently.

Use an industry solution

With SAP Business ONE, you can add industry-specific features for certain industries. For example, there are specific solutions for medical device industries. These solutions are compliant with the industry-specific requirements. Therefore, you don't need to reinvent the wheel, and you can benefit from the experience of other successful projects.

Perform a thorough analysis

A thorough process analysis is always advised in case your processes reach a level of complexity which require a more detailed approach. For example, even if there is an industry-specific solution, it is likely that your business has specific processes in place that are unique. This uniqueness may establish a **competitive advantage** and you want to make sure that the system will map those features correctly.

Problems with this simple example

In the following walk-through, we will utilize the ad hoc prototyping method. You will see that even though the Lemonade Stand enterprise is the simplest example, it already incorporates a significant level of detail. An analysis would surely help to make this a better implementation, and this will be done in the next section.

Future way for SAP implementation

Future ERP system implementations will be more streamlined. SAP is already guiding its partners in the direction of establishing **industry-specific solutions**. Therefore, in the future, you will be able to select industry-specific solution templates and a qualified and experience partner in this industry. Actually, all this is already happening.

Your own project

What can you get out of this chapter? If you are currently implementing SAP Business ONE, or are planning to implement it in the future, the next section will help you understand the overall scope for an entry-level configuration. You see, I like to put things into perspective. The essential configuration steps touch many different areas. The reason for this is that the system is integrated and all features are connected in some way.

You may use the questions I introduced in Chapter 1 to identify the areas in your business that are **disconnected** and may benefit from better integration. It may be a good idea to prepare a piece of paper and write down the main processes of your business. Organize the processes into sections such as sales, service, purchasing, warehousing, and inventory. You may also add processes for web sales, serial number management, and other custom functionality that you have. As mentioned before, the most powerful aspect of our implementation toolset is asking the right questions. As you go through the implementation steps, you may write down questions about your business as they come up. For example, you may ask **what our sales stages are.** Use the questions I provided as a starting point, but attempt to ask questions that address the **disconnected** areas specific to your business.

The Lemonade Stand case study

I start the SAP Business ONE client and arrive at the login screen. As the system is currently not configured, I don't choose to log in. Instead, a click on the **Change Company** button on the right side of the screen will lead us to the right area:

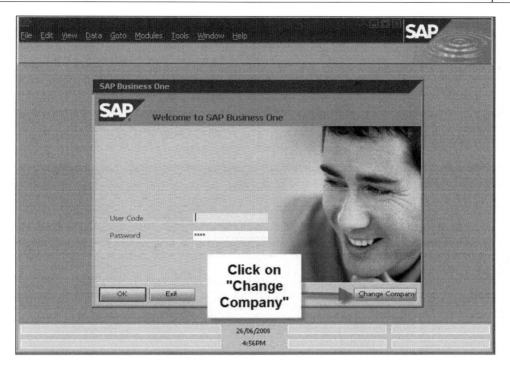

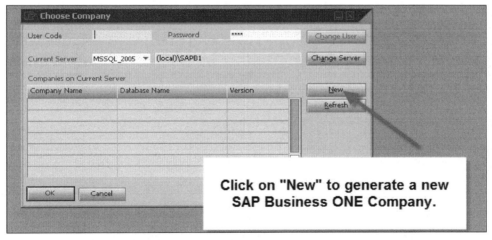

Now, click on the **Refresh** button to make sure all the current companies are listed. If you have existing companies, make sure that no company is selected before you click on **New**. If a company is selected, the **New** button will use the selected company as a template for the new one we will create. In my example, I have no company. Therefore, clicking on **New** will open up a configuration wizard.

The wizard will provide a series of screens, which will allow us to enter the parameters required to configure a new **empty** company:

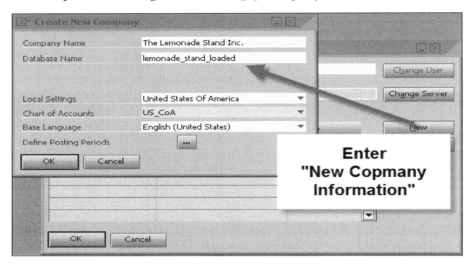

Once you click on **New,** a new screen opens. Here, the following parameters need to be entered.

Company Name

This is the name of the company we are planning to configure. In this sample, I have chosen **The Lemonade Stand Inc.**. As already mentioned, we can later use our company as a template to generate another new company. Therefore, in an ideal world, we can create multiple companies based on a preconfigured template. This holds a lot of potential as we will be able to possibly multiply the configuration efforts later in the process. Therefore, it makes sense to pay attention to every possible detail that may later play a role when working with companies.

Database Name

This is the SQL Server Database name, which will be used when the database is generated. This database will reside on the database server. In this example situation, the database can reside on the same computer where we are using the client software. I have chosen a name that will somehow indicate the purpose of the database—**lemonade_stand_loaded**. You may notice that I have not used spaces or any other special characters. This is a good practice as this name will be used by SAP and possible other programs to run reports.

Local Settings

The **Lemonade Stand Inc.** company will reside in the US. Therefore, I selected the appropriate setting of **United States of America**. SAP Business ONE is a solution that can be used worldwide. Therefore, there is a long list of available local settings.

Chart of Accounts

I have chosen the default Chart of Accounts option **US_CoA** for the case study. Since we want to get it up and running, I will not focus on this point too much. However, I would like to mention that the CoA (Chart of Accounts) design is a key part of a system implementation. This will be done in collaboration with your company accountant, based on how you would like to run your business.

Base Language

Again, there are many options and I have chosen **English** as the most appropriate setting for our case study. What's the difference between **Local Settings** and **Base Language**? The local settings define the region where your company will operate. This will determine country-specific default settings (such as . or ,) in numbers. However, you can use a preferred language independently.

The country-specific selection options also indicate that the SAP system is designed for countries worldwide, and not only for a specific region. Later, we will see the option to configure the system for a single- or multi-currency operation.

Define Posting Periods

The posting periods define the periods that the financial books are organized in. This will separate and organize your business transactions into periods, where each period has a set of transactions that occurred within that period. When a period is **closed**, the next period becomes active and any new transactions will become a part of the new period. For this case study, I have chosen **Months** as **Sub-Periods**:

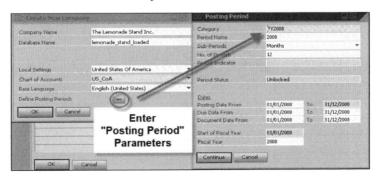

Finally, when the posting periods are defined, you need to confirm the settings by clicking on the **OK** button and the company database will be created. This is shown in the following figure. During this process, the system may indicate the progress on the progress bar with a short information label about the current task being completed. In the screenshot below, it shows **Creating account table...**.

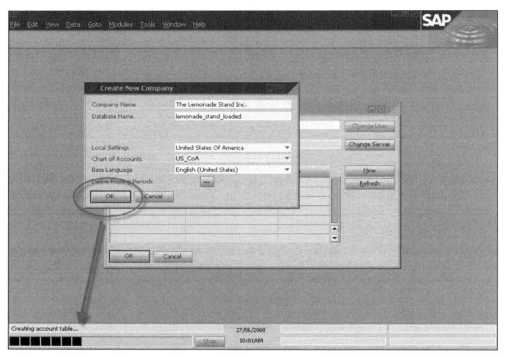

Now that the company database is created, we can log in and start configuring the parameters:

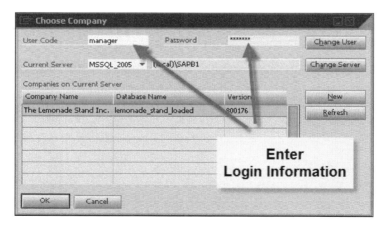

The default administrator user in SAP Business ONE is **manager** and the password is also **manager**. Please make sure that the company database is selected. If no company shows up, click on **Refresh** and then select the company you created. Then, enter the username and password, and click on **OK.** The system will log you in.

Once you are logged in, the system will remember the company you selected the next time you log in. Therefore, you don't need to select the company every time you log in.

Walk-through configuration

At this point, it is essential to identify the core parameters we need to set for getting started. When first encountering the SAP Business ONE interface, you will be presented with a standard tree-type navigation menu called **Main Menu** (seen below). This **Main Menu** provides access to all of the functionality in SAP Business ONE. No other tool or program is needed. In case you are curious, it is possible to configure the interface for different types of users. For example, a sales user may not be interested or even allowed to access any of the finance or administrative parts of the application. Therefore, you can adjust the visible components on a per-user basis.

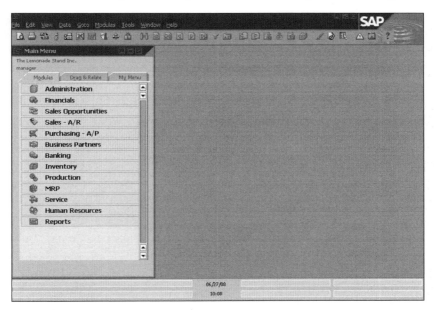

In order to demonstrate the interface capabilities, I will now deactivate all of the menu items that are not immediately needed for the system configuration. You can see the **Forms** icon in the top menu bar (circled in the following screenshot). When we click on this button, the **Form Settings – Main Menu** section opens up. You can deactivate the **Visible** checkbox for all of the items except **Administration** and **Financials**:

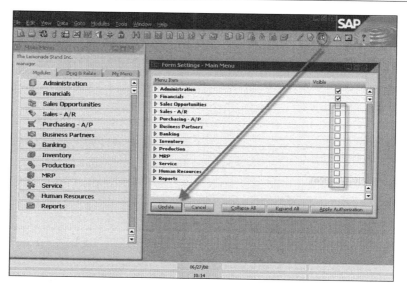

When you click on **Update**, the **Main Menu** only displays the relevant sections. Note that the **Form** icon in the top menu bar is dynamic. This means any currently active form in the application can be adjusted with this button. For example, if we open a sales order and then click on the **Form** icon in the top menu bar, the sales order form can be configured. Additionally, if you encounter a situation at any point during this case study where a particular menu is not available, please double-check the **Form Settings - Main Menu**. It may be possible to easily make the items visible:

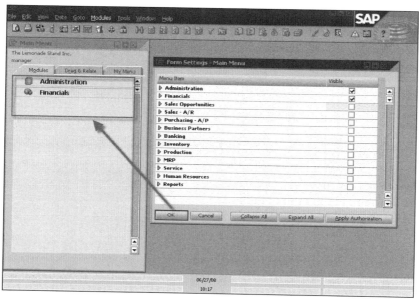

As you may have guessed, the only menu item required to configure the system can be found in the **Administration** section of the **Main Menu**. Let's further investigate this section:

The available sections are discussed next.

Choose Company

Remember how we configured our first company **The Lemonade Stand Inc.**? Here, you can choose a company in case you are running more than one. Why would you have more than one company? Well, there are many reasons. When implementing a system, you may configure a company with all the relevant settings before migrating data from your previous system. Some settings cannot be changed once data is added in the system. The reason for this is that data is tied to transactions which have multiple consequences in the system, such as numbers calculated for your accounting. Therefore, you may have a company, **The Lemonade Stand Inc.**, which you use for data loading and testing. In addition, you may also establish a company which only has the **skeleton** without any data where adjustments can easily be made. Think about it. This also enables you to easily start a new company with the same configuration parameters that you already developed and configured. All you need to do is change the **company information** and a new company is up and running. This is the second reason why you may want an additional company. For example, you can start a new business which you want to manage separately from your established business. While you don't need to create a new company for this as it is possible to manage this in one company, you may decide to create a new company to separate it completely if the entities are legally separate. Later in this book, we will investigate the consequential financial consolidation issues you may face when running separate companies.

 At this point, I encourage you to use the available help in the SAP Business ONE system for investigating every available field of interest. Instead of explaining every available field, I would like to focus on the essential parts. This means not every field is considered when configuring. Also note that additional companies don't require new licenses. You can use the licenses you have for more than one company as long as the companies are on the same server and the actual users are the same. Users get **names licenses**, which means a license is assigned to a specific user.

Exchange Rates and Indexes

This section highlights that SAP Business ONE is suited for international applications. You can manage single- or multi-currency systems. In our example, we only focus on the USD currency. Therefore, no particular action is required to continue. Local ledgers are managed by the local currency. All transactions are posted in parallel with the local currency and system currency. In case they are set differently, an exchange rate has to be specified. **Default Currency** will be used as the currency by default for new G/L accounts that are created.

Company details and settings

I don't want to bombard you with too many screenshots. At this point, you should be able to understand the **Main Menu** system and navigate to the different sections.

Company details

Here, you will provide information about the Lemonade Stand with regards to the company name and address. Besides the obvious data to be entered (such as address information), there is a crucial parameter that will impact how transactions will affect the accounting. It is in the **Company Details** section and here on the **Basic Initialization** tab page. **Item Groups Valuation Method** is of particular importance.

What is the valuation method?

There are three valuation methods available in SAP Business ONE. They are:

- Moving Average
- Standard
- FIFO

All of these methods are explained in the `help` file. However, for your understanding, the valuation method determines the way inventory is valued. With the **Standard** method, each item in the inventory will receive a **standard** price. In this method, the inventory valuation is simple because the same standard price is always the basis. However, this does not always apply in the real world. Prices may fluctuate seasonally for certain types of inventories. In that case, we may choose to use **FIFO**, which values the inventory based on the actual cost that was required to purchase the item. Finally, **Moving Average** calculates the average price based on all purchase prices.

It is important to understand this setting as the underlying transactions generated by the system will be impacted by the choice we make.

I worked with a customer who could not understand why the values in the Chart of Accounts did not match up at the beginning of his SAP Business ONE usage. After evaluating the system closely, we found that each inventory transaction was set to use the **last purchase price**. However, since it was a new system there was no **last purchase price**.

Essential configuration parameters

To further configure the settings, we now need to establish the framework to manage incoming funds. The House Bank Accounts must be set up with the relevant information. To navigate to the right form, choose the path **Administration | Setup | Banking | House Bank Accounts**. The **House Bank Accounts – Setup** screen opens up and allows the House Bank information to be entered. This includes **Bank Code, Branch , Account No., G/L Account**, and more. The G/L Account Determination is crucial because this is the bridge that translates your transaction data into the **double-entry** based accounting back end.

This again highlights that the G/L Account design is crucial for every system. In this example, I have chosen to use the **default Chart of Accounts for the US**:

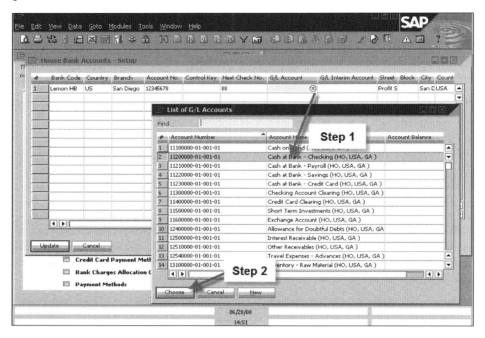

For this example, I have chosen not to manipulate the CoA by entering a new account. This is easily possible if we click on the **New** button. Next, we will be taken to a new screen where a new account can be entered. To explain how this may look, let's open this screen and investigate the existing account structure for a second:

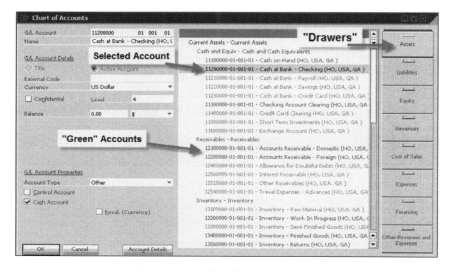

The **Chart of Accounts** form organizes the accounts in a simple **drawer** concept. The **Assets** drawer is selected. Therefore, the list of accounts is filtered and only the **assets** accounts are displayed. The selected account is highlighted in orange. The account I have chosen as our House Bank Account is a **Checking Account**. It is classified as an **Active Account** and a **Cash Account**. I will introduce a more thorough explanation of the different account types and the CoA organization in the next section. The CoA can be automatically generated and may include a long list of accounts. How do we know which account is actually used as part of the G/L Account Determination? You may have already guessed this since I have highlighted those accounts in green in the previous screenshot. This turns out to be very helpful and is a new feature in SAP Business ONE 2007. Therefore, if you have SAP Business ONE 2005, the screen may look the same. However, the green highlighting of accounts already used in the **G/L Account Determination** will not appear.

Can G/L Determination Accounts be changed later? This is a good question to ask in case the implementation of the system bypasses the importance of the CoA design, and during the operation it becomes obvious that changes need to be made.

G/L Account Determination

When choosing the default CoA, most of the G/L account determinations are already set. These accounts will be highlighted in green in the CoA Management window:

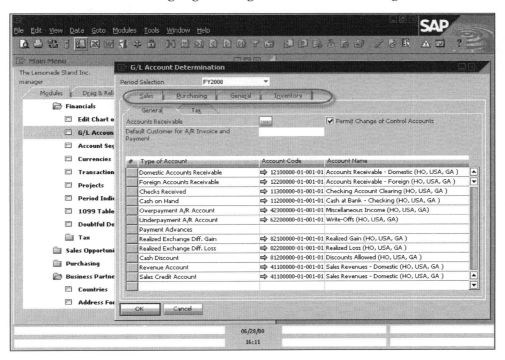

Default payment terms for banking

The next step is to set the payment terms for banking, customers, and vendors. Most commonly, you would define cash, check, electronic bank transfer, and so on. There are sections to manage payment methods in the **Administration | Setup | Banking** section and the **Administration | Setup | Business Partners** section.

When setting the **Payment Methods** for the bank, only **Bank Transfer** is available:

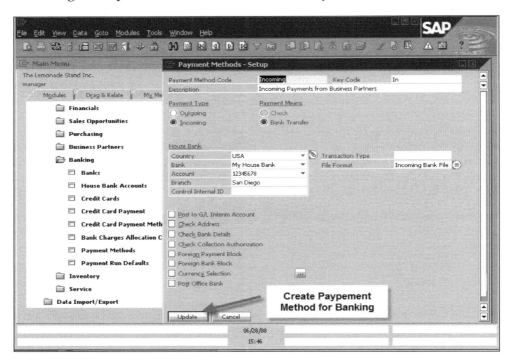

Tax

Every company must comply with local tax regulations. Setting up the tax rates, which will later be applied to the transactions, is a part of the core setup.

In the **Administration | Setup | Financials** section, we find a separate item called **Tax**. This opens up three options to set up tax-related information. We assume our location to be California, and therefore will set up the California state Tax as **7.25**.

Tax rates can be managed via **Jurisdictions**.

Payment terms for customers and vendors

I will now take the opportunity to introduce the two modes available to use the SAP system. By default, each form is on the **Add** mode. This means we can add new information. However, we may sometimes decide to search for information before we add it. We use the **Find** button to do that, which I have highlighted. When we click on the Find button, the **Add** button changes to **Find**. The form fields will then be empty and the user can enter a search key such as * in the **Payment Terms Code** field. Pressing the **Find** button in the following screenshot will either present a list with the available options, or automatically display the data in the form if the search key leads to a single record. In our example, it turns out that **Cash Basic** is a payment term that is automatically set up when the system is generated.

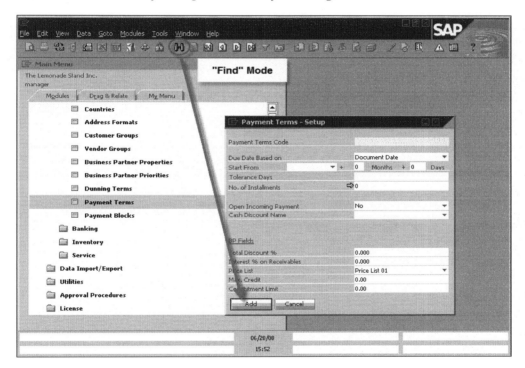

Setting the stock system

Stock levels in a financial system, such as SAP Business ONE, are evaluated by assigning a monetary value to items arriving and leaving the warehouse. These incoming and outgoing transactions will determine financial transactions on the accounting level represented by monetary values.

SAP Business ONE is a continuous stock system where stock values are represented in **real time**. The stock management system is a **continuous stock** with the valuation methods of Moving Average, Standard, or FIFO. How can we define this in the system? There is more than one area where relevant settings can be applied.

In the following section, you can find settings related to this in the **Administration | System Initialization | Company Details | Basic Initialization** tab. We have already checked **Use Perpetual Inventory** and selected **Standard** as the default valuation method for new item groups. More settings can be applied in the **Administration | System Initialization | General Settings | Inventory** tab. **G/L Account Determination** has a tab page where inventory-related accounts can be mapped accordingly:

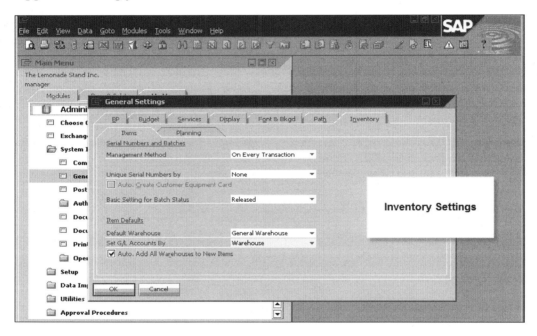

Finally, we can apply the remaining information required for the back end in the **General Settings**. The following screenshot also shows the additional functionality that can be activated. For example, the **Activate Approval Procedures** checkbox will allow us to implement an approval procedure for business documents.

Why is this important?

As a business owner, you may want to approve purchase orders made by employees. The approval procedure is a good tool that you can use to approve documents.

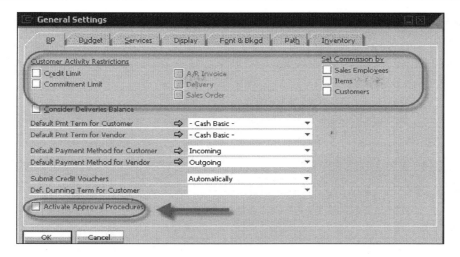

Another key setting, which is a bit hidden, is **Manage Freight in Documents**.
When this is checked, all business documents will have a separate section in the
footer for **freight**:

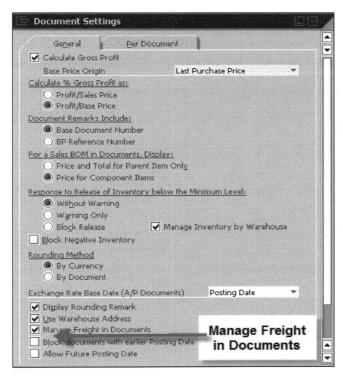

Try this out on your system and check **marketing documents** before and after.

Getting ready for transactions

At this point, you have learned about most of the essential steps to configure the system. You have seen that the system works on the **Add** mode and in the **Find** mode. Therefore, be cautious when trying to find information. You may accidently add information.

There is more terminology specific to SAP Business ONE, which I will explain now.

Business partners and marketing documents

A business partner is any type of address with a contact who can either be a supplier or a customer. In fact, there are three types of business partners in SAP Business ONE which allow us to organize the global BP, that is Business Partner, categorization. The three types are customer, vendor, and lead. The business transactions among these entities are documented in the **marketing documents**.

Office integration

The main skeleton is now set and it is time to make some adjustments that are specific to our case study. You have seen that we have touched many, but not too many, forms to make the configuration entries which will drive the system. You may have also gotten an understanding about where the potential pitfalls, such as underestimating the CoA design, are. I have also shown areas where more configuration settings are possible to gain even more control (for example, document approval). There are even more aspects to consider when implementing a production system. Here is a few examples from the complete list:

- Office Document integration via Paths
- Outlook integration via SAP Add-On
- Document forms design
- Printing strategy
- User access privileges

Don't rush—details will always catch up

Consequently, it is important to get things done without hesitating. The cost of doing nothing may exceed the project's overall cost to implement SAP Business ONE. However, make informed decisions and don't rush. A piece of advice I can give, based on many years of consulting, is that every project in which the customer attempts to be extra fast **WILL** take extra time to implement. Customers in this category may say things such as "**We are a fast-moving company**", "**We are small, but we will grow quickly**", "**I need the Demo today**", and so on.

Business partner master data

In order to better report our customer base, I will categorize the **business partners** (**customers**) into four groups. The groups are **Street-Walker**, **Registered-Customer**, **Reseller**, and **Distributor**. These groups are also an indication of where we will be trying to sell our product. Of course, we think big. That's why we will have a **Distributor** group.

By default, only **Customers** are available to categorize business partners. I will now add the relevant groups. Go to **Administration | Setup | Business Partners | Customer Groups** and add the lines as shown in the following screenshot:

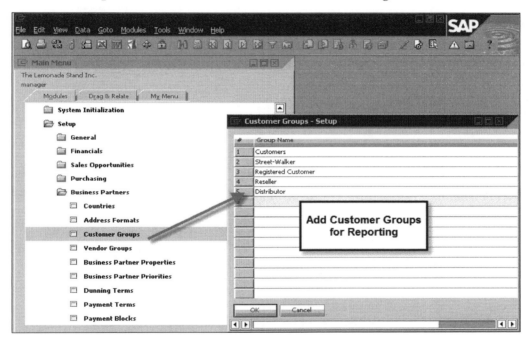

Add sales people

We have categories for our customers. We may now assign sales people to specific customers, in case we have returning customers who need more attention. We can then find out which sales person is the best. In addition, we will see how well information can be collected in SAP Business ONE. That is the key element of SAP Business ONE. You don't need a separate CRM solution to manage your customers and leads. It is all included, and with some simple settings, we have complete integration.

Where can I add salespeople? Just like the business partner categories, we get access via the **Administration | Setup** menu. There are even more settings here. Please evaluate and find relevant settings:

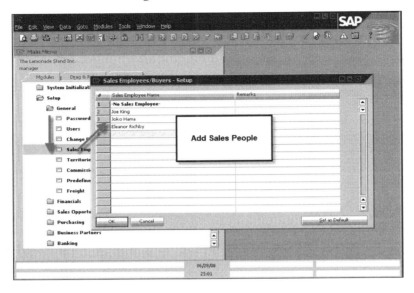

Item groups

I will now set up the item groups which we initially planned for. They are **Raw Materials**, **Raw Materials Perish**, and **Tools and Equipment**:

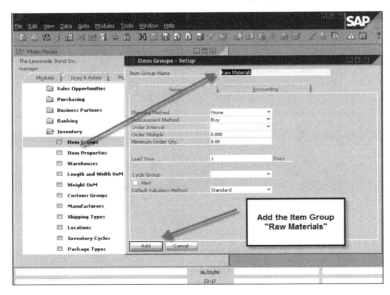

I added all of the required item groups. Let's practice a bit with the **Find** mode:

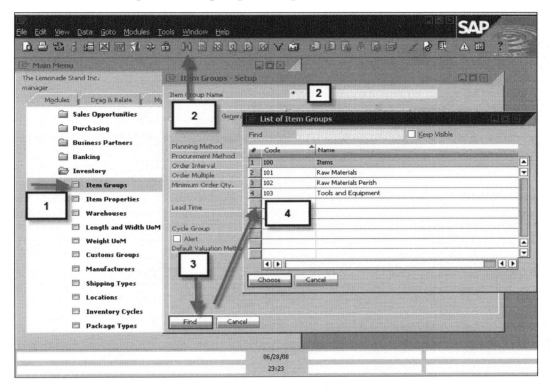

First, you need to navigate to the correct menu at **Adminstration | Setup | Inventory | Item Groups**, and then click on the **Find** icon in the top menu bar. Then, enter * in the **Item Group Name** field, and click on **Find**.

I am highlighting this because it may take some time getting used to differentiate between the **Find** and **Add** modes.

Almost done

To sell products, we need price lists. Since we have plans to sell our products on more than one channel (**Street-Walker, Reseller, Distributor**), we need price lists for them. To set up price lists, let's look in the menu:

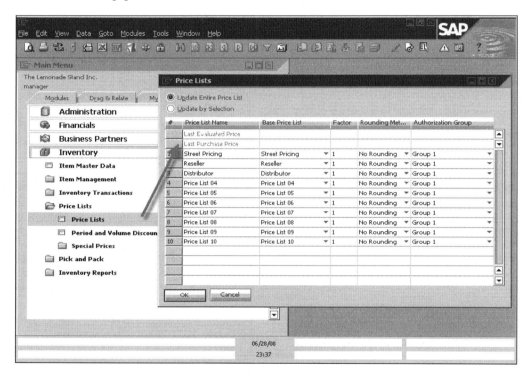

There are two price lists highlighted in grey (seen in the previous screenshot). These are **Last Evaluated Price** and **Last Purchase Price**. These prices are automatically generated by the system and cannot be renamed or changed.

Sales stages

SAP has an integrated CRM feature set. The core idea is to gain control over the sales process and track the sales peoples' activities. In a larger-scale implementation, this will give the business owner control. When a sales person leaves, all of their information is still available in the system and nothing is lost. In addition, it will be possible to create a **sales pipeline**, which will give us an overview of how the business is doing over time. It is then possible to plan not only the material resources via **MRP (Material Requirements Planning)** in the **MRP** section, but also plan the sales resources:

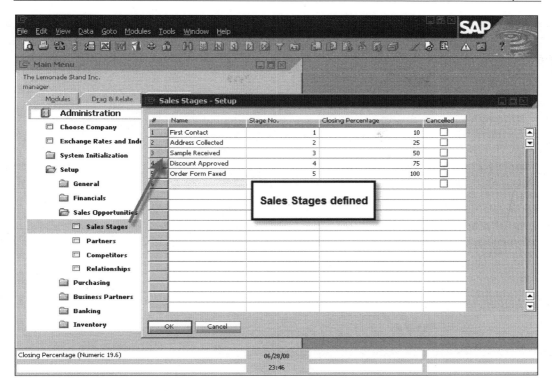

Entering master data

It is now time to enter master data. Master data is the data that we use to run the business. This includes business partners, item master data, and BOMs. **BOM** is short for **Bill of Material**. Basically, a BOM is a combination of raw materials that are automatically drawn for each BOM. A BOM is usually a final product. However, a final product can be made up of a series of hierarchically organized BOMs. When MRP is activated in the system, each BOM transaction will trigger production orders or purchase orders. When used in conjunction with individual lead times for items, it is possible to plan complex scheduling tasks with ease.

The **Business Partner Master Data** screen can be seen in the following screenshot:

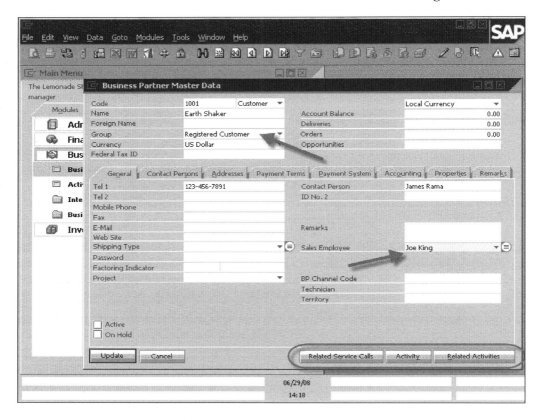

Please note the highlighted buttons at the bottom of the screen. **Related Service Calls**, **Activity**, and **Related Activities** are areas showcasing the integrated CRM functionality. When entering master data, and later adding order and proposals, we can use this information within the CRM functionality. In addition, any CRM-related functionality, such as calls, meetings, and notes, can be immediately used from within the customer master.

A further exploration of each tab will allow you to enter specific information related to each BP. I have already entered information in **Contact Persons**, **Addresses**, and so on.

Please note that each BP has one **Bill To** address and multiple **Ship To** addresses.

I have also added a vendor named **Local Grocery** to allow raw materials to be purchased.

I will now create the raw materials and combine them into a BOM. When creating the raw materials, I assign the vendor I created as the **Preferred Vendor**.

For the purpose of this example, I have simplified the form for the BOM:

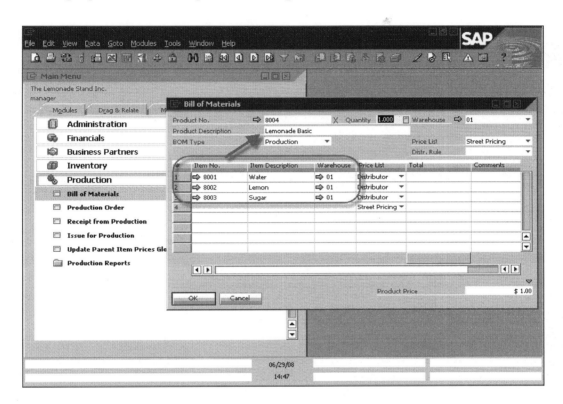

You can now see how raw materials are combined to create a final product. I will no longer provide a screenshot for every data entry I make. I believe you have collected enough information to confidently navigate to each screen and enter data.

Transaction digestion

I will give you one quick tip to allow orders to be entered with direct payment. Please enter a default customer in the **G/L Account Determination | Sales** tab. For this purpose, I have created a customer for Bridge Street, where we will be selling the lemonade first. Transactions are entered using the **Sales AR** Menu using the **A/R Invoice + Payment** form:

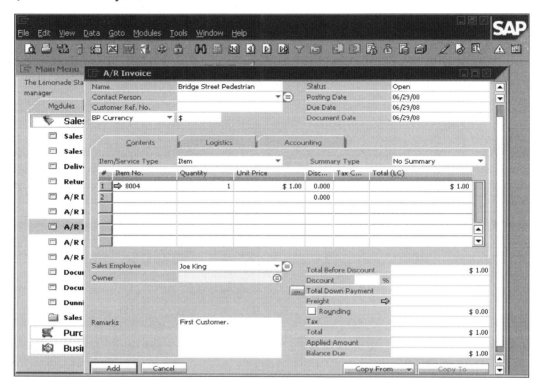

Since we are not officially writing a quote and then converting it to a sales order with appropriate payment means, we used the **A/R Invoice + Payment**.

When entering an invoice via A/R Invoice Plus Payment, it is assumed that we will immediately receive the payment. Therefore, when entering the data in the form, SAP automatically prompts us with a **Payment Means** form:

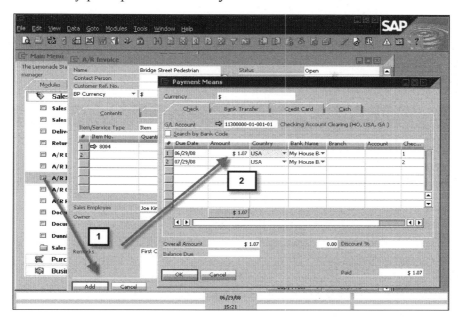

OK. We just entered the first transaction. In order to understand the underlying consequences, let's investigate the CoA (seen in the following screenshot). How did this first transaction impact the numbers in the underlying accounts?

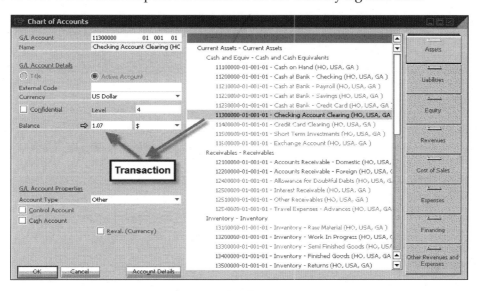

This looks good. We received the money and it shows up in the relevant account. However, it is not quite right yet because to sell the lemonade, we really need to purchase the raw materials first. Let's see how our inventory looks. How does the inventory tracking system honor the situation that we sold something that was not available?

In the following screenshot, we see the default warehouse accounts for a quantity of **-1**. The key setting that allowed this to happen can be found in **Administration | Setup | Document Settings | General Tab**.

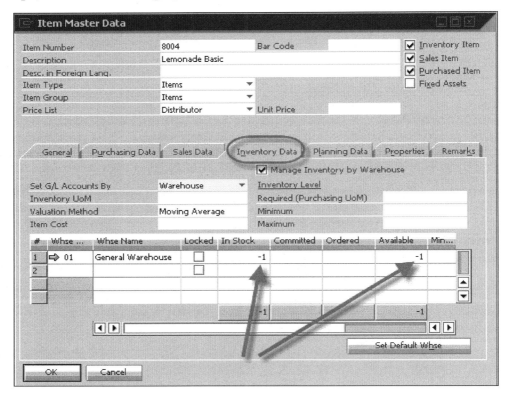

You can see the settings in the following screenshot. We specifically allowed the release that may cause a negative stock:

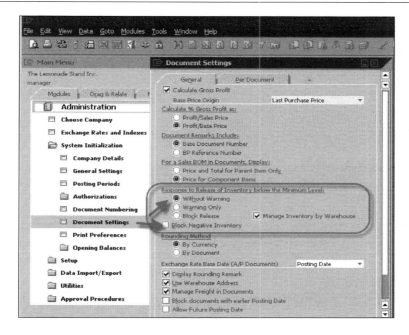

To continue working with the system, we will now purchase the relevant raw materials and produce the **Lemonade Basic** in sufficient quantities. I will create a PO and use the SAP Business ONE feature to directly convert the PO (Purchase Order) into an **A/P Invoice**. When clicking on the **Copy** button on the right-hand bottom side of the screen, you will see the available options:

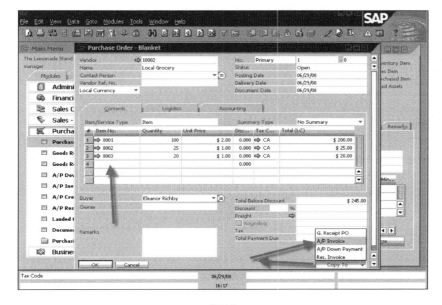

I create a PO and copy it to an Invoice. When running the inventory status report, it is obvious that the stock levels of each raw material have increased. However, the finished good **Lemonade Basic** still accounts for **-1**. Why is that? The finished good **Lemonade Basic** has to be produced first because it is a BOM:

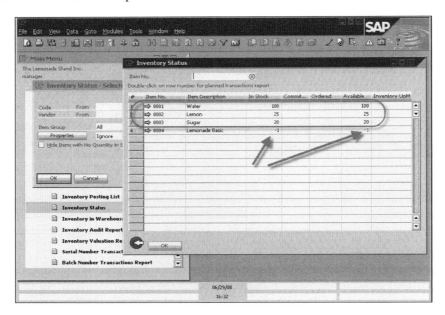

A production order will help generate the required inventory. I entered the default status of **Planned**. In the inventory status report, this would be accounted for with the status of **Planned**. This would be an indication that the production is planned. However, to receive the product **Lemonade Basic** from production, we need to change this status to **Released** and complete the **Receipt from Production** form. Enter the production order number **1** in the **Order Number** field, and all of the relevant details will automatically be displayed. I did not provide screenshots for this as you will be able to find this on your own as a practice test.

A subsequent check in the CoA shows that the numbers now look better.

Summary

In this chapter, we did an express configuration. There are different ways to implement a system and an appropriate method should be selected based on the underlying complexity. We used the ad hoc prototyping implementation of the core system. The following information could be obtained during the configuration:

- The system setup is simple and straightforward
- Due to the high level of integration, many aspects are touched during a single transaction
- Checking the CoA is essential when digesting transactions

You should now be able to quickly configure the core system and understand the relevant settings that may impact how transactions are accounted for. Please note that you should obtain qualified consulting help to finetune the overall settings for your business.

3

Reporting and Analysis: Getting Ready for Growth

The main benefit of an integrated solution is better information to support crucial business decisions. Simply obtaining information may improve the way your business operates. For example, if your employees know that their Internet browsing activity is tracked, the quality of the sites they visit will improve. The same applies to your business system. In this chapter, we will see the key aspects of a reporting strategy. As part of that, we will touch upon all of the features in the SAP Business ONE application that are relevant for reporting. In the process, the following areas will be covered:

- Reporting architecture and its forward-looking vision - How does it fit in? I will explain the key role reporting plays within your SAP solution.

- Real-time reporting - The information in SAP is real time. What does this mean for your reporting strategy? We will look at how information can be categorized in SAP.

- BI - What is BI? We will look at the core aspect of what BI means for your reporting strategy.

- The difference between data and information – Let's not forget that we are seeking information. Data is not equal to information in this sense.

- UDFs – We will take a thorough look at UDFs. UDFs are key aspects of every SAP implementation, and you will be able to understand their purpose and create your own.

- Reporting strategy – How can you apply the concepts in this chapter to your own project? I will help you understand the key aspects of a successful reporting strategy for your business.

- SAP Business ONE reporting tools explained – We will use SAP reporting tools to create queries using Query Generator, Query Wizard, Drag and Relate, and the Alert system.

- The chapter closes with a brief positioning of the other more high-end reporting tools which will be covered later in this book.

Reporting architecture

What is reporting? Reporting is the analysis or **slicing and dicing** of business data to identify key performance indicators. These key indicators are used to navigate your business through the ever-changing challenges it encounters during operation.

The true value of a system, such as SAP Business ONE, can be evaluated when it comes to reporting against the data that was collected during its operation. Remember the settings we discussed in the **Financials** section, such as the **Chart of Accounts** settings? This was the financial skeleton that we established, which will eventually hold all of the financial data. This system has to comply with the local legal requirements and it uses the so-called **double-entry** bookkeeping system. In this system, each transaction is represented by a monetary value associated with a credit and a debit that are of equal value.

The accounting skeleton collects all of the relevant data based on the transactions entered in the system with the underlying **G/L Account Determination** settings. Consequently, all transactions will be documented in the Chart of Accounts as per our settings in the "G/L Determination Settings".

This is the first crucial aspect to understand when it comes to reporting. SAP Business ONE provides a reporting system based on **double-entry bookkeeping accounts**, plus the system settings that help us collect key performance data about the business.

Reporting requires a forward-looking vision

The art of reporting lies in a forward-looking vision that prepares the system with additional fields and parameters to collect relevant data as we operate our business. For example, we may sell lemonade as a part of the business. However, it may be a good idea to categorize the type of lemonade we sell to later analyze which type of product had the best sales. In addition, we may categorize the location where we sold the final product. To further apply our case study, we may also want to run a report on a per-salesperson basis to gain information about the salespeople's performance. It is often quickly decided who the best customers are. Business owners commonly take pride in knowing this. However, it is a good idea to include all of the available information and analyze the data. For example, who may look like a good customer because of the fact that they are responsible for most of our workload, may not lead to most of the businesses' profit. A customer may return products often, or complain about them. This may cost the business excessive time and money. Let's consider the infamous 80-20 rule as an inspiration. This rule basically claims that 80% of the customers are responsible for 20% of the profit and 20% of the customers are responsible for 80% of the profit. Understanding the 20% that drive our business and collecting the right information so that we can learn more about them and improve our services is the challenge at hand. It is an interesting fact that in order to design an efficient reporting system against past data, we need to have a forward-looking vision that enables us to define the data collection framework in the system.

Real-time reporting

The SAP Business ONE solution has an integrated financial skeleton and a Business Indicator Architecture which will be the basis for our reporting. All of the business information is collected in a single system without the need for synchronization or re-entering.

In today's digital age, it is easy to collect too much information. This often leads to data graves with information that cannot be used. It is therefore important to collect the **right information** for analysis.

The SAP Business ONE system provides reporting tools that collect the **right information** for the following areas:

- Financial reporting based on legal requirements
- Business management reporting
- Compliance requirements

What is BI—business intelligence?

An ad hoc definition of business intelligence is "the aggregation of data from different sources and presentation of this data in an integrated format to provide new information."

It is a fact of today's business world that the amount of data collected exceeds the information which will be extracted from this data. However, modern tools (such as Crystal Reports) provide sophisticated means to access the data, process it, and present it in a desired format.

Business intelligence comprises the process of using tools (such as Crystal Reports) and automating the reporting process.

The difference between data and information

Let's focus a bit more on data and information. Data is not information. What does this mean? Let me explain this with relation to the SAP Business ONE system. Only entering sales orders and collecting data in the SAP system will not provide all of the information we need to make informed decisions about our business. We need to think ahead and design the information framework that will collect data based on the way we want to run the business. Let me give you an example which will make this concept clearer. For example, as part of the Lemonade Stand Inc case study, we may want to collect information about the following areas:

- Best salesperson
- Sales per street
- Returning customers
- Most sold lemonade flavor
- Orders with special instructions

Therefore, by using a forward-thinking SAP configuration, we can make sure that all of the relevant information will be automatically collected.

In SAP Business ONE, this essentially means that we add fields in the relevant forms that allow us to specify the required information. For example, we may add a so-called **user-defined field** to most of the SAP forms.

User-defined fields

User-defined fields (or UDFs) are a simple way to add custom fields to the SAP Business ONE forms. For example, we may want to collect specific information that is not presently accounted for in SAP. It is then possible to easily add a custom field which will allow us to collect the designated information. It is a simple feature that has a great value. In most systems, we need to write a custom program to modify an existing form. I have worked with many accounting and business management solutions, and during the years it has become clear that there is great risk in programmatically changing an ERP system. It basically renders the system non-compliant to any updated or maintenance patches released. Therefore, I recommend the use of programming to implement custom features with caution. The SAP way of using UDFs for simple form adjustments is a good feature because it allows us to make changes without programming. Therefore, the system is still **release-ready**. This means SAP will continue to support it.

API programming and certified add-ons

I would like to leave one last thought about programming at this point. When considering programming, use a well-defined interface that keeps the system **release-ready**. SAP provides the API interface to allow the add-on functionality, which ranges from simple credit card authorization to sophisticated manufacturing solutions. By complying with the API requirements, the path is set to keep SAP support. Add-ons are certified by SAP. This should be your first indication about the quality and lifecycle of an add-on.

How to create a UDF?

Let's stay on track and finalize our discussion about UDFs. UDFs can easily be created. I will actually show you how in this section.

It is so simple to add your own field that you need to be careful not to create too many. To create our own UDF to collect specific instructions for larger orders of lemonade, I will add a field called **Instructions**. Please navigate to the **User-Defined Fields - Management** screen, which can be found via **Tools | Customization Tools | User-Defined Fields - Management**. This will open the **User-Defined Fields - Management** screen, as shown here:

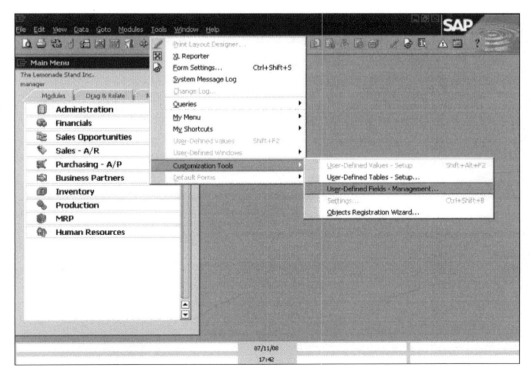

The **User-Defined Fields – Management** screen (seen in the following screenshot) shows the areas were UDFs can be added. In short, you can add UDFs for most business objects. When you add a UDF, and assign it to **Marketing Documents**, this UDF will only be available for marketing documents. This makes the most sense as it allows us to collect information specific to marketing documents.

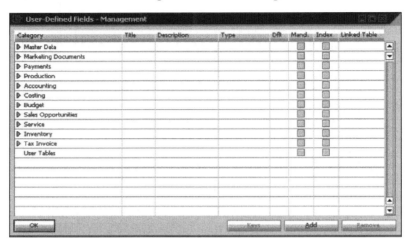

Adding a UDF to Marketing Documents

I am adding a field called **Instructions** (as seen in the following screenshot). This field can be used to enter specific instructions for a **lemonade order**. For example, we may receive an order for a party and need to deliver lemonade in larger quantities, complying with the customer-specific taste and delivery requests.

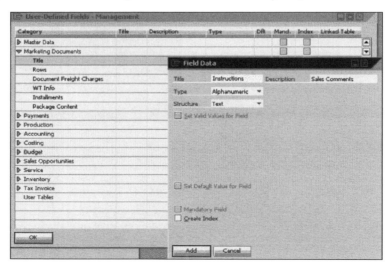

When opening our first sales order, which we entered as part of the case study, we can now see that a new field is available on the righthand side of the form. This field allows us to enter **Sales Comments** that can be used as instructions:

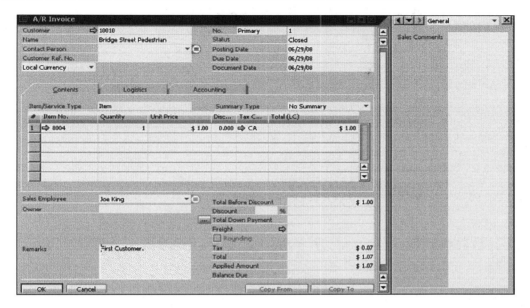

How can the new field be used for reporting?

We may run a report that would show us the orders that have specific instructions assigned versus the orders that are standard. This is important for our production planning since standard orders (without instructions) can be scheduled directly, whereas orders with special instructions require further review and manual scheduling.

Developing an efficient UDF concept

Now that we know how easy it is to create UDFs, let's briefly expand and see the larger scope of this relatively simple technology. In order to additionally fine-tune our **lemonade production**, we could automate the creation of **production orders** for our standard lemonade flavor. However, the orders that have custom instructions need special attention. You will see that just by adding the **Instructions** UDF, we can categorize the production orders. In addition, we can create UDFs in the **Production Order** section that implement a workflow and create a simple production routing system. This is actually a good example which shows where simple technology components can be combined to create a sophisticated solution. Consequently, you now understand that UDFs can be used to improve the data you collect for reporting, and also for simple workflow routing.

In case you are curious, here is a brief recap on how to implement workflow routing by using a simple method. Create a UDF for each status that your production goes through. This could be Get Raw Materials – Clean Production Environment – Squeeze Lemons – Add Sugar – Fill in bottles. Then assign a status of Complete – Not Started to each step. The default status should be Not Started. While going through production, you assign each step to Complete as you go through.

You may run a report for different departments. For example, when the last step is complete, a quality control report could show all of the production orders when the last step is complete. The quality control engineer could then go through the list and add a quality control performed signature to each production, and then assign a status of Complete to the overall production order.

Consequently, by using UDFs and reporting techniques to report on values entered in the UDFs, we can extract information and also create a workflow-type information flow in the system.

Components of a reporting strategy

A reporting strategy in SAP Business ONE has two main aspects:

- Establishing the data collection framework
- Report delivery based on information requirements

Establishing the data collection framework for your project

The most crucial part of reporting is obviously to collect the right information in the first place. As part of the toolset I provided you at the beginning of this book, you understand that asking the right questions is important. This is true for your reporting system too. The questions you ask should focus on the key performance indicators that are specific to your business. Basically, you need to write down all of the reports that you need, and then find out if the system provides this information by default. UDFs should be added to address non-default information requirements. Therefore, the data collection framework follows this process:

- Define information requirements by asking questions
- Define UDFs to accommodate information requirements
- Select reports

Report delivery based on information requirements

With all of the required information available in the system, the reports can be grouped together. For example, I grouped the reports based on the delivery frequency and the target audience for the report:

- Monthly reports (for example, sales analysis)
- Weekly reports (for example, sales pipeline)
- Daily reports (for example, alerts)
- Ad hoc reports (for example, Drag and Relate)
- Reports to further analyze hidden information (for example, XL Reporter)
- Web dashboards (for example, Crystal Web report)

Each report serves a specific information need in accordance with the established business metrics represented by key performance indicators in the reports. This sounds complicated, but it is simple when categorizing the reports based on the list above and identifying the key values that are important to run your business.

SAP Business ONE reporting tools "hands-on"

Now, let's finally log in to SAP and run some reports. The simplest form of a report in SAP is a plain query that is saved with a title. This can be run at any time in the system. Therefore, if you know how to design a query, then this is a fast and simple solution. In case you do not know how to create a query, let me show you how.
I am explaining this to ensure you are making good use of your SQL skills when using SAP Business. In most business solutions, it may be hard to find the right tables and columns to run a query. In SAP Business ONE, you can switch on **System Information** via **View | System Information**. Then, as you browse with the mouse over fields in a form, the table name will be displayed in the footer section of the SAP Business ONE interface.

I have added a screenshot that shows the table name and column name for the Business Partner Master record. You can see that the cursor is in the **Code** section. In the footer, it shows **OCRD, CardCode**. This means the information is in the OCRD table, and the column for **Code** is **CardCode** in the database table level:

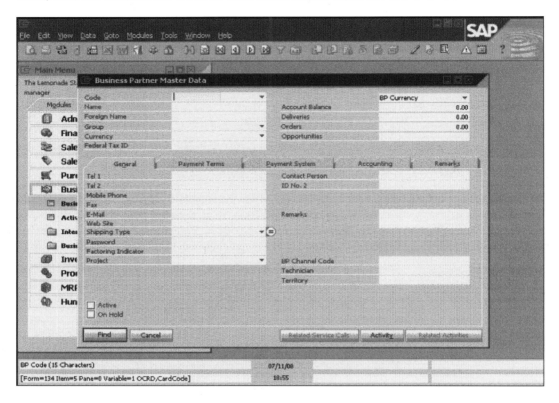

I have created a simple query (as seen in the following screenshot) that shows all of the business partners. You can fine-tune this even more based on your requirements. If you know how to run SQL queries, then please continue your own adventure with this area. I recommend creating views from complex queries in the SQL Server, and then use simple queries against those views in SAP.

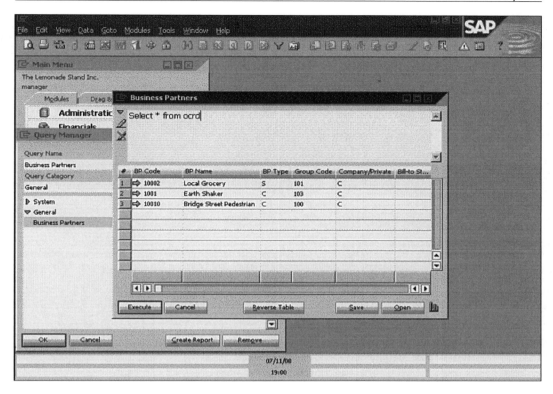

If you do not understand this, you may ask for another way to run reports appropriate for mere mortals without an SQL background. Well, SAP Business ONE has a concept for this too.

SQL for managers

SAP offers two additional ways to create SQL queries using wizard-type tools: **Query Generator** and **Query Wizard**. The Query Generator works at the table level and helps you create a query, including conditions. The Query Wizard is of a higher level and allows tables and columns to be selected on a business context level by providing more descriptive information about each table. You should experiment with both the Query Generator and the Query Wizard to find out what works best for you. I believe that these tools are a great teaching aid when learning how to create queries. You can first attempt to create the query on your own. If you encounter problems, use the Query Wizard and see what the query should look like in order to work.

Using the Query Generator

Open the **Query Generator** (seen in the following screenshot) and enter **OCRD** in the left section. If you remember, this was the table name provided for business partners. Now, what if we only want a report with business partners from a specific zip code? Well, you hit the *Tab* key once you enter **OCRD** in the left section. Based on this information, SAP displays the columns available in this table in the next section on the right side. Now place the cursor in the **Select** section in the upper-right white field. Then click on **CardCode** and **CardName**. SAP automatically adds the names here. Next, place the cursor in the **Where** section and click on the column which will provide the **Where** criteria. I selected **ZipCode**. However, I want to enter the zip code dynamically and not create a new report for every zip code. Therefore, I clicked on the **Conditions** button. This opens a side panel on the right. I clicked on **Equal** and **[%0]**. This will ensure that the SAP system will ask for a zip code value every time we run this report.

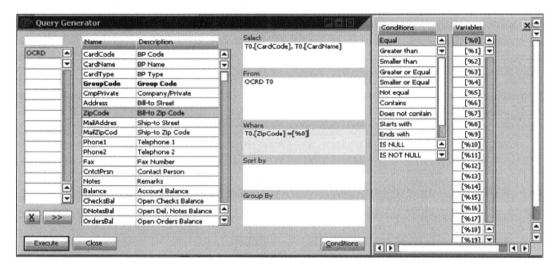

I saved the report as `Business Partners by ZIP` and I will now run it. A small window opens, which provides an entry field for the ZIP parameters:

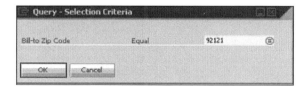

Once a zip code is entered, the query runs and returns the result. In the result window, the underlying query that produced the result is always displayed. Take a look at the following screenshot:

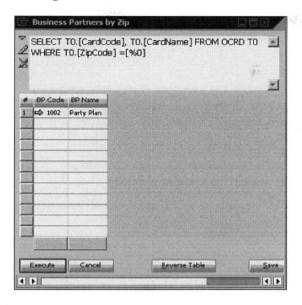

By using this method, it is possible to create pretty sophisticated queries and reports without advanced SQL knowledge. In addition, by investigating the generated queries, you can easily increase your SQL knowledge if you like. In case you do not want that, then I recommend looking at the other available reporting options such as the Query Wizard.

Using the Query Wizard

Although the Query Generator was a good help, when it came to generating a query that required parameters, the Query Wizard helps us in identifying related data in different tables. When a database is defined, not all data is saved in a single table. I would like to provide a simple example that showcases this by using a query against the item table called **OITM**. The OITM table has all of the information about all items. However, it only has the **Item Group** code expressed as an id number called **ItmsGrpCod**, and we do not get the Group Name with a simple query. We need to find the related table that has the Group Code and the Group Name. Let's activate the **System Information** feature and open the **Item Master Data** form in the **Inventory** menu. With previously described method, move the cursor over the form and find the table name **OITM**. Next, open the Query Wizard and enter **OITM** in the first column.

In case you are not sure which table to use, you can also hit the *Tab* key with the cursor in the empty **Table** box and all of the available tables will show up along with an explanation of the relevant table. We entered **OITM** directly into the first row and the **Description** is updated with the value **Items**, indicating that we correctly entered a valid table name and that it represents item information. Now, the trick is to select the first row in the **Table** column and click on **OITM** again. This will display the related tables in the lower section (as seen in the following screenshot). We will select **Item Groups**. In other ERP systems, you may need to request for technical documentation to get this type of information.

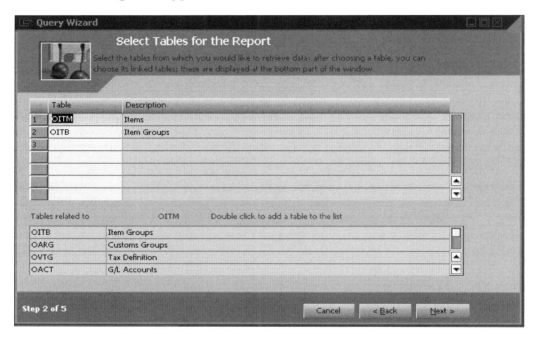

The next step is to select the columns that we want to match and display. Since it is our goal to get a descriptive Group Name and not a number-like Group Code, I am using the common column **ItemCode** to match the two tables and display the **Group Name**. For the purpose of the example, I am displaying the Group Code twice. The first value comes from the **Items** table and the second comes from the **Items Group** table. You will see in the query result that they match up:

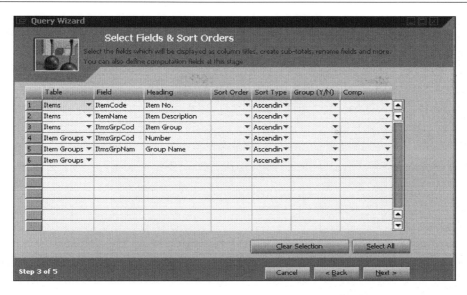

In the next screen of the wizard, I will now match the column as shown in the following screenshot. This is a visual guide for designing an SQL query. If you have ever studied SQL and forgot some of the techniques, this wizard will refresh your memory. As a matter of fact, you do not need to know SQL. However, the resulting query will be presented once you are done. In addition, the process of first selecting the tables and then specifying the conditions and relations will help you understand the required steps to actually design an SQL query. Therefore, if you have technical personnel willing to do some of the reporting themselves, they can easily get started with the SAP Query Generator and Query Wizard:

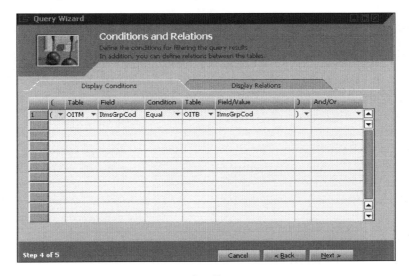

The final query is presented. When confirming with the **Finish** button (seen in the following screenshot), the query is executed and we can see the result. Do not forget to save this query. I saved it as `Items_Groupname`.

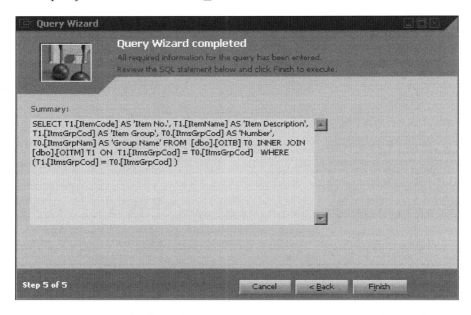

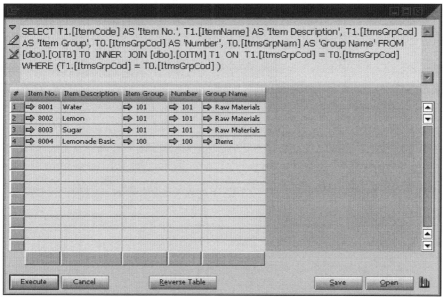

Drag and Relate

As you can see, there are many ways of reporting and it is up to you to choose the appropriate tool. In case you are on the phone with a customer and need a report that is not available in SAP Business ONE, you may also use the so-called Drag and Relate functionality. This is somewhat groundbreaking because you can use the form interface elements and drag them against common business objects to see related information. Sounds complicated again? I am using the term **business objects** on purpose to make you think in terms of objects that hold a specific type of information. Examples of such objects can be found when actually using the **Drag and Relate** functionality.

The basis of the Drag and Relate functionality is an open form in SAP Business ONE. I will open the item master for you and select the **Lemonade Basic** product. This is our only finished good. When I click on the **Drag & Relate** tab page in the **Main Menu**, all of the available business objects show up.

If you want to quickly see any invoices that were issued against this item, open the **Sales – A/R** business object. Click on **Item Number** and hold the mouse button. The box with the **Item Number** then becomes a floating box and you can drag it over the **A/R Invoice** business object. When you release the mouse, you will get an immediate **Drag and Relate** report about the invoices related to the selected item.

Look at the following screenshot to see how it is done:

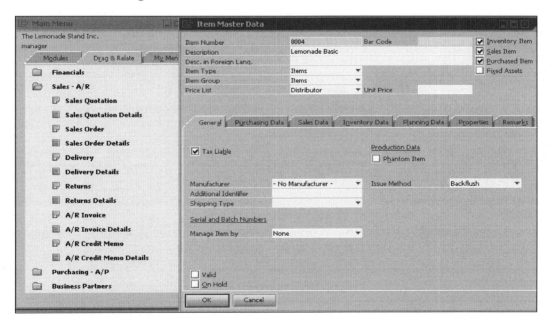

When should you use the Drag and Relate information? I usually use this to obtain information in a system that has no specific reports set up for the information I require. In addition, if the information you are looking for is a one-time lookup type, you may not want to create a query and save it. You may just drag and relate quickly and move on once you have the information you need.

The Drag and Relate concept also allows you to obtain information based on open data in a marketing document. When dragging the fields, you get immediate information about related data for the particular document. You do not need to run a lengthy report where you need to enter parameters and then analyze the results.

Another example is a situation where you have a customer on the phone and you want to quickly see the related transactions for this customer as you talk to them.

A Drag and Relate activity cannot be saved though. It is strictly **ad hoc** style. If you think about it, this concept basically transits the SAP Business ONE system into a dashboard, where every form can be immediately reported on within the context of a specific data set.

A bit of caution is advised for Drag and Relate if your database is large. In such a case, a simple Drag and Relate could generate a very large query which will take a long time to complete and slow the system down.

Alert system

In SAP Business ONE, you can define **alerts**. An alert is a business event that meets a certain defined criteria. An example of an event could be that a salesperson exceeded the maximum discount allowed. You can define an alert which will notify the manager of the salesperson if such a thing happens. Another example is a situation where a customer orders items that exceed his or her credit limit. You can then get an alert and discuss with the customer the option to prepay certain parts of the open orders.

As you can see, the alert system is a bit like a workflow trigger system. You can trigger business processes, such as order verification, by using alerts. This will help keep your business in line with your policies and make sure that there are no surprises in the key areas.

There are two types of alerts: pre-defined alerts and user-defined alerts. Pre-defined alerts are already defined in the SAP Business ONE system. However, you can create any type of alert that complies with your individual business rules. These alerts would be user-defined alerts.

Technically, an alert is a simple query that checks that the business rules are met. For example, we may create a query to check the maximum number of orders. If the maximum number of orders is exceeded, then the query returns a result and the alert would notify the assigned employee.

With the knowledge obtained in the previous chapters, you now know that you first identify the business objects involved in this business rule. You then identify the relevant tables, and finally specify the conditions. Therefore, you can use the previously explained query tools to develop the query, and then assign the query to an alert.

At this point, let's focus on the pre-defined alerts that come with SAP Business ONE. You can find them by navigating to **Administration | Alerts Management**. Enter * in the **Name** field and hit *Enter*. You will then get the list of pre-defined alerts. I am selecting the **Deviation from Discount (in %)** alert. This alert, as the name suggests, will notify the selected user if the discount granted in a marketing document exceeds a set limit.

In the following screenshot, it can be seen that I set the discount percentage to **25%**. The **Documents** tab page allows us to easily assign the documents that we will **monitor** using this alert.

See how the discount can be set based on your requirements.

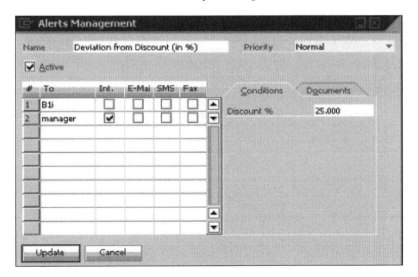

Using the **Documents tab page**, you can set the documents which will be **monitored** by this alert:

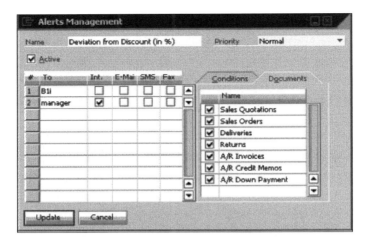

One final step is required to activate the alert system. Go to **Administration | System Initialization | General Settings** and then select the **Services** tab page. This is where you can configure the way the alerts will work in the system.

Two crucial settings must be specified: **Send Alert for Activities Scheduled for Today** and **Display Inbox When New Message Arrives**. These settings, along with the **Update Message (Min.)** parameter, will get this going. I set the update to **5 Minutes**. This means the system will check every five minutes if the alert criteria is met and will then inform the designated user about that.

How does this work under the surface? Since the alert system uses pre-defined and custom queries to identify if the criteria for the alert are met, there must be a query hidden somewhere in the system. Let's try to find it. Open the **Alerts Management** window, and while **System Information** is activated, browse over **Query** and note that the table is called **OUQR**. When you select this table using the Query Wizard, you will see that there is a query called **Locate Exceptional Discount in Invoice**. You can copy the **QString** column and you will have the underlying query for this alert. Why would you do that? Well, if you have a requirement that is similar to an existing alert, but not quite the same, you can use this method to get started with a query and then make adjustments to fit your needs.

As you can see, the alert system is a workflow-concept based on queries and custom criteria that reflect your business rules.

At this point, it has become clear that reporting in SAP Business ONE goes through all levels of expertise and addresses the needs of managers and technical personnel. I have even explained features such as Drag and Relate and alerts that do not immediately look like a reporting tool. However, a closer look did uncover that most SAP Business ONE features are on some level based on key reporting concepts and technologies.

XL Reporter and Crystal Reports

The two high-end reporting tools available in SAP Business ONE are XL Reporter and Crystal Reports. I am explaining these tools together to better distinguish their functionality for you. In short, XL Reporter runs from within SAP Business ONE and will export report data directly into Excel. Crystal Reports will allow you to retrieve the results and then export to the most common formats.

XL Reporter comes with a long list of very powerful pre-defined reports. Those are dashboard-style reports that make heavy use of graphs in Excel. The advantage is that you have all of the results in Excel. The disadvantage is that you need Excel to run these reports. Crystal Reports will not provide all of the Excel power for further processing of data. However, with Crystal Reports the result can be retrieved via a local Crystal Viewer or a Web Dashboard.

Therefore, if you have a high-performance desktop computer and are proficient in the use of Excel, then I highly recommend using XL Reporter. Crystal Reports has the same data visualization power without the Excel Processing Functionality. For large-scale implementations, Crystal Reports can be deployed on a separate server. Therefore, it can offset the required processing load from the desktop computer to a powerful server.

At the time of writing this section, SAP has released a new add-on for SAP Business ONE which will integrate Crystal Reports. As you may know by now, SAP has purchased Business Objects, which was the former owner of Crystal Reports. Based on the latest roadmap for SAP Business ONE, Crystal Reports is a strategic platform for reporting. This means all SAP reports will soon be available in native Crystal Reports format.

XL Reporter add-on

Please note that prior to SAP Business ONE 2007, the XL Reporter feature was activated via a separate add-on. This required a separate installation and activation. Since 2007, this add-on is incorporated with the core package and the add-on is activated automatically.

Summary

In this chapter, we analyzed the strategic position of reporting. You learned how to define the information collection skeleton using UDFs, and how to apply the available SQL tools in SAP to generate your own reports and alerts. Since all reports are based on SQL queries, you are ready to tackle all of your reporting needs.

Therefore, reporting is more than just calling the reports that come with the system. It is a way to make sure you get the information you need to evaluate the key performance indicators of your business.

4

Creating a Project Plan using the SAP Accelerated Implementation Plan

This chapter will explain all of the tasks required to design a solid SAP Business ONE project plan. I will first explain some project management basics, and then quickly help you in a **hands-on**, step-by-step process to design your own plan.

The following topics will be covered in this chapter:

- Introduction to project managment: Your project's goal, budget, required personnel, as well as time and task groups organized in milestones - I will provide a quick introduction to project management so you have the right tools to understand how an SAP implementation can be managed.

- Introducing the SAP ASAP methodology – Here, I will explain how SAP recommends organizing and managing an efficient SAP project.

- Preparing an SAP Accelerated Implementation Plan – This is the ultimate toolset for you to manage your SAP Business ONE project. At the end of this section, you will have your own project plan.

Overall, the goal of this chapter is to create a plan in a template format so that it can be used as a starting point for every SAP Business ONE project out there. Before we start diving into the SAP Accelerated Implementation Plan, let me provide some background information about project management.

Project management background

Project management is the balancing act of optimizing the agreed-upon goals within a prescribed time using limited resources. The limited resources are most commonly represented by financial, personnel, and material resources. If you read this carefully, you will notice that the purpose of project management is to reach an **agreed-upon goal**. The goal has to be well-defined so it can be reached. If you do not define a clear and crisp goal, the end result will also be a bit fuzzy. In general, it can be said that **project management** allows you to reach a complex goal by completing a series of simple tasks.

Let's define the goal

Imagine a world where **everything** is possible. What would your business look like in an **ideal world**? Can you see the problem with this? **Everything** and an **ideal world** are not very specific goals. We need to connect our real business needs and be specific. Let me define the goal for our case study. You can take this as a guideline for your own business. For example purposes, I would like to assume that we have already completed a thorough market analysis. Based on this analysis, the strategic goal of our company has been defined. Remember that the more detailed our goal is, the more detailed our project plan will be. Therefore, the likelihood of reaching the goal goes up. The goal of our project plan is to create a task list with milestones, which will prepare a platform for the **Lemonade Stand** to grow into a modern distribution center that uses outsourced manufacturing resources. I would like to have a small distribution center with 3 to 5 employees, and be able to grow by adding new warehouses and locations. I would also like to optimize our inventory and reduce repetitive tasks. In addition, the new brand name "**Handmade by Nature**" should be established alongside our marketing slogan—**Lemonade against Global Warming**. This is a good example of a goal that is lacking detail. Therefore, I will further define that the above goal should be reached within 12 months and within a specific budget. For your project, always include the most important constraints that impact any project—time and money.

Project codename

The high-level project goal has a longer description. For companies that run many important projects simultaneously, it makes sense to establish a **project codename**. This codename is usually very short and summarizes the vision of the project. Creating a **codename** is a fun activity and allows everybody to become curious about the project. If you have any ideas for good project codenames, write them down. You can use them later. For example, **Lemonade Live 2009** represents a good codename for our project. It suggests that we will be going live with the new system soon.

Task lists

How do we reach this goal? In order to reach our goal, the project is organized in milestones that can be reached by completing tasks. The SAP Business ONE AIP is the process of subdividing a complex combination of tasks into logical groups that are all easy to manage. The overall project will be a success only when all of the relevant task groups have easy-to-follow, step-by-step tasks. Therefore, it is important to avoid tasks that have no clear definition. In that case, you need to split those tasks into a set of simple tasks. Simplifying tasks also helps to clarify potential communication problems between different departments. A checklist is a good tool to make sure that a certain set of tasks is completed. A good example may be a pilot who completes a checklist. The pilot is not an engineer who maintains the airplane. However, by completing the checklist, the pilot provides the information needed by the **engineering department** about the status of the plane.

The limited resources

A key aspect of project management is to balance the **limited resources** against your goal. As a starting point, always include time, money, and human resources as potential limited resources. However, there could be additional constraints specific to your project. What are the constraints for your own project? Think about it for a moment and write down your ideas. Additional constraints may be compliance requirements imposed by government regulations, or seasonal requirements.

Progress reporting and controlling using checklists

The only way to reach our goal is to complete the relevant tasks without exceeding the defined limited resources. In order to measure progress and make any required adjustments, we need to regularly review the tasks completed and the budget that has been consumed. This process is often called **project controlling**. I recommend using checklists to measure progress. Each item on the checklist must have a certain set of characteristics to be considered successful. For example, you can establish a **baseline** concept to measure your actual project cost and resource usage against the planned parameters. The baseline represents the values you had planned and started with, while the checklist provides the actual values. This way, you can quickly see if your target values are met and make required adjustments accordingly.

Project management resources

To further investigate the profession of **project management**, I recommend that you visit the PMI (Project Management Institute) web site for similar resources. The PMI is a professional organization that is dedicated to project management. Please search the web for **PMI Project Management** to find more information about the professional skills related to project management. Their web site can be found at http:// www.pmi.org.

Step-by-step SAP project plan preparation

Now that the basics are set, it's time to get started. In order to follow the next steps, you will need a letter-size notebook, a file folder, and Microsoft Project or Excel along with a folder on a file server, or a laptop. There is a computerized, digital side of project management, but there is also a physical, paper-based side. During the completion of the tasks in our project, we will create and receive processed documents that were generated while working on tasks. Those documents will be stored in an electronic form on a central server and will also be printed. The printed documents will be saved in our file folder.

Consequently, the project plan does not stand by itself, but comes with real printed documents. For this purpose, I recommend establishing a dedicated file folder. The file folder needs to accommodate different sections and allow the insertion of printed documents in each section. It is organized alongside the milestones that we will establish in the project plan. Each milestone will generate characteristic files, which will document the status and progress made in a format which addresses the information requirements of the particular tasks covered during a milestone. The concept of a structured project plan with associated documents is a framework called the **AIP (Accelerated Implementation Plan)** for the SAP Business ONE application. The approach of managing project documents can go through great lengths ranging from a simple physical folder, to a full-featured digital document management platform. In this book, I am assuming a startup situation where you will establish your own folder. I will provide screenshots of Microsoft Project later in this chapter.

Hands-on activity

Based on this introduction, please write down the following information on a piece of paper from your letter-size notebook:

- Your goal, budget, and personnel
- Project codename
- The scheduled time you have allocated for this project

This shouldn't be a long description, but rather a bullet-point list which will provide the cornerstones of the later project plan. In order to create the project plan, I will now introduce you to the SAP ASAP methodology, and then prepare an SAP AIP with you.

How to speed things up?

In today's world, everything needs to be fast. However, isn't it a fact of life that it will take you extra time if you want to bypass the next logical step? This is also the case with project management in general, and SAP specifically. When it comes to larger projects, you can speed things up only to a certain point by bringing in additional manpower. For example, building a house takes time due to the nature of the process and it cannot be done in one day by adding an infinite amount of resources. Certainly, you can counter back that it is actually possible to build a house in one day using **prefabricated house kits**. OK. That's where the AIP comes into play. It is sort of an assembly kit for the SAP project.

The perfect project

So how can things be sped up? SAP has developed a set of documents and guidelines which are combined with best practices for specific industries, which will assist in planning the perfect project. This limits the surprises and aligns the budget with the scheduled resources and timelines.

However, what makes the perfect project plan different from our own project plan? Think of it this way: If you work on a project and make mistakes, you will make sure that you don't repeat those very same mistakes in the future. At least, I hope so. The same is true for the SAP projects. In an industry where bad news spreads more rapidly than good news, SAP developed a system to make sure that new projects can benefit from the previous mistakes of similar projects. For example, extensive time and budget consumption are common issues. We want to make sure that we optimize those factors.

The SAP procedural model

The procedural model was one of SAP's first attempts to establish a methodology that was designed to create an easy-to-manage project plan, which will cover all aspects of the project. Before the procedural model was established, projects suffered from the organizational deficiencies that SAP was trying to overcome. For example, before SAP, companies would think heavily in terms of departments, and would lose sight of the complete processes that covered more than one department. With SAP, the goal was to create more integrated processes. However, the departments would only participate to re-enforce the old model of separation. The procedural model helped to create an integrated process. Let's take a peek at a visual representation of the SAP procedural model.

The big SAP "procedural model"

The **procedural model** was developed for **big SAP**. When I say **big SAP**, I am referring to R/3 and mySAP. I bring this to the table to give you an overview of how things are planned in larger projects. It helps you understand how to change your plan if you have a larger team involved with your SAP Business ONE implementation. In addition, SAP Business ONE is often implemented for smaller satellite offices that actually need to integrate with a larger headquarter which may run a larger SAP solution. In this case, you know a bit about their project methodology. You see that the procedural model is colour-coded. The first section is in green and represents the organizational and conceptual design phase. In this phase, the project is prepared. All departments will designate their project team and relevant project leaders. The project leaders will collect information within their department, and then collaborate with the other team leaders. The team leaders and their project members in the departments will be briefed about the overall process. This way, everybody is clear about how the project will be organized. If you look in the green section of the procedural model, you can see Design Interfaces and Enhancements. This means the departmental project teams will not only define their own processes, but will also work on how they **interface** or **exchange information** with other departments.

So for larger projects, it's all about creating teams that focus on specific tasks and also having those teams interact via team leaders. During the progression of the project, it is important to establish regular **quality checks** to make sure the overall project scope is still in order.

The SAP Accelerated Implementation Program

The SAP Business ONE AIP is a modified version of the SAP procedural model, which was adjusted and simplified based on the most commonly found SAP Business ONE project environments. Mainly, the changes honor the fact that Business ONE projects are smaller in size than the common mySAP projects. The reason I brought both of the methodologies to your attention is to highlight the fact that even though the SAP AIP for Business ONE model is different from the mySAP Procedural Model, it is still built on the same idea. In addition, with SAP Business ONE possibly being implemented from very small- to large-sized companies, some organizational project management aspects should be included in the SAP AIP, depending on the size of the implementation. For example, you can implement SAP Business ONE for a small startup with two people. However, it can also be implemented for larger companies with up to 250 employees. The project plan needs to honor both scenarios.

Project milestones based on the Implementation Blueprint

The SAP Business ONE Implementation Blueprint has five essential milestones or phases.

These five phases are:

1. Handover from Evaluation
2. Analysis and Design
3. Installation andCustomization
4. Handover
5. Training and Continuous Improvement

I will now briefly explain all of these phases. Each phase is important. However, our project plan will focus on Phase 2.

Phase 1: Handover from Evaluation

The handover from evaluation phase means setting the scope of the implementation. Based on the information you were able to gather during the decision-making process, you should have an idea about what SAP Business ONE will do for you. SAP provides demo databases for different industries that you can use to test the system. Most commonly, a series of demos are prepared. During this phase, your requirements and expectations are matched with the capabilities of the system on a high level. In addition, the timeline is established.

Therefore, let's list the relevant tasks for our project plan with reference to Phase 1:

Handover

- **Describe business processes and functional requirements** – This is a brief description of the **core** processes of your business. It is meant to be brief and to the point. The SAP system will have to cover all of the core processes.

- **Develop a time schedule** – This is the time schedule you have planned for the project. For example, you may want to start and finish the project at certain times to complete the project before the end of an accounting period. In addition, you may want to complete the main tasks of the project during off-season times.

- **Describe the structure of the company and responsibilities** – Write down all of the project participants and key players. Based on their involvement, participants can plan their schedule.

- **Use the customized demo database** – During the evaluation phase, you should have used a demo database to make sure that the system's functionality accommodates your style and work environment. For example, many systems have similar features. However, it would be crucial to see if the way SAP handles a process complies with how you want to do things.

- **Identify unconventional business processes** – Most businesses already know if they have specific processes that are very uncommon and yet important. You should make sure to write down these uncommon processes and include them in the project plan.

- **Identify activities and the amount of data to be migrated** – Here, you basically identify the data (if any) you want to migrate. Businesses will often have existing customer data with contacts which needs to be brought over.

Kick-off meeting

- **Present implementation methodology** – During the kick-off meeting, the implementation methodology will be introduced to all project participants. This essentially explains everybody's involvement.

- **Review available resources** – This is a summary of available resources that contribute to the project progress.

- **Review the time schedule** – The **kick-off meeting** is a good point to verify the validity of the assigned time. Participants often have suggestions about how time can be optimized.

Create a project binder

The project binder is a physical document folder, which will hold the physical documents that are generated during project execution.

Hands-on again—starting your implementation blueprint

Please gather your dedicated project file folder. This folder has the following information that you have already prepared:

- Your goal, budget, and personnel
- Project codename
- The scheduled time you have allocated for this project

I recommend that you take the file folder and review the bullet-point list that you already created, and then continue as follows: Look at the first task—*Describe business processes and functional requirements*. Use your favorite word processor, or simply write down how your business works on a piece of paper. Don't worry too much about how SAP may handle things at this point. Just write down how your business works and point out some key areas where you think your business is special or unique.

Project binder and documents

The project binder is a physical representation of the progress and the history of our project. It basically includes things such as the handwritten notes you made with information about the project goal. You may also have documents from the vendor from whom you purchased SAP. It is a good idea to archive the relevant documents in this folder for later reference, if need be. Therefore, the project binder should, at a minimum, contain a letter-size notebook with handwritten notes about the project. Each page should be dated. It could also contain a printed project plan and additional office documents.

Documents for tasks

As a part of the project plan, I included the main documents that you will obtain as we progress. For example, as I mentioned earlier, you will start by writing a high-level description of how your business works. This will be included with the project binder in the **Phase 1** section. Note that the list of documents is only a guideline. You must add any additional documents that are relevant.

Phase 1 documents

- Company's core process description
- Risk assessment
- Proposal history
- Contract

Phase 2 documents

- Issue log
- Timelined organizational diagram
- Departmental process description
- Meeting minutes
- Test scripts per department

Phase 3 documents

- Hardware configuration
- Service-level agreement

Phase 4 documents

- Go-Live checklist

Phase 5 documents

- Training plan
- Continuous improvement plan

Project plan for Phase 1

Based on the tasks that you have to complete in this phase, I created the project plan outline that you can see in the following screenshot. The screenshot shows an outline for Phase 1. You can see that the project is organized in a hierarchical manner. Phase 1 has a subset of tasks that need to be completed in order to accomplish this part of the project. The **+** sign indicates that there are associated subtasks. However, by hiding the subtasks, it becomes easier to get an overview of the overall project structure.

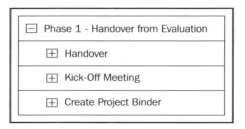

 Open Microsoft Project or Excel, and write down the phases and tasks I am listing here. As a result, you should have a full project plan. In addition, create a divider in the file folder that represents each phase of the project. Consequently, you will have a project plan and a physical folder that can hold printed documents for each phase.

In order to show the details for **Phase 1**, I opened up all of the subtasks in the next screenshot. You can add the same details to your plan and make adjustments based on your individual requirements.

⊟ **SAP Business ONE Implementation Plan**
⊟ **Phase 1 - Handover from Evaluation**
⊟ **Handover**
Describe business processes and functional requirement
Develop a time schedule
Describe the structure of the company and responsible
Use the customized Demo Database
Identify unconventional business processes
Identify activities and amount of data to be migrated
⊟ **Kick-Off Meeting**
Present implementation methodology
Review available resources
Review the time schedule
⊟ **Create Project Binder**
Phase Organization
⊟ **Phase 1**
Company Core Process Description
Risk Assessment
Proposal History
Contract
⊟ **Phase 2**
Issue Log
Time Lined Organizational Diagram
Departmental Process Description
Meeting Minutes
Test Scripts per Department
⊟ **Phase 3**
Hardware Configuration
Service Level Agreement
⊟ **Phase 4**
Go-Live Checklist
⊟ **Phase 5**
Training Plan
Continuous Improvement Plan

Phase 2: Analysis and design

This is the key phase of the project. In this phase, the actual configuration of the system takes place. The configuration is based on the requirements you communicated and the way those requirements were matched with the SAP settings. With software projects, it is important to understand that the system will only do what you configure it to do. The system will generally not make any assumptions about your business. Therefore, it is crucial that you are able to clearly describe your requirements.

Dividing the analysis into subjects

Organizing the tasks into subjects will help you manage the requirements on a departmental level. How is this done? Just open the SAP interface and look at the menu. Basically, the menu is organized into **subjects** or **departments**. Those will be the sections we look at. What does this mean to you? The sections in the SAP menu will be the project sections in our project plan. This means that if you do not perform any "**production**", this section can be left out in your project plan. It also concludes that if you have a key process that is not available in any of the sections, it is probably not available in SAP with the standard installation. This will require programming or selection of a qualified add-on solutions.

Project plan for Phase 2

Based on the established strategy to enter all of the tasks into a project planning tool, please continue this process based on the tasks as outlined in the following screenshot:

- ⊟ **Phase 2 - Analysis and Design**
  - ⊟ **Process Analysis and Design**
    - **Clarify and elaborate on all business process defined**
    - **Define Business Process needs in detail**
    - **Establish Schedule for Workshops**
  - ⊟ **Divide into subjects**
    - **Sales Process**
    - **Purchasing Process**
    - **Inventory Management**
    - **Production Process and Material Requirements Manage**
    - **Financials and Chart of Accounts**
    - **Sales Opportunities**
    - **Service**
    - **Banking**
    - **Reporting**
  - ⊟ **Solution Architecture**
    - **Define Authorizations and Data Ownership**
    - **Define Hardware Requirements**
    - **Review Data Conversion Needs (Amount and Type of**
    - **Review any Integration Points with any 3rd Party Solut**
    - **Review critical success factors**
    - **Identify limitations in SAP and discuss workarounds**
  - ⊟ **Explore solution possibilities such as**
    - **User-Defined Fields**
    - **Formatted Searches**
    - **Queries**
    - **Use of SDK**
    - **Define specifications**
    - **Create Project Plan and Assign Tasks**
  - **Update Project Binder and Review**

 The **Update Project Binder and Review** task is a part of each phase and assures that you save all of the physical documents you created during the completion of **Phase 2** in the project binder.

Phase 3, 4, and 5: Installation and Customization, Handover, and Training

Since the key part of the project is **Phase 2**, I will not extend any further into the other phases at this point. However, I will complete those phases later as we progress with the case study. In order to provide a complete project plan, I have added the relevant tasks for each phase in the following sections.

Project Plan for Phase 3

This phase primarily covers the tasks ranging from physical hardware installation of the SAP Business ONE Server with all related IT tasks to actually configuring the SAP system based on the information gathered in **Phase 2**. While all of the work in **Phase 2** is focused on **how** we can configure the system based on the requirements, in Phase 3, we conduct all of the consequential settings based on the information retrieved in Phase 2. Therefore, in phase 2 we decide how to run the system and also document the right settings. In Phase 3, we apply this to the system. Look at the following screenshot:

```
☐ Phase 3 - Installation
    ☐ Hardware and Software
            Size Hardware based on Users and Transactions
            Purchase Hardware
            Operating System
            SQL Server Database
            SAP Version Selection and Patch Level
    ☐ IT Installation
            Install Initial Version and Updates
            Create Database
    ☐ Data Migration
            Migrate Master Data
            Receive Raw Data and Prepare for Migration
            Test imported data
            Sign-Off on Imported Data
    ☐ SAP System Configuration
            Implement Business Process Requirements
            Create Users and Authorizations
            Create UDFs and Tables
            Customize Forms and Printout Templates
            Create Queries as defined
            Create Reports as defined
            Create Alerts as defined
            Define Approval Procedures
            Create Screen Layouts via user settings
        Update Project Binder and Review
```

Project plan for Phase 4

Phase 4 focuses on designing a Go-Live procedure that fits in with your profile. For example, many companies decide to go live on a Sunday. Therefore, they will make sure all minor issues will be fixed by Monday morning. This reduces the risk of having to deal with last-minute issues during business hours. In addition, arrangements are usually made to have the IT personnel available for this phase. There should also be a fallback plan in case Go-Live fails for some reason. Take a look at the following screenshot:

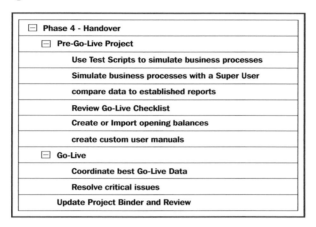

Project plan for Phase 5

This phase deals with training and the continuous improvement plan. Training is not only required for how to use the system, but also for additional resources provided by SAP. SAP provides a customer portal where additional information (for example, for software updates and SAP Notes) can be found. The continuous improvement plan can be scheduled based on requirements. This is sometimes accomplished by the means of a quarterly review. The SAP users collect all ideas and issues in a central document. Then during a quarterly review meeting, those new features are discussed and implemented based on preference. Check out this screenshot:

The project plan—the main outline

Based on the five phases, we uncovered the appropriate project structure for our SAP Business ONE Implementation project. In the following screenshot, you can see that I have a simple five-phase structure. If you follow the sequence of tasks I have presented for each phase, and enter them in your own project plan, your project document should look the same as mine. Each phase requires that the previous phase be completed, which is why I have defined the **Predecessors** column. For example, Phase 2 has Phase 1 as its predecessor, which starts in row 4. This way we can estimate the overall project length. As you can see, the estimated time for the average SAP Business ONE project is about 88 days. Please use this method to assign predecessors. In addition, assign your own time based on the schedule that you established with your team. You can then roughly estimate the duration of your SAP project. However, this number is only a guideline and depends on a series of factors. The following factors may impact the time for your project:

- Time available for project management
- Training requirements and completion
- Requirement to develop a custom add-on
- Market situations (for example, your company may have to meet business deadlines)
- Milestone decisions and progress

An important fact to remember when planning the project is that it is a good practice to set realistic moderate milestones. As it is the nature of an SAP project that all departments of a company are involved, there is a good chance of delays taking place.

	ⓘ	Task Name	Duration	Start	Finish	Predecessors
1						
2		⊟ SAP Business ONE Implementation Plan	88 days?	Mon 2/2/09	Wed 6/3/09	
3						
4		⊞ Phase 1 - Handover from Evalution	13 days?	Mon 2/2/09	Wed 2/18/09	
36						
37		⊞ Phase 2 - Analysis and Design	32 days?	Thu 2/19/09	Fri 4/3/09	4
67						
68		⊞ Phase 3 - Installation	24 days?	Mon 4/6/09	Thu 5/7/09	37
97						
98		⊞ Phase 4 - Handover	9 days?	Fri 5/8/09	Wed 5/20/09	68
110						
111		⊞ Phase 5 - Training and Continuous Improvement	10 days?	Thu 5/21/09	Wed 6/3/09	98

The project plan and issue log management

You now have the right plan with a physical binder, where you can add you own notes along with other relevant documents. The binder may be organized into sections, where each section represents a major task group. For example, you can establish a section for each phase, and then a separate the section for each **subject** that you find is important for your business. Consequently, you may now have a physical binder with five phases. Phase 1 has a high-level description of your business. Phase 2 has all of the **subjects** that SAP has to offer. Plus, you have a project plan either in Microsoft Project or Excel with a top-down list of all of the tasks explained in this section. There is one more thing that I would like to recommend. We call it the "Issue Log Management Sheet". This is an Excel spreadsheet where you list all of the issues that you come across when progressing through your project. This helps to keep track of issues and how they were resolved. This **issue log** becomes especially important during **testing**. Once we are going through the test scripts and trying to use the system, we will probably find issues with forms and functionalities. We should establish a platform to manage those issues. This is done via an issue log system.

Summary

In this chapter, we laid the groundwork for the SAP Business ONE Implementation. We looked at the SAP Implementation Guide and put it within the context of the SAP Procedural Model for larger projects. Structuring the project during the phases and creating task groups based on SAP **departments** allows the scaling of an implementation project for your environment. This could range from a small one-person team to a larger team with project managers on a per-department basis. You also learned how to add your own sections if your implementation has specific requirements that are not covered in this chapter.

In addition, I stressed the point that you may want to establish a physical binder for your project. All of the documents related to the SAP project will be collected here.

With this concept, you have the tools at your disposal to organize a multitude of tasks in your SAP project. This way, you can control and make sure that your SAP Implementation is a success.

5
Business Process Analysis and SMBs

In the previous section of this book, I compared the SAP Accelerated Implementation Method with a prefabricated house kit. The purpose of this house kit was to speed up the project and make use of knowledge acquired from similar implementations. In order to expand on this example, it could be said that the SAP functionality can represent all of the furniture and appliances we will put into this house in order to move in. Wait a second now. Something is missing here. We have the house and it is fully furnished like the best model home could ever be. What could possibly be missing? If you look at the small and medium business landscapes today, you can see that there are many small businesses with just one employee, whereas there are also businesses with more than 100 employees that also belong to the small business category. In addition, there are major functional differences. While some businesses are retail-oriented and only serve their neighborhood needs, other small businesses have many locations. For example, automotive suppliers, often establish their production sites close to major automobile manufacturers all over the world. Consequently, the **house** that we should build for the **neighborhood retailer** may look different from the **house** we need to build for a **worldwide automotive supplier**. We need an **architect** who will design the house. The architect will design the **prefabricated house kit** for our type of business. Likewise, the business process analyst will close the gap and design the architectural blueprint for our SAP implementation.

Being a business architect for your own SAP solution

In this chapter, you will temporarily assume the position of a business architect to design the architectural blueprint which will be used to accommodate all SAP functionalities. The decisions you make as an architect will have long-lasting effects. For example, if we built a high rise, our architectural plan will be quite different from a one-story building. The following sections will provide the opportunity to apply your new knowledge to your own business situation. In order to do that, I suggest you to get an A3-size piece of paper and a pencil. As we continue through this chapter, I will let you know how to use this paper in order to prepare the **prefabricated house kit** for your business. I will use the **Lemonade Stand** case study to apply the techniques. You can take the case study methods as examples for your own work.

Business process analysis is used for strategy

At this point, you understand that business process analysis is a strategic component. It is used to design the long-term platform that your business operates on. However, while designing long-term strategies and goals, we need to consider many smaller aspects of the implementation. All of the different departments with their distinct needs must be addressed. For example, the sales department may look at an item very differently than the maintenance department. The sales department looks at the item categories and its attributes as they are perceived by customers. The maintenance department may look at serial numbers and maintenance cycles, as well as knowledge base information about issues related to an item. Business process analysis is also used to address this **communication** issue.

Business process analysis is used for requirements analysis

In **Lost in Translation** one of my favorite movies, Bill Murray plays an aging actor who arrives in a major city in Japan to create a whisky commercial. During the course of the events to create the commercial, he is confronted with many cultural differences that seem odd to people like us who are from the western world, but for the Japanese culture, they are not so unusual. Therefore, when crossing cultural boundaries and using a translator, there is a great chance that although we communicate using the right words, there are many little differences in meaning which will lead to the situation where information is **lost in translation**.

When working with integrated software, such as the SAP Business ONE application, or similar so-called ERP systems, the potential to come across the very same problem is great. For example, look at the very different departments that are integrated and **talking to each other** in SAP. The finance, production, and sales modules for example. It is no news that finance people may not entirely speak the **same** language as sales people do. Who would be surprised if there was content that was **lost in translation**?

Consequently, that's a bit of a problem. The system has to overcome this challenge as the very design of an integrated system requires that all modules **talk to each other**. This is the entire point of an integrated system.

How to talk to your ERP system

There is more. How can we find out about the functionality the integrated SAP Business ONE system has to offer? How can we communicate with an ERP system to recieve the right information about what it can do, and then communicate back to what it should do? As you can see, there is a lot of communication to be made, and we 'd better not lose any valuable information on the way. The concepts and techniques I am presenting here are designed to help you define the exact requirements of your business. We are not discussing any type of programming, protocols, or similar technical aspects here.

This chapter will cover the tools and techniques used to make sure that you can efficiently communicate with SAP, or any other ERP system, without being lost in translation.

In order to explain the methods available which will ensure the ERP system functionality matches our requirements, I will cover the following:

- Learn why BPR (Business Process Re-engineering) is important - You will temporarily assume the role of a business process analyst. We will see why business process analysis is beneficial for your business.

- How to use BPR for your own business - In this section, you will get a toolset-type framework of models and guidelines which will help you complete your own BPR project in an SAP environment.

- How to prepare a time-lined organizational chart – This section explains why even a simple organizational approach can have important, long-term benefits for your project. This will be accompanied by an example time-lined organizational chart for the Lemonade Stand.

- Explain what a process is – Here, we will focus on the EPC (Event-driven Process Chain) concept. This method is used by SAP to describe how the system works. It is a very simple concept.
- How to create models for the Lemonade Stand – At this point, we will discuss the framework and the relevant models we can use. Let's put it to work with the Lemonade Stand case study.

Using business process analysis tools for your business

Business process analysis tools are used to define strategic direction and to nail down the detailed requirements for departmental process requirements. With regards to this **strategic** aspect, I will show you the **time-lined organizational chart** technique. This will help you design your own strategy. I will then expand on this and show you the process analysis models you can use to define your requirements so that no information is lost.

Let's get started with the time-lined organizational chart.

Time-lined organizational chart

The **time-lined organizational chart** helps you document the organizational structure of your current business alongside its key success factors. Your future plans for the business are also considered. By doing this, we will make sure that a **platform for growth** is created. This means that as the business grows, we can use the SAP system as a platform for this growth and avoid the need to re-think the way the system was implemented every time we face changes.

"Lemonade Stand"—key success factors

In order to explain this method, I would like to apply the technique to our Lemonade Stand case study. Let's write down the most basic success factors of the Lemonade Stand:

- Direct customer interaction
- Custom lemonade for larger orders
- Natural ingredients

I established these **key success factors** based on the uniqueness of our offering. I believe that most customers purchased the lemonade in our case study because of the key factors above. By understanding these elements, we are able to expand our current business and reach our future goals.

Defining your own "key success factors"

Alongside this case study, you may now use the A3 paper you have prepared to write down the key success factors of your business. Write them down in the upper-left corner of the A3 paper. The key success factors are a bullet point list of characteristics that differentiate your offerings from the competition. This is where the customer perceives unique value when deciding to go for your products. What characteristics does your business have?

As we move on, we will add information to this A3 sheet. See the following screenshot to get a quick overview of what we will cover in the following sections. We will first start by identifying the **success factors,** and then define the strategic direction. The key component is the organizational chart, as it will help us determine the core structure of our business. Finally, the core processes will be defined. The return of investment factors are the monetary representation of our core processes, and will help us justify the possible process improvements. As the path we are following from **success factors** to **ROI factors** resembles the letter **Z**, I like to refer to this method as the **Z-strategy**:

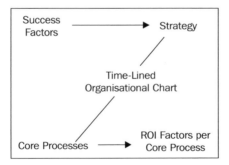

The Lemonade Stand strategy

Based on the key success factors, I would like to further define a fictitious strategy for the Lemonade Stand case study. The strategy builds upon the **key success factors** to develop a long-term strategic direction, which will further strengthen the uniqueness of our offering.

In today's business world, we need to walk the thin line of using highly specialized anonymous tools, while at the same time offering a personalized service for our customers. We want our customers to feel that they are taken care of in a very personal way. The Lemonade Stand will implement a focused and specialized sales organization. In addition, a sales process for Storefront Sales, Event Sales, and also Internet Sales will be designed.

The Lemonade Stand will not incorporate the requirements and regulations of the **Food and Beverage** industry into its operational core expertise. The Lemonade Stand will meet those requirements through qualified outsourcing solutions.

The core expertise of the Lemonade Stand operation will be in the **Distribution Center** area. The Lemonade Stand will implement a platform that uses the latest, state-of-the-art distribution center technologies in order to gain a competitive advantage.

Combined with a focused individualized sales strategy, the Lemonade Stand will uniquely meet the customer and market requirements. This platform will grow using the distribution center features. Based on the success factors in our example, we would like to establish the brand name **Hand-made by Nature**.

Your own "strategy"

You see that the strategy design in this example focuses on establishing what we **make** as a business and what we **buy** from other business partners. Please utilize these two cornerstones as a guide to define your own strategy. Please refer to the **key success factors** you wrote down in the upper-left corner of your A3 sheet when writing your own strategy. Now, write down the strategy in the upper-right corner of the A3 sheet. You now have an A3 sheet of paper with the key success factors of your business in the upper-left corner, and the **strategy** of your business in the upper-right corner. The **strategy** is aligned with the key success factors and will build a long-term platform for your business.

The Lemonade Stand "time-lined organizational chart"

In our Lemonade Stand that we implemented in the first three chapters, the following organizational structure will have evolved. We did not consider any strategic direction at that point and therefore treated all modules as equal:

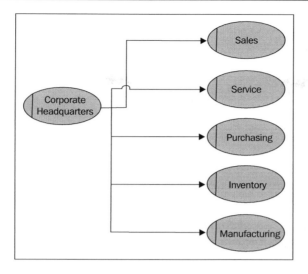

It essentially reflects the SAP modules and their available functionality. With the newly established strategic direction, we can now better specify the representation of the organization.

Based on the strategy I laid out during the strategy definition, an updated organizational diagram is due:

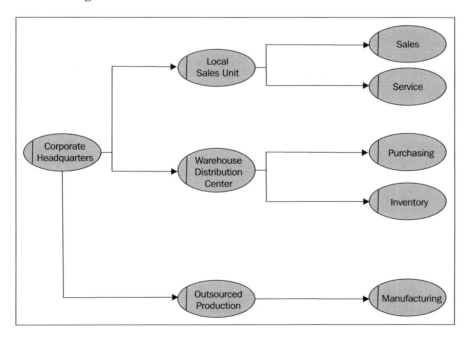

You can see that the organizational chart looks quite different from our initial design. This chart makes it clear where we want to go with our business. Let's now take this chart as a basis for defining how we want to implement the system today. By doing this, we can make sure that our future expansion plans do not interfere with our initial design and implementation. In fact, our initial design and implementation strategy will fully support all of the changes we have in mind.

There are two important design decisions we will make for the system implementation. They are:

- Web-based storefront design for sales – We need to make sure that SAP Business ONE has the right tools to establish a web e-commerce sales channel.

- Distribution center – We will need to make sure that SAP Business ONE can evolve into a high-end distribution center platform. This will include barcoding with shipping, and receiving using portable computer scanners. We will also need to accommodate integration points with UPS, FedEx, and so on, for shipping rates and tracking. In addition, we need inventory optimization to make sure our inventory investments are optimized.

Your own "time-lined organizational chart"

You must have noticed that the organizational diagram I created is entirely based on ovals that are connected using arrows. Each oval represents an organizational unit. Based on the key success factors and the core strategy that you have noted down on the A3 sheet, use the oval notation to define your own organizational diagram. Keep in mind that you are not looking at how it is organized today, but rather how you would like to have it organized in the next five years. The chart that you design should go in the very middle of the A3 sheet. You see, this is evolving from the upper-left **key success factors**, to the upper-right **strategy**, and then arriving in the middle. When designing your own chart, keep in mind what you will want to **make** and what you will want to **buy** from other business partners. What you buy can most likely be **outsourced**. For example, you can have a **warehouse and distribution center** outsourced alongside manufacturing. This would mean that your company only focuses on the design of the product and invests in the raw materials which will be manufactured. As you can see, it is a good idea to focus your efforts on your area of expertise and then **outsource** or buy the other parts.

Since the design of the **time-lined organizational chart** is heavily built upon the **strategy** you developed, let's look a bit more at why **strategy** is important. This may be a slightly reiterative process. Therefore, you will find by looking at your chart that you want to adjust the strategy a bit, and vice versa.

Painting a coherent picture from a set of yellow sticky notes

Having an established strategy in place, all of the different requirements and changes that we confront every day, can now be put into a larger strategic context. For example, now that we know we will establish a distribution center alongside specialized sales, we will not need to worry about how we will need to comply with the **Food and Beverage** industry's production regulations. However, we can collect information that is relevant for the distribution center, and for our sales on the way, and use it to improve our strategic goals. We can collect information in a meaningful way, and then utilize the **experience** that we gain to drive **innovation** that fits our strategy.

Think about it, by just starting up the Lemonade Stand, we were able to accomplish some short-term goals. However, isn't it also a fact that no Lemonade Stand sticks around for a long period? With a strategy in place, we will collect information that supports our long-term goals and also improve the **value chain** step-by-step.

Based on this realization, it becomes clear that the process of documenting **what** we are planning to do versus **how** is going to be a continuing process.

To summarize, the **what** defines our strategy while the **how** explains the way we will implement this in the SAP system. Keep in mind that a strategy does not get developed in one go. You may collect bullet-point-type information and put things together over time.

The "international language of ERP"

Now that we have a strategy in place, we need to find out if an ERP in general, and specifically SAP Business ONE, can do the job. We now need to put the available functionality in SAP to the test. How can we do that? The obvious way is by just opening SAP Business ONE and clicking through the available screens. However, this may not be sufficient because a screen is only meaningful when used in a business context. It may otherwise be meaningless to the outsider. In addition, by just looking at the available fields on the screens in the **inventory** section, an inventory employee may get some information about how the system maintains inventory. However, that may not satisfy the information requirements of the C-level managers. C-level managers are CEOs, CFOs, etc.

SAP uses a method called an **EPC (Event-driven Process Chain)** concept to address this situation. It consists of very basic symbols. This notation solves the problem we have when only looking at the screens. As the name suggests, we essentially have **processes** and **events**. Each event produces input for a process, and a process produces output for the next event.

I will now introduce you to the EPC notation, and use it to develop a sales process. I will also use this method to design the high-level distribution center requirements.

The EPC "Event-driven Process Chain" notation

Look at the EPC notation below. It is incredibly simple. Since we can communicate with our ERP using this **language**, and we are happy to learn that we can almost instantly **speak** the international language of ERP.

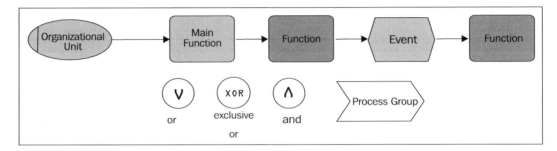

Now that we know how to communicate with the system, let's briefly define what a process really is. This is a good point to introduce this definition as the EPC notation is designed to document processes, and SAP was designed to implement those processes. It is worth noting here that the concept of EPC can be used to automatically generate screens and code. This concept is called **EPML**. You can go to `http:// www.epml.de` to find information on this interesting approach. There are also tools available that can generate EPC representations of SAP logs. Therefore, you can document the way your company works **backwards**–and thereby generate the EPCs based on how the system is used. It would be interesting to see how the initial EPCs compare to the actual EPCs to draw conclusions for improvements.

What is a process?

It would be easy to say that almost everything is part of a process. However, this would lead to process **reengineering** projects that are huge in size. It is a bit of a misunderstanding that I come across many times when talking to customers. The process analysis is **comprehensive**. However, it should not cover everything only to create a never-ending project. Always keep in mind that this method is designed to improve an implementation and not to paralyze it.

The art of process optimization, with regards to an implementation, is to focus on the **core** processes. In our example based on the defined strategy, we can easily derive the core processes from our strategy and time-lined organizational chart.

The sales process and warehouse distribution process are the key strategic components of the Lemonade Stand, and therefore also serve as the core processes.

This establishes the term **core process** as an integrated functionality derived from our strategic direction.

Designing the "core processes" for your business

On our A3 sheet, we currently have the key success factors in the top-left, and the strategy in the upper-right corner. From those items, we derived the time-lined organizational chart in the middle section of the sheet. Now, continue and write down the **core processes** on the lower section of the sheet. The **core processes** can be directly obtained by looking at the organizational units in the middle. Focus on the organizational units that are within your organization. Let me use the Lemonade Stand case study to help explain with an example. You can then go back and use this information to write down your own **core processes**.

Sales process and distribution center core processes for the "Lemonade Stand"

The future lemonade operation will have three main distinct sales areas, namely **Retail Stores**, **Internet Sales**, and **Wholesale**. These three areas will be established, as shown in the following figure. Those will be the customer types that we will need in order to implement in the system:

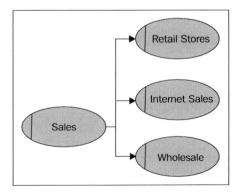

The main interaction with customers will be straightforward at this point. Each time we are interacting with a customer, in SAP Business ONE language a business partner, we will update their contact information, or create a new business partner if it is a new contact. Once this is done, we will continue the sales process or take a service call. In case the business partner is calling for the first time, I would like to offer them a sample. Once they have received a sample, a proposal will be completed. See, nothing complicated is going on. I fully trust that simplicity is the key to success. However, simplicity is not a silver bullet. That's why I introduced you to the important aspects of strategy and operational goals that continuously develop and improve the **uniqueness** of your company.

Based on the workflow we designed, the EPC can be defined. Please reference the following chart to see how the EPC notation was used to write down the core process workflow. Notice that this is not very detailed, but rather appears high-level. This is intentional as we are defining the core processes on a high level first.

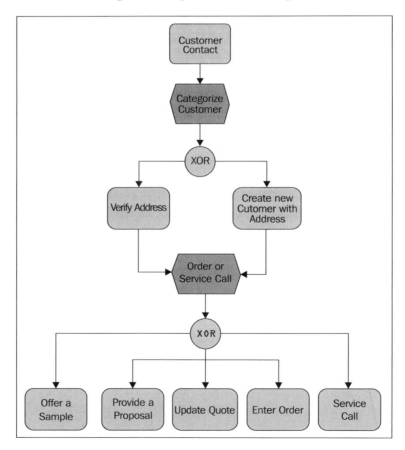

Finalizing your own "core processes"

Use the A3 sheet and write down the core processes based on your strategy. Use a name for each process, such as **Sales Process** and **Distribution Process**. Then prepare a high-level EPC notation for each process while focusing on the essential **events** from start to finish. Your business may be complex, however, focus on keeping this simple and at a higher level. Nevertheless, list all of the core processes you have in mind for your business. While doing this, always consider that you should not worry about **how** things are done, but rather on **what** will be done.

You now have a full strategy paper in front of you. Based on this A3 sheet, you will be able to branch out and allow each department to define the process chart at the required level of detail. This will be done using Visio, or any other popular flowcharting and process analysis tool. Based on your budget, you can use paper and pencil, Visio, Aris Toolset, or Casewise, for example.

Project status—where are we now?

Before we continue, I will spend some time measuring our current accomplishments against the project plan. In order to show you how this works in a real world, I will start by presenting the current process analysis charts. Depending on the size of your company, this may be done by a departmental project manager or yourself.

Let's recollect the tools we have and then use them. The following tools are established in our project:

- SAP Accelerated Implementation project plan
- Process analysis tools and A3 strategy paper

Phase 1—Handover from Evaluation "Lemonade Stand"

The project plan had five phases. **Phase 1 — Handover from Evaluation** included the **kick-off meeting** and the creation of the project binder that holds the physical documents which were created during the implementation. We have accomplished all of the milestones in Phase 1. Therefore, this phase is complete.

Phase 1—your project

When you determine the status of your own project, realistically evaluate the accomplishments. At this point, I recommend you verify that the **kick-off meeting** was done and all of the available resources have been assigned. Verify that you have the project binder in order. If you have all of that, you are ready to proceed to Phase 2.

Phase 2—Analysis and Design "Lemonade Stand"

As indicated before, this is the key phase of the project. That's also why I introduced the process analysis tools. Those tools make sure that we can communicate and document the specific requirements we have. In addition, the time-lined organizational chart assisted in the creation of the strategy. The strategy helps to direct our focus on strategic success factors when performing the core process analysis.

Phase 2—your project

Before I proceed with the Lemonade Stand status report regarding Phase 2, I would like to make sure the information is put in perspective so you can use it for your own project. I designed the process diagrams for the case study in a way so that they fit available SAP Business ONE features. Therefore, you can use the process diagrams I am showing as a starting point for your own process charts. Please consider this when evaluating the case study.

Phase 2—Process Analysis Results "Lemonade Stand"

The time-lined organizational charting resulted in the following organizational structure of our Lemonade Stand. You saw that due to the strong regulatory requirements, we decided to **outsource** production and focus on warehouse and distribution center functionality. Please review the organizational chart below:

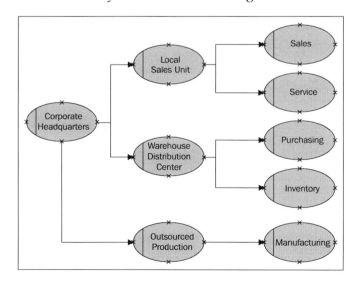

In order to proceed with this, we now know that we do not need to prepare a detailed process for **Manufacturing** since we are outsourcing this functionality. However, there are two aspects that need our full attention as we are planning to develop a set of competitive advantages. They are sales and warehouse management.

The sales process chart

The sales process chart is currently defined as outlined below. You can see that I have added a new notation called Process Path here for **Service Call**. This notation indicates that the **Service Call** has its own process chart. The reason why this was introduced is to keep a chart simple, while at the same time allowing us to branch out and create a new chart. I have also added some processes on the right. In addition, I added **Update Sales Stages**. Based on the process description I provided earlier, we want to establish **sales stages** during the sales process. When interacting with a customer, the relevant sales stage will need to be updated. Please review the updated process chart and compare with the initial version:

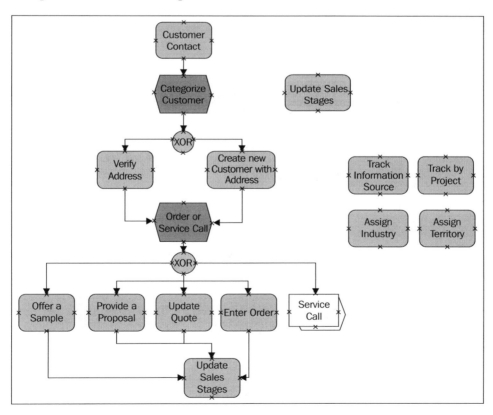

The service call process chart

The service call process chart (seen below) is linked back to the sales chart via the **Sales Order** process path icon. You see that you can create a set of simple process charts and link them back together versus creating one gigantic chart that may be confusing.

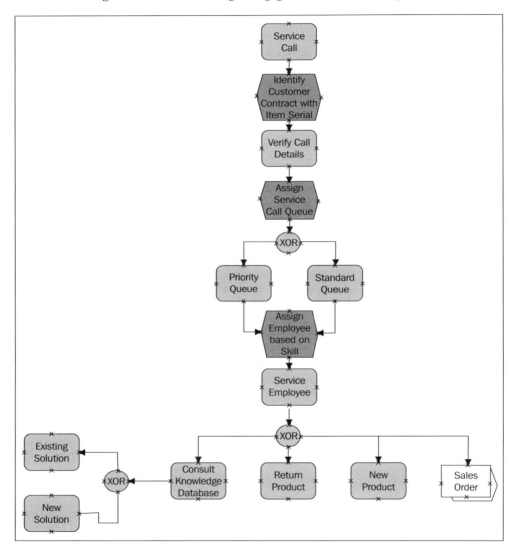

The purchase order process chart

The purchase order process chart is not complete yet. Therefore, I am listing a simplified version as follows:

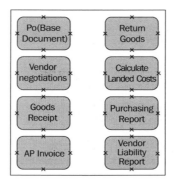

You can see that I only listed the processes. You can do this in case you have not nailed down an actual process, but start collecting functionalities in a list format. This will be the basis for a flowchart once you get there.

The MRP Process

The Material Requirements Process looks as follows. Here, I have taken all of the processes and lined them up in the manner that SAP uses them. Since SAP provides a wizard for this functionality, the chart is simplified as outlined below:

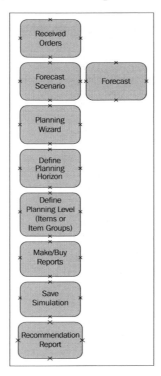

 I will explain the MRP wizard in detail later when we implement the process charts in the system.

The warehouse process

The initial configuration for the Lemonade Stand will have two warehouses. The **Main Warehouse** will hold the inventory. The **Drop-Ship Virtual Warehouse** is a special virtual warehouse in SAP that accounts for shipments made directly to the customer without having been shipped to our **Main Warehouse.** In addition, we will configure packaging assignments in the SAP system, which is represented by the **Packaging Assignment** box in the following figure:

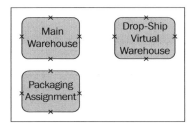

Putting it all together for your own project

You can see that we have a process chart for each section in SAP. For your own project, proceed in the same manner. Create a chart for each section. If you do not have sufficient information, just start by listing the required features and have this list evolve into a process chart at a later time.

Phase 2 "Analysis and Design" completion

Our case study now has all of the right information for each department according to our Phase 2 "Analysis and Design" requirements. In addition, you have all of the right tools available to further document any requirements you might have in your own business. At this point, let's consult the project plan and evaluate what we need to do to continue our implementation. As part of Phase 2, we have the following project task groups listed:

- Solution architecture
- Explore solution possibilities

Solution architecture for "The Lemonade Stand"

The process charts established the detailed requirements for our overall business workflow. However, this did not yet consider any access privileges for employees. It is crucial for our business to identify who has access to what. This will ensure that documents can only be created by employees who have dedicated privileges to do so. The core SAP licensing system actually promotes this concept. SAP only authorizes **named users** for the SAP Business ONE system. Thereby, a user can be assigned their access privileges to view relevant documents. For example, a sales user may view and edit all of the documents that are required to make a sale. However, they may not edit invoices, issue deliveries, etc.

Define authorizations and data ownership

Assigning privileges for small companies with two or three users may be easy. However, if you add additional salespeople, and also have a separate inventory operation, privileges can be hard to structure. In order to structure this information, I suggest we use a graphical representation that builds on our organizational units, and then expand this by adding the documents each department processes:

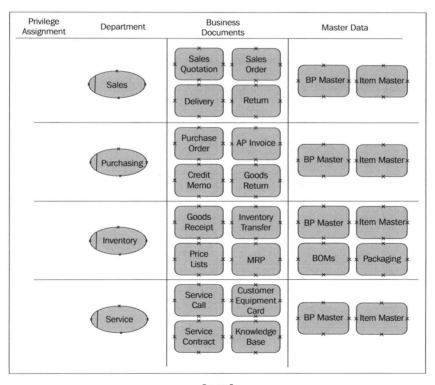

If you review the previous **workflow privileges** graphic, you can see that I have listed the organizational units. Then, on the right side, I also listed the business documents that are being processed in each department (organizational unit). In addition, each business document uses master data. I listed the **Master Data** on the very right of the workflow privileges chart. This chart resolved the following information requirements:

- You can easily assign employees to a department, and thereby determine the business documents that they will have access to.

- You can see interdepartmental communication requirements. You can better optimize your workflow if interdepartmental communication requirements are minimized. For example, it is not good if the service department needs to call the inventory department many times to resolve an issue.

- You can see the **Master Data** that your company needs in order to work. If you closely evaluate the Workflow Privileges chart per department, and look at the **Master Data** column, you can see that **BP Master** and **Item Master** show up for every department. **BP Master** represents all of the customer and vendor address information, including terms, etc. **Item Master** manages the products you sell, including warehouse location and quantities.

Master data

A system like SAP requires master data, such as business partner information, item information, and so on, to be set up. Master data is the data that your processes use and change via **events**. Remember the process notation is called EPC. Therefore, the series of events uses master data to change documents such as quotes, invoices, etc.

The master data in SAP Business ONE is fairly straightforward and has the following elements:

- Business partner master – The BP master data manages customer-related information, such as address and contact information.

- Item Master – The item master describes the items that are managed in the system. These are essentially finished goods, but could also be raw materials.

- Bill of Materials - BOMs are a specific combination of raw materials or finished goods that make a new product. The BOM thereby describes all of the items that the parent item is made of.

- Price lists can be managed in SAP based on a **base price list**. This **base price list** allows a price to be assigned to all items. New price lists can then be based on the base price list. The new price list would adjust all prices based on a factor to modify the prices. For example, a retail price list could be the base price list. The reseller price list would then take the retail price list and multiply each item by 0.8 and have a discounted reseller price list. Price lists may also define volume discounts per item. This means that an item may cost $20 per unit. However, if you buy 30 units, you get a discounted price. I will show you how to set this up in SAP once we open SAP and implement the price lists.

- Packaging allows pre-defined **packaging** sets to be defined. For example, our lemonade could come in a six-bottle box or a larger 24-bottle case.

Summary

Today's world is highly specialized. However, only being specialized is not sufficient. We need a strategy to focus on the value chain that makes our company a success. Strategic guidance will provide organizational flexibility and allows valuable information to be collected in order to improve the way we work and adjust to changing requirements.

During the course of this chapter, I introduced you to the following tools and methods:

- Time-lined organizational chart – This technique allows you to create a strategic vision for your company.

- EPC – The Event Process Chain is the **international language of ERP systems**. You are now able to speak **ERP**.

- I introduced you to the workflow privileges chart technique. This method allows cross departmental workflows to be documented and user privileges to modify documents per department. In addition, I briefly touched on **master data** and explained its key role in the ERP architecture.

Consequently, you are now able to define a proper strategy using the right techniques, and you will not run risk of miscommunications regarding your crucial requirements. Using these tools and methods, you can now be sure that no information will be **lost in translation**.

6

Implementing an Integrated Sales Strategy

Recently, as I was in the process of ordering a new laptop from my preferred IT vendor, the old laptop from the same manufacturer failed. You know how it is. These machines seem to know when you are turning to a new one. I called the service line and was asked by an auto-attendant to enter my phone number. The result was impressive as it indicated that my records were found. I was forwarded to the next available support agent. Now, it was even more surprising to hear the first question of the service technician, "Can I please have your phone number?" Well, even though I was initially prepared to provide this information, it was a bit frustrating that I had to do it again, even after their phone system seemed to have found it already. It took a while again to find the records and I was then told that I need to call another department that handles extended warranty. This department told me that the spare part I needed was not available. While on the phone, I researched their web site and found an alternative item and suggested to get that instead. The service person put me on hold and came back to confirm that the alternate item is sold by another department and not the extended warranty department. This experience made me switch my preferred IT vendor and I purchased the new laptop from another company.

It seems that the **sales** and the **service** areas were not properly **integrated**. Even though the most modern technology was at work, it only contributed to frustration rather than efficiency and improved sales.

What you will learn about SAP Business ONE sales in this chapter

The company in my initial example seemed to have all of the required information and a 360-degree customer view, but was unable to translate this into proper action. It is like placing a new Porsche engine into an old Volkswagen. You can't make full use of it if you don't change the procedures to be aligned with the potential. In this chapter, we will focus on establishing a 360-degree view with the proper action plan to turn customer interaction into sales. You will also learn about the sales methodology in SAP as we will go through the following topics:

- History of CRM – A brief overview of the reasons behind the development of modern CRM (Customer Relationship Management) systems will clarify the importance of an integrated system. We will identify problems related to the traditional **best-of-breed** approach.

- Positioning sales in the company – Identify the areas in your company where sales is influenced. We will look at **customer touch points**.

- Developing a CRM strategy – Align your processes to develop a CRM strategy. For example purposes, we will develop the core component of a strategy that uses 360-information and translates customer touch points into sales-specific workflows.

- Sales success factors – We will look at the sales success factors that you can use in the SAP Business ONE application.

- Sales workflow by example – To better understand how it works in SAP Business ONE, you will experience the key features firsthand as they relate to the sales success factors. During this process, you will understand the 360 +ONE strategy.

- Future of CRM – We'll take a look at how the future of sales may look. You can then decide if SAP is a part of it.

History of CRM

The example I provided earlier showcases the very reasons why integrated CRM systems were developed. A closer look reveals the following problems:

- No integrated service call management – The service department was not communicating with the **extended warranty department**.

- Service was not connected to sales – None of the service departments knew about the current proposals for a potential new order.

- No reports showing customers with a new sales quotation and a service call – Sales personnel never caught up and apparently were not informed about service calls. Otherwise, it could have led to faster purchases. For example, I could have received a call that went as follows: "You are planning to purchase a new system. We noticed your current service call and would like to assist getting your business up and running again..."

- Inventory levels were not available to adjust sales components based on availability – Alternative items were not available in the service department.

- Warehouse management inflexibility – The actual warehouse management functionality was not available to deliver an item from the local warehouse.

The problem is rooted in the traditional best-of-breed approach. This approach leads to each department independently selecting specialized software. CRM attempts to overcome the issues above and integrate all of the areas where the customer interacts with our company into one application. As we have seen in the example, the customer interaction actually stretches through almost all of the departments, from opportunity management to sales, service, inventory management, and warehouse management. Therefore, if you are planning to establish a sales force based on a new application, it is a good idea to consider an integrated approach.

In SAP Business ONE, all of the departments above are integrated into one system. Let's put the solution to test and see how it can handle the sample situation I described in the initial example.

Positioning CRM in your company

We just saw that an efficient CRM system is integrated with many departments. The overall transparency and real-time information we gain is often referred to as the 360-view of the customer. However, there is an issue. Let me provide you with an example. In nature, animals that have a 360-view are mostly at the very end of the food chain, while the leading species seem to have their eyes focused in a specific direction. I am using this example to emphasize that just having 360-degree information will not translate into success by itself. The 360-information needs to trigger a workflow with a specific, narrowed-down focus. In our example, the service call I placed could have triggered an alert for the sales person who is working on my proposal. The sales person could have then called me to follow up. This is one example how 360-information could have helped the specialized departments in achieving their goals.

Customer touch points

In order to identify the relevant information, and to also the trigger points that generate alerts and workflows, we start by establishing the customer touch points. Those touch points in our example are as follows:

- Service department
- Extended warranty department
- Sales or quoting department
- Inventory department
- Warehouse department

For all of the areas where a potential customer interaction takes place, a workflow must be established which will improve the overall customer experience. For your own project, you may use the flowcharting technique that we talked about in the previous chapter to create a blueprint of the customer interaction (for example, from initial phone call to service).

CRM is a strategy

Once you have a blueprint that documents customer interactions based on touch points, you can develop a sales strategy.

The sales strategy has the following components:

- Integrated information based on consistent data – All of the relevant departments should have the same information, and preferably in real-time.
- Defined workflows based on touch point events – This determines what will happen if a customer interaction takes place.
- Collaborative team work - This ensures that synergy effects are utilized. It also describes the end of the single sales person, since sales comprises of more than just sales.
- Strategy name and title with the manager responsible

Integrated information and data discipline for reporting

SAP Business ONE is based on a single database. All of the departments share the same data. Real-time information is available beyond departmental boundaries. It is important that all of the relevant data is automatically maintained as users work with the system. For example, in case you intend to use e-mail newsletters, you should make sure that e-mail addresses are collected and maintained as business partner information is entered into the system. Therefore, e-mail should be a mandatory field. You may define the exact information that you want to collect and use on a per-department basis. The collected information is also the basis for your reporting and sales metrics. We will see how the metrics for sales progress can be used via sales stages later in this chapter.

Defined workflow

Collecting the right data via mandatory fields is the basis to trigger workflows based on threshold values and performance indicators. For example, we could create an alert to a salesperson when a customer with a large opportunity is placing a service call. The handling of the service call may impact the next steps for the opportunity. In addition, we may alert a salesperson that an alternative item is available if an out-of-stock item is being quoted.

Collaborative team work

As we have seen, it is beneficial for departments to share information and work in sync with each other. Therefore, we establish a collaborative environment based on enterprise information. This way, synergy effects can be used to improve sales, service, inventory, and warehouse management processes. The information basis in our example is the SAP Business ONE database.

Summarizing the success factors for a CRM strategy

Based on the highlighted strategic components, the following functional success factors can be derived:

- Integrated system comprising all departments
- Data discipline
- Workflow
- Collaborative functionality for enterprise data

I am listing the success factors here because I will focus on these aspects during the SAP case study.

The "360 +ONE" sales strategy

This strategy comprises many departments and requires integration points on a departmental level. Therefore, it is recommended to establish a strategic sales lead in your company. This is essentially a manager who focuses on the goals of the sales strategy and also promotes it. As part of this promotion, the strategy should be assigned a name. The name should somehow reflect the core idea of the strategy. Therefore, let's list the core components of our strategy and select a proper name:

- 360-information
- Triggered workflow
- One-degree focused action

Therefore, I would call our strategy the **360 +ONE** strategy. You can do the same thing for your own project. List the key success factors and components, and identify the keywords that are motivating for all parties involved.

Implementing the 360 +ONE sales strategy with SAP Business ONE

In this section, we will use the SAP Business ONE admin functionality to configure sales stages, and then use those stages to manage opportunities. By evaluating the opportunities window, we will learn about the information that can be managed in SAP in this area. We will continue to enter marketing documents (quotations, sales orders, and so on) for an example opportunity. As we move on to manage this opportunity, you will learn how SAP Business ONE can overcome all of the described shortcomings from the example in the beginning of the chapter.

Integrated sales workflow

Here are the steps of the integrated sales workflow, which we will cover in this chapter:

- Consistent workflow **sales stages**
- Show sales stages
- Show opportunities window
- Create an opportunity

- Use warehouse information and inventory levels on line item level for quoting
- Create a quotation
- Alternate products
- Price lists
- Define volume discounts
- Schedule next follow-up call
- Drag and relate service calls
- Find service calls for an opportunity (optional alert)
- Run reports

Consistent workflow—sales stages

In SAP Business ONE, there are two main areas to look at when evaluating the screens for functionality. In the **Administration** section, you can find menus and forms which will allow you to enter data or check settings, which will then **drive** the user area. For example, in the **Administration | Setup | Sales Opportunities** section, there is a menu item called **Sales Stages**. This allows the sales stages to be set up, which will be used by our sales personnel when using the system. For our case study, I am implementing five sales stages (as seen in the following screenshot):

- **First Contact**
- **Address Collected**
- **Sample Received**
- **Discount Approved**
- **Order Form Faxed**

These sales stages are aligned with our case study—the Lemonade Stand Inc. You can design your own sales stages for your own project. This would be a good time to evaluate the sales stages that you intend to use for your company.

Take a look at the Sales Stage - Setup window in the following screenshot:

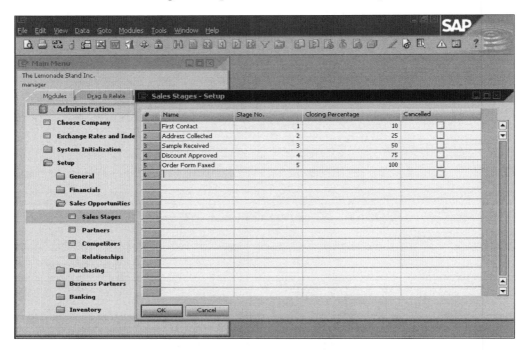

If you compare this with our initial sales process from the first section of this book, you can see that I had already decided the sales stages in my mind. It is beneficial that SAP has the above screen and allows this basic information to be entered in a simple manner.

If you take a closer look at the screenshot above, you will learn that in addition to **Sales Stages**, we can also manage **Partners**, **Competitors**, and **Relationships**. We don't need to use these information components, which is why I am not using them in our example. However, you can review them based on your own requirements.

Sales opportunities

A sales user would never use the **Administration** section to enter data. A regular sales user just expects a system that adequately maps his sales process. Therefore, let's open the **Sales Opportunity** form in the user section. A closer evaluation of this screen provides an entire set of available features that we can use. The following areas can be identified:

- Business partners can be assigned a **Business Partner Territory**. This allows regional sales departments to be developed. By just adding an opportunity and assigning a territory, the relevant regional sales department can get an alert.

- The sales opportunity is classified based on the assigned sales stage and the closing rate for the sales stage. This allows forecasting and budgeting. For example, if we have more opportunities in a region, we can adjust our inventory accordingly. In addition, we could optimize our marketing in other regions to catch up with the demand there.

- We can attach documents. This allows documents that are relevant to an opportunity to be collected and managed. This could be marketing brochures or technical information.

- We can define **Interest Range**, which means although a customer may be interested in a specific main product, he may also be interested in another product. Based on this information, we can optimize our offering and plan inventory accordingly.

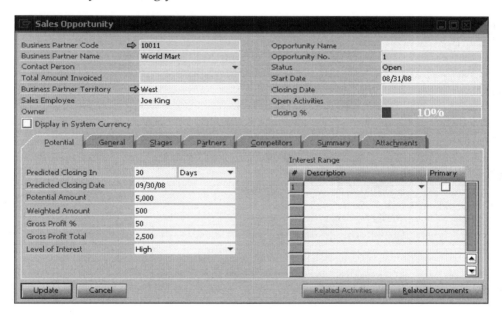

In the **General** tab page (seen in the following screenshot), we can see that we can also define and use the following information:

- **Project** – This allows sales opportunities to be tracked based on a project. For example, we can see if a trade fair activity or Google marketing activity generated sales opportunities. This will help us make better investments in marketing activities and trade fairs.

- We can specify the **Information Source**. This will allow us to establish a tracking system to know how a customer found us. This will also help in improving our marketing funds. For example, we can track how many new sales opportunities we generated based on our latest Google ad.

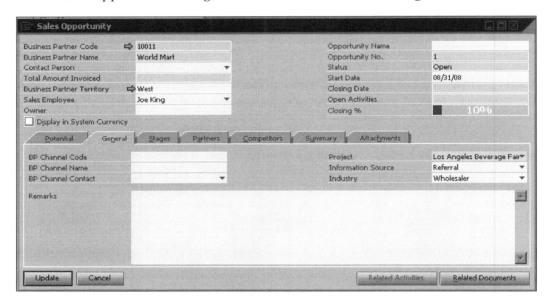

You see that we are utilizing an opportunity by entering information which will help us make better decisions regarding marketing and inventory planning. There are many other important decisions that can benefit from the collected information. Here are some additional benefits:

- Identify regional demand variations
- Identify sales personnel performance based on sales stages
- Identify high-quality lead sources
- Measure the success of trade fair activities

- Identify preferred products
- Report on products that customers had a secondary interest in
- Number of leads worked on by a salesperson
- Number of conversions from lead to customer per sales person
- Meeting time spent in relation to customer project
- Discount levels provided on average sales

The list is not complete as there are many more potential reports that you can run to gain insights into the operations of your company. In case you require additional information, you can add your own user-defined field.

Sales stages

The core feature for any CRM is the way sales stages are implemented and used. Sales stages help to structure the progress from initial contact (first call) towards the sale. By doing so, the relevant information needs can be covered and utilized with greater focus. In addition, by structuring the process into stages, each stage can be simplified. Consequently, a complex sales process is subdivided into simple tasks. As a result, you can easily train sales personnel.

Another benefit of having sales stages is the ability to better forecast future demand (this could be higher or also lower demand). By optimizing our inventory levels based on the estimated demand, we can save money and optimize investments. The analysis of sales stages may also uncover weaknesses in the sales process. For example, we could have a large number of leads with very view coming to a close. This would indicate that the lead collection is working. However, the transition from first contact to negotiating sales proposals may need improvement. Another scenario could be that a large number of projects are in progress. However, due to intense resource requirements, not enough new projects are coming in. Using the sales stages system, you can overcome these situations and plan ahead.

Overall, the structuring of the sales process into stages is beneficial. This complies with the success factors described before, namely **workflow**. In the **Stages** tab page (seen in the following screenshot), all of the documents provided for this business partner are tracked and can be referenced. In addition, the progress is tracked.

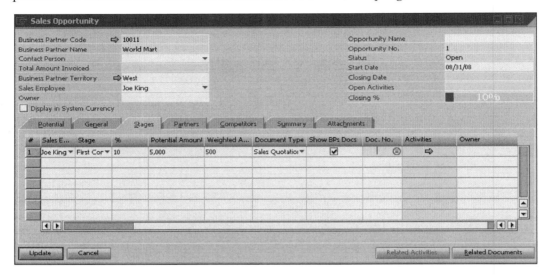

In the example screenshot above, **First Contact** is selected as the initial sales stage. As a part of this, a sales quotation can be created. This will be directly associated with the opportunity we manage here. You can create a sales proposal by selecting the **Document Type** as **Sales Quotation**, and then clicking on the icon in the **Doc. No.** field. Please note the checkbox in the **Show BPs Docs** column. When you check this option, a filter is applied. This filter ensures that only documents for the selected BP(business partner) are listed when you click on the **Doc. No.** field. Therefore, you will automatically see documents that are relevant for the BP that you are working on. This is a good source of information, as it helps you to learn about the current sales activities your company has with the potential customer.

Sales quotation

The quotation screen automatically pulls the business partner information and populates the relevant fields. You can now enter the item number and prepare the quotation. However, please note that in our introductory example, we identified a beneficial connection to the inventory levels. If you remember, the service department was not aware of inventory levels for certain items. In addition, alternative items were not available.

It would be good if we could see, on the proposal level, what the inventory levels for an item are. For example, if an item is not in stock and the customer wants to get it by the next day, we need to inform the customer ahead of time. The initial **sales quotation** screen does not show this information:

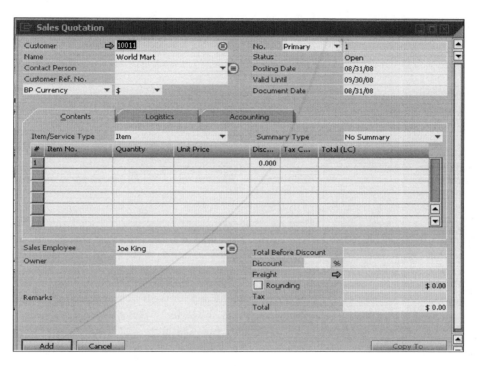

However, by selecting the **form layout** icon in the top menu bar, we can adjust the information that is presented and available here. Therefore, in order to show the relevant fields, the columns **Whse**, **In Stock**, **Committed**, and **Ordered** are checked (seen in the following screenshot) and will be **Visible** from now on.

- **Whse**: This column will show the warehouse.
- **In Stock**: This will show the number of units that are available in stock
- **Committed**: This shows the number of items that are still in the warehouse, but are already committed to other sales orders
- **Ordered**: These are the items that we ordered for our inventory, but have not yet arrived

I added all of these columns believing that we can make good use of this information during the sales process:

The updated **Sales Quotation** form (seen below) shows the information. You can see that for the selected item, the customer has requested **25** units. However, upon reviewing the inventory levels, we notice that there is not enough inventory available to cover this requirement. It would be good if we could identify similar or alternative items that are in stock and available for immediate delivery, which would satisfy the customer's need in the same way.

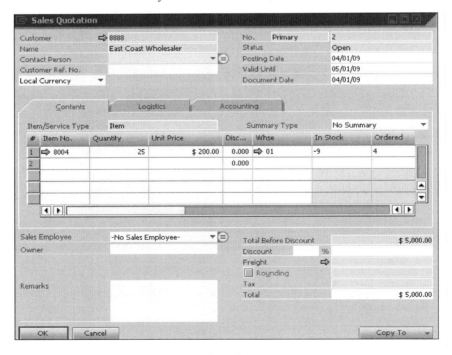

Configuring alternative items

The configuration of alternative items can be done by navigating to the
Inventory | Item Management | Alternative Items menu (seen below). You start by
selecting the item that you want to define alternatives for. In the example, **Lemonade
Basic** is selected. We will create a new item in the system. This new item could be a
promotional package that we market to all customers and leads. In addition, we may
keep sufficient inventory levels to satisfy the demand that was generated. Therefore,
customers could benefit from better pricing and availability. The alternative items,
definition can be categorized with a match factor. In the example, I specified a match
factor of 100%.

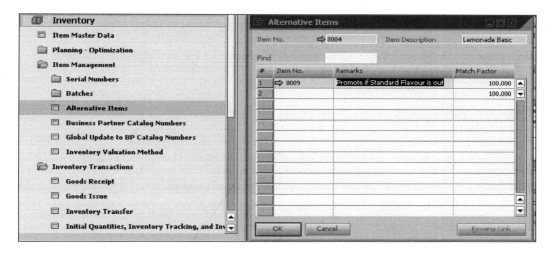

Let's now review how this would work in our sales quotation.

The previous sales quotation is open again and it is obvious that the selected item, **8004**, is not in stock. However, if you right-click on the item, a menu pops up that allows **Alternative Items** to be selected (as seen below). The selection of **Alternative Items** will reveal the item we defined in the previous step.

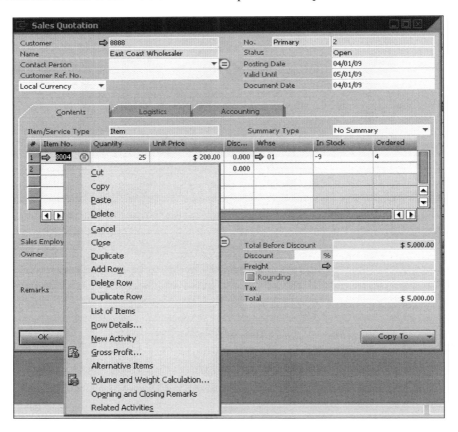

The alternative items are presented in a list alongside their inventory levels and match factor. This helps the salesperson to immediately offer the customer an alternative item that is in stock. In our example, you can see that **Lemonade Summer Edition** has 200 units in stock:

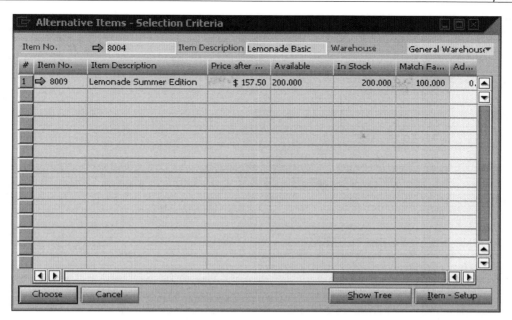

Configuring volume discounts

Based on the previous processes, we now have the right item in the proposal and are ready to deliver it. However, since the customer is ordering a larger quantity, we could provide additional incentives if certain quantities are met. Therefore, you will now learn how **volume discounts** can be configured in SAP.

The configuration menu can be reached via **Inventory | Price Lists | Period and Volume Discounts**. The **Period and Volume Discounts** form will now open up. The first aspect to note is that volume discounts are defined per price list. In our example, the **Distributor** price list was selected. Upon selecting the price list, all of the items that are available to be sold with this price list are shown. A double-click on the grey line number for the item will open the **Period Discounts** form. In order to open **Volume Discounts for Price List**, you will need to again double-click on the grey line number.

You can now define the quantities and the relevant discount as a percentage. It is interesting to see that by ordering 25 units, the customer could already obtain a discount of 50%.:

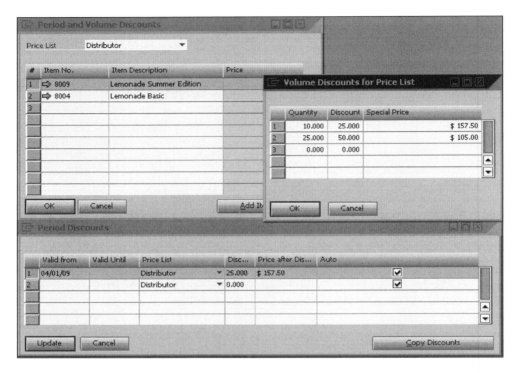

Collaboration activities

We entered a new sales quotation as a part of the opportunity management. With the available functionality, we were able to identify that the selected item is not in stock and selected an alternative item that is in stock. By selecting the alternative item, and entering the quantity of 50, the volume discount will automatically be presented in the **Discount** column of the proposal for this line item. Please note that the discount could also be manually adjusted. This could give the sales person additional flexibility to negotiate with the customer.

As a next step, the sales person schedules a follow-up call for the proposal to finalize the order. In the following screenshot, you can see that a phone call was scheduled and assigned to a salesperson. It is important to note that this scheduled appointment could be set for another salesperson who is in charge of managing the subsequent sales stage.

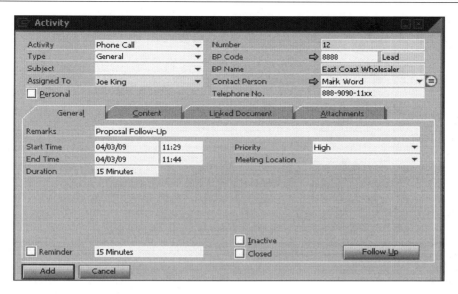

The salesperson who was assigned to this scheduled activity will now see an entry in his calendar. A double-click on the calendar entry will reveal the details (as seen below). This includes a direct link to the **Sales Opportunity** form via the **Linked Document** tab page. Therefore, a full collaborative enterprise environment is at work here, where information can be shared and used among departments.

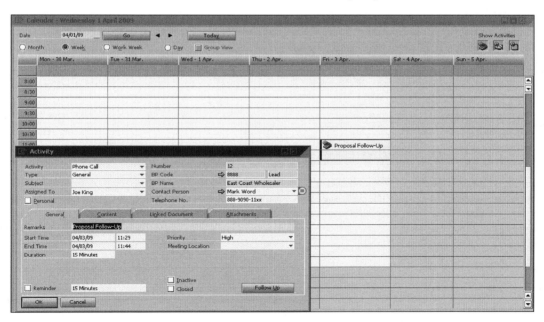

The assigned salesperson can send an e-mail notification and select the relevant delivery method ranging from **E-Mail**, **SMS**, **Telephone**, and **Fax**:

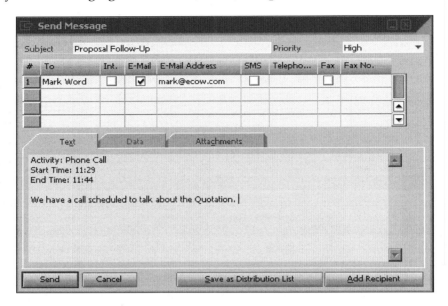

Sales opportunities and service calls

The relevance of service calls and sales opportunities was shown in the beginning of this chapter. If you remember, the service department I called was not aware of the new sales opportunity that was open with my account. Therefore, we will now review the current service calls for the opportunity we just entered. This is accomplished using the Drag and Relate functionality. You basically drag the form field that holds the business partner code from the **Sales Opportunity** window to the drag and relate target called **Service Call** in the **Service** section (seen in the following screenshot). It is interesting that the result indicates the customer has actually called to return a previous order. Therefore, we need to evaluate the reasons and make sure we don't invest additional resources prior to this getting resolved.

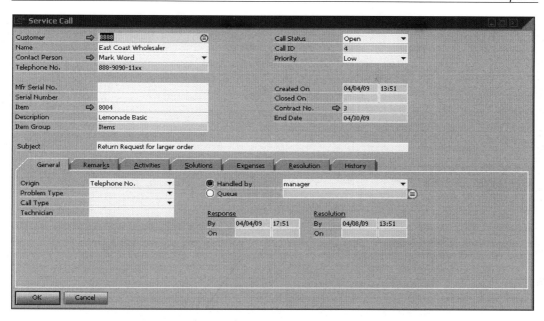

Summary of the SAP CRM workflow

The sales opportunities functionality can be integrated with all of the departmental functionality. This includes:

- Sales stages
- Quotation and sales management
- Inventory levels
- Pricing and volume discounts
- Alternative items
- Service calls
- Collaborative calendar functionality
- E-mail and similar

The following schema shows the workflow and how the different screens are related:

Sales opportunity reports

One thing to look for in a new system is the availability of reports. What reports are available by default? You know that in a SQL database, almost any report can be generated. However, the crucial part is what reports are available by default. This is where the information that is maintained in all of the SAP forms comes to light. We can use the information to analyze sales stages, sales personnel performance, sales by territory, and marketing budget as it relates to sales.

You can evaluate the sales stages by opening the "Sales Pipeline Report" (seen in the following screenshot). This shows a report in a pipeline format. Each section represents a sales stage. Apparently, in our Lemonade Enterprise Database, we only have transactions related to sales stages 1, 3, and 4. Therefore, the pipeline diagram only shows this information.

One important aspect of this information is that it allows you to continue serving customers even when salespeople leave. You can simply continue maintaining the opportunities and manage the follow-up calls.

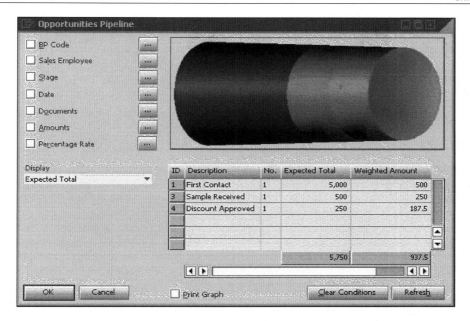

Critical analysis of the SAP Business ONE sales functionality

The integrated system approach allows required information from all customer touch points to be utilized in order to improve the sales methodology. In addition, the information can be translated into specific workflows that enable sales personnel to bring specific opportunities into greater focus.

The integration with inventory, and the utilization of sales stages, can be used to manage growth. For example, the predicted sales can directly determine future inventory levels. This also works the other way round. By focusing on items that are in stock, we can align the sales process towards items that are available and in stock.

In a later chapter, we will integrate a web-based technology with this process. Therefore, the existing platform is ready to expand its reach to more customer touch points using the Web.

Summary

In this chapter, we learned about CRM as it relates to SAP Business ONE. We began with historical reasons for an integrated CRM. We then continued to position sales-related activities as part of an integrated enterprise workflow. Touch point analysis was used to identify the areas in your company that contribute to sales directly and indirectly.

Based on this information, we developed the 360 +ONE sales strategy and implemented the core aspects using SAP Business ONE.

As a result, you can clearly see the benefits of an integrated system. It is not only technology that is important, but also the way it is utilized to trigger workflows in order to improve the customer's experience. The example workflow we implemented helped to overcome all of the shortcomings introduced in the example mentioned at the beginning of the chapter.

7
Logistics and Supply Chain Management

In the previous chapter, you learned about the importance of aligning your sales efforts with inventory levels. This is especially true if your inventory reaches a point where significant amounts of capital are involved. In our case study, we saw that one item had insufficient inventory levels, whereas another item that we promoted had higher inventory based on the increased demand we anticipated due to the promotion.

A recent study by AMR (*How to predict demand amid economic upheaval?*, InformationWeek's issue, Page 29, 02 March 2009) shows that 7% of all retail products are out of stock at any given time. Furthermore, 15% of goods that are on promotion are out of stock according on this study. When capital is scarce, you need to align your inventory investments with demand and implement forecasting methods.

Let's say we keep about $50,000 in inventory for our promotion. According to the AMR research study, we will be 15% short of stock, which will equal $7,500. In order to compensate for this shortage, we may increase the inventory. The above situation describes a common problem. Stockouts are dealt with by overstocking. Over time, this leads to extensive additional capital that is bound in inventory.

Imagine that the distribution center for the **Lemonade Inc.** enterprise grows and the inventory levels are reaching $1,000,000. Considering the numbers from the AMR study, with 15% inventory shortage and a potential overstocking investment, we could easily bind an additional $150,000 just to compensate for poor planning. Based on these numbers, it is worthwhile to closely evaluate the available options that help plan and optimize our inventory using SAP Business ONE.

Goals of this chapter

In this chapter, we will cover the warehouse and distribution center aspects of an SAP Business ONE implementation. As we are implementing a full-scale distribution center, we will start with the basic SAP Business ONE feature set. However, we will then move on to implement parts of the 360 order-to-cash configuration for an advanced distribution center functionality. This is essentially a proven combination of add-ons that enhance the standard SAP functionality for a specific industry. By studying this example, you will learn what SAP Business ONE can do when using the standard. You will also quickly understand how to select industry solutions in the form of proven combinations of SAP add-ons. The following topics will be covered during the course of this chapter:

- Summary of logistics trends – I will provide a brief overview of current trends that may impact the design of a competitive logistics system. In addition, I will explain the key terms commonly used when discussing logistics.

- Project status – Where are we now? It is always important to understand where we are in the project. Therefore, you will see the tasks we need to focus on, based on the project plan that was established.

- Apply the tasks related to inventory and warehouse management to our case study – You will see how SAP manages inventory-related tasks, and also how warehouse management is implemented.

- We will continue to evaluate the most crucial components of the SAP 360 order-to-cash industry solution, which is designed for modern warehouse and distribution centers. Essentially, the message that I am giving here is that SAP Business ONE is a business management engine, which provides a platform for industry-specific solutions by means of add-ons. Please note that the add-ons in this chapter are developed by third-party, SAP-certified software vendors.

Logistics key terms

The following key terms attempt **to bring production closer to the customer**. This is accomplished with better information and technologies that integrate the physical component of logistics (the product) with the non-physical component (information). An example is the industry trend to extend the inventory planning functionality from the warehouse to the actual Point of Sales (POS) at the store locations. This will resemble a live view of demand at the store location, and can directly impact the way inventory is planned.

Current trends and success factors

The Internet provides the infrastructure to send information anywhere in the world almost instantly. This applies to anything that can be digitally transformed into files. However, physical items cannot directly take advantage of this infrastructure, and that's exactly what **logistics** is about — (moving physical items to the customer). Therefore, the **logistics value chain** comprises the entire process of acquiring raw materials to receive, produce, and deliver to the customer. What happened to digital information with the availability of the Internet also essentially happened (a bit in the background) to the **physical Internet,** so to say. UPS and FedEx are good examples of companies that have established a **physical Internet**. They have created a network of delivery **hubs** that deliver packages. In addition, this is combined with digital information, such as **tracking numbers**, to support and enhance the **physical network**. Therefore, a modern logistics system must comprise of:

- Efficient resource utilization
- Collaboration of networked hubs
- Transparent information in real time

Logistics success factors

Today's logistics solutions focus on **green** technology, and therefore optimize factors such as **energy optimization** and **resource utilization**. For example, as a side effect of optimizing inventory, the entire logistics chain is optimized with regards to resource utilization. A delivery truck does not travel the road anymore only to overstock items, and thereby waste fuel, resources, and warehouse space. So you see that optimizing an inventory has a multiplying effect on all of the subsequent supply chain members. In the past, we only worried about investment optimization and inventory turn-around time, but it is getting a major success factor depending on how we manage the environmental impact of our supply chain. As a part of the technologies I am introducing here, I want to make a point of measuring those new success factors against the technology used. The following critical success factors are established for modern logistics systems.

Green-information-collaboration

Minimizing transportation, and therefore **gas mileage**, is the most obvious requirement. In addition, what is known as **globalization** not only appears to contribute to optimized international trade, but also to a more rapid fluctuation in upward and downward trends. This leads to a warehouse potentially being over and under utilized. In order to address this situation, we can plan on **sharing** our warehouse with other partners who can utilize the infrastructure. Technologies, such as barcode and RFID, make the location and tracking of inventory more transparent. This is the basis to utilize digital information in a standardized way so that all trading partners can contribute to the overall logistics process. The following important criteria were identified:

- Warehouse-sharing capability to accommodate demand fluctuations
- Use barcode and RFID for information collaboration
- Inventory optimization as the starting point of logistics value chain

Inventory optimization = investment optimization

The main aspect of a warehouse is obviously the inventory. Therefore, the focus of our system must be on the optimization of inventory levels. This way, we ensure that the capital bound in our inventory is worth the investment. Inventory that is not sold, or is sold only after a significant storage time, has a high turnover time. Therefore, we need to push for the lowest possible turnover time. In order to meet the requirements of our customers, we need to have sufficient safety stock. This is the stock level we believe is necessary to meet the customers' demand for our products.

A rock-and-water example is commonly used to explain this situation. In the following schema, you can see that the inventory level or **Water Level A** tends to exceed the demand in all aspects. Based on your current knowledge, this only means we are paying unnecessary **interest** because there is too much capital bound in our inventory.

Now if we look at **Water Level B**, we can see that the inventory was lowered. However, we will now need to cope with the situation that the seasonal demand peaks are not addressed. Basically, we are losing money here as well because we will not be able to supply products during peak demand times.

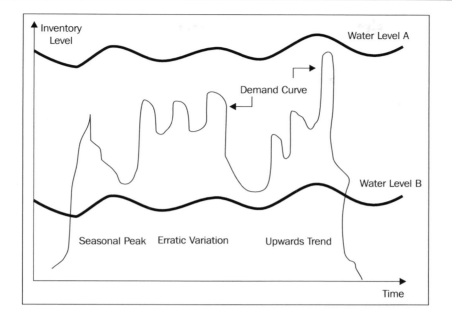

Lead time management

Lead time is the time it takes to move an item from the supplier's warehouse to our warehouse. When considering seasonal peaks for our products, we need to include lead time to plan for our stock levels. For specific items that may be ordered from overseas suppliers, lead time can have a significant impact on our inventory. A wrong decision may bind large amounts of capital, and may lead to inaccurate inventory levels if the wrong products are forecasted.

Warehouse management

A warehouse is the physical location where our inventory is stored. It is the center of the logistics value chain as **receiving**, **inventory management**, and **delivery** takes place here. With the already mentioned terms, such as **green**, **inventory optimization**, and **lead time management**, the technology used in the warehouse is crucial to properly address the requirements. The warehouse information system essentially has to be fully integrated with the main ERP system to function properly. The following technologies are used to accomplish this:

- Barcode
- RFID
- EDI

Barcode system to minimize errors

Most errors in a warehouse happen while **receiving** items. This means that when the delivery truck stops at the warehouse and delivers products, we need to establish a method to make sure that mistakes are minimized. Most commonly, a barcode system is used to automate the receiving process. A barcode is a specialized font that allows digital devices to easily scan and translate the barcode font back into a font that the system can read. For example, this book is printed with a font that you can easily recognize. The barcode font expresses each letter or number with a set of lines. In reality, this is just a representation that can easily be read by a digital barcode scanner.

RFID—the next generation barcode

Radio Frequency Identification Devices (RFID) are similar to barcodes in the way that they provide information about the product in an encoded format that can be read by designated devices. However, RFID can store more information. Therefore, it is a more expensive solution. To obtain the information, RFID readers can be placed at the entrance of the warehouse. Then, as the products and pallets are delivered, the RFID reader will **automatically** account for this in the inventory. The same will happen when the items leave the warehouse. This way, real-time inventory is available. However, this technology is not very common in an entry-level setting.

EDI

Electronic Data Interchange is an industry standard to describe electronic documents. These electronic documents allow intercompany transactions to be automated. For example, larger distributors often require their suppliers to use EDI. When the supplier delivers an item to the distributor, an electronic document is sent from the supplier to the distributor. This document is automatically processed in the distributor's system. Essentially, what would have traditionally taken lots of paper work and manual steps to complete a transaction among trading partners is now automated. In our case study, we are working with an outsourced manufacturing company to create the lemonade. As we work with this manufacturer, it would be a good idea to automate the process using electronic documents instead of sending proposals, orders, and delivery paper notes back and forth.

Project plan progress

This is a good time to evaluate the project plan, our file folder, and additional electronic files we have collected so far. According to the project plan, we are in phase 2—Analysis and design—**purchasing, inventory management, production process, and MRP**. These items also include tasks related to warehouse management. As you can see, the details we cover in each section are based on our specific needs. After a review of the Visio charts we create, and our A3 strategy paper, this section will cover an area that we will focus on strategically as it is our declared goal to establish a modern distribution center.

Based on the current trends in logistics, and the key technologies outlined above, it will be our task to implement SAP in such a way that we have the key success factors optimized.

Therefore, we need to fulfill the following needs:

- Optimize inventory levels – This will essentially optimize the main factor, namely **investment optimization**. By optimizing inventory levels, all of the depending members of the logistics chain are optimized.

- Automate warehouse management – Receiving and shipping must establish a method to verify package contents upon receiving and shipping.

- Enable collaborative information—the complete **logistics value chain** must be transparent with regards to information that is available. For example, at any time, we must be able to obtain a tracking status and get related auditing information.

The following technologies must be used to accomplish this:

- Barcode – We will use barcodes to automate the receiving and shipping process. This way, we can reduce mistakes, such as shipping items on sales order that don't match the items ordered. The same is true for **receiving**.

- SAP MRP – We will use MRP (Material Requirements Planning) to establish forecasts for our inventory levels. This way, we can make sure adequate stock levels are available in the warehouse.

- SAP PO processing – From negotiation to ordering and receiving, the PO (Purchase Ordering) functionality must be tightly integrated with the MRP and warehouse management functionality. For example, the results of MRP must trigger relevant purchase orders. The same is true for receiving and shipping items in the warehouse. The right documents must be generated.

- SAP warehouse management – The warehouse management system has to manage the **receiving** and **shipping**. In addition, the way we organize items in the warehouse must be optimized. For example, we can establish methods to efficiently store items. This includes counting stock levels, location management, and so on.

Note that the logistics value chain in this example ranges from demand planning, based on customer order history, to delivery. This logistics value chain can easily be extended to include a POS (Point of Sales). A POS is a computer that allows the sale to be completed in a store environment. However, as retail store management is a bit of a separate subject, I will not cover this aspect here. In addition, based on our core strategy, the implementation of a POS solution for store environments is not a part of the core implementation.

What to do now in your own project

Consequently, for your own project, you may define your own end-to-end logistics value chain. In case your business does not match the key success factors of our example, don't panic. A good way of thinking about your own logistics process is the concept of **bringing the customer as close to your production as possible**. This way, you will optimize the way your logistics chain operates. Use the A3 strategy paper and Visio charts to identify the key success factors. Now, select the technologies in SAP that would address and implement these success factors.

Case study—inventory optimization and warehouse management

We will now implement an on-the-edge distribution center solution based on SAP Business ONE. During the course of the implementation for the case study, we will first implement the SAP standard features, and then evaluate the use of a qualified industry-specific add-on. The add-on will compensate for the limitations we found in the SAP standard. This way, you will see how SAP works in its standard implementation. In addition, you will lean about limitations and how to overcome them.

This is what we will do now:

- Show the inventory management features and explain how demand planning is done in SAP using MRP.
- Automate warehouse management using SAP. This goes with an introduction to the SAP PO processes that include negotiation, ordering, receiving, and shipping.

Therefore, we will implement the complete cycle starting from customer demand signal, progressing to PO, receiving, inventory, warehouse, and finally to delivery.

Inventory forecasting with SAP Business ONE

It is now time to take a closer look at the SAP MRP – (Material Requirements Forecasting) functionality. I will show you how it works and what it can do. We will then conclude with what it will not be capable of, and then find a way to compensate for that.

SAP MRP

The SAP inventory planning functionality is nested within the **MRP – Material Requirements Planning** menu item. MRP helps the user plan for relevant raw materials based on orders in production and orders placed. In addition, custom forecasts can be created. These will be used as a part of the MRP process. The process of MRP in SAP Business ONE is driven by a **wizard-style** interface. This means the user is guided through the entire process, step-by-step.

A closer look in the **MRP – Material Requirements Planning** menu area reveals that we have three menu options:

- **Forecasts**
- **MRP Wizard**
- **Order Recommendations**

SAP MRP forecasts

The MRP forecast screen shows the parameters that the user can use to enter manual forecasts:

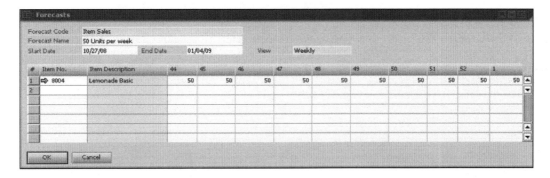

We can enter forecast information based on a date range for multiple items within that date range. This appears to be sufficient for now. However, it is not an option to enter forecasts for items per warehouse. We can create **Lemonade – LA Warehouse** and **Lemonade – Atlanta Warehouse**, and then provide a forecast on a per-warehouse basis. Basically, this indicates what has become evident when working with SAP Business ONE. We can define multiple warehouses. However, there is always one main warehouse to which the core functionality primarily applies.

Item master settings for MRP

Before any item is considered by the MRP wizard, we need to set up MRP as the **planning method** for this item. To do that, you need to open **Item Master Data** and select the desired product. Then, navigate to the **Planning Data** tab page and select **MRP** as the **Planning Method**. You can also specify the **Order Interval**. This is a good way to define how often this item will be revisited. For example, if we plan this item every month, we need to make sure that the safety stock is sufficient for the time frame. Please review the following screenshot to see how the **Planning Method** and **Order Interval** are set:

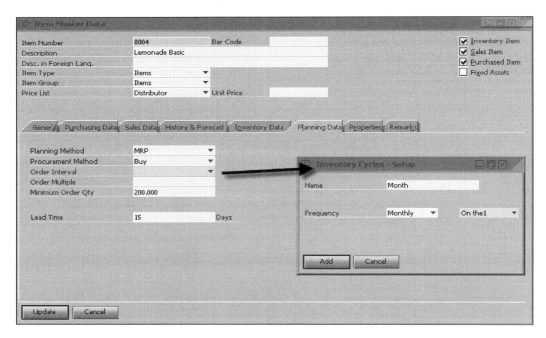

In the **Item Master Data** screen (seen below), we also need to pay attention to the **Inventory Data tab page**. Here, we see how the item is currently accounted for in the warehouses that we have defined. In the following screenshot, two sections are highlighted. In the lower right, you can see the **Set Default Whse** button. This allows the currently selected warehouse to be set as the default warehouse. In the screenshot example, **General Warehouse** is highlighted by clicking on row number **1,** and then clicking on the **Set Default Whse** button.

Note the **Manage Inventory by Warehouse** checkbox. If this is checked, the min/max values for an item can be set on a per-warehouse basis. Then, as shown in the screenshot, the min/max values will be set on the line level for each warehouse. You can see in the screenshot that the **Min. Inventory** and **Max. Inventory** columns show up for each warehouse. If we uncheck the **Manage Inventory by Warehouse** checkbox, those columns will disappear from the line level and will be activated on a per-item basis. In this case, the min/max level will be maintained on a per-item basis.

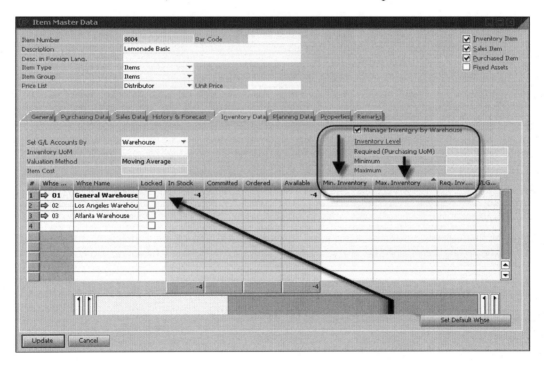

Change Log—a hidden but sophisticated feature

At this point, I would like to highlight a valuable, often-overlooked, feature in SAP Business ONE. When we click on **Tools | Change Log,** while the item master for the current item is open, we can see a history of changes that were made to this master item. This provides excellent tracking and auditing functionality. You can see who made the changes and when. For example purposes, the last two changes are highlighted in the screenshot below. By clicking on the **Show Differences** button in the lower right of the **Change Log...** window, the change log is displayed. You can see that **manager** set the **Default Whse** for this item to warehouse **01**. Keep this in mind in case your system is modified. You can often track who made the changes.

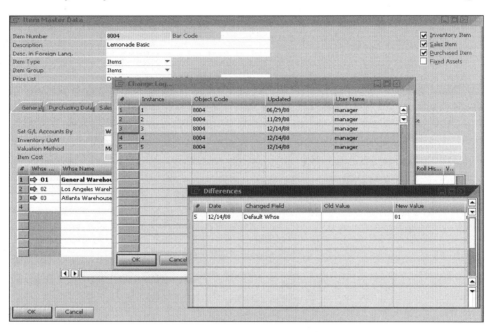

Document Settings—the driver for inventory and warehouse management

Let's take a look at the admin section related to inventory and warehouse management. If you navigate to **Administration | System Intitialization | Document Settings**, you can see that there are highly important settings in this form. It is a good idea to carefully review each setting and modify it based on your business needs:

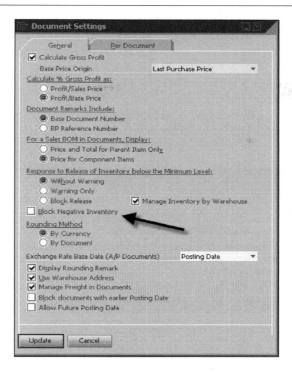

The important settings, with regards to inventory management and warehouse management, are as follows:

- Response to release of inventory below the minimum level - If you don't carefully select this option, transactions may be blocked because the minimum level of a master item is reached. This sometimes causes issues with new implementations.

- The **Block Negative Inventory** checkbox - If any transaction causes negative inventory, the transaction would be blocked. This may not be desirable for all implementations. I recommend unchecking this so we do not have this problem during further testing.

- The **Manage Freight in Documents** checkbox - If you activate this setting, a freight column appears in the footer section of **Sales Order** documents. For example, if you manage freight on a per-line item level, you don't want this here and you should consequently deselect the checkbox.

SAP MRP wizard

You now have an understanding of how all of the dots are connected from the background settings in the admin section, which **drives** the system to the item master **Planning Method** settings. So, we can now run our first MRP wizard. Each item that has MRP as the selected planning method can be considered in the MRP wizard. But to plan accurately, a custom forecast should be entered for items you want to plan for.

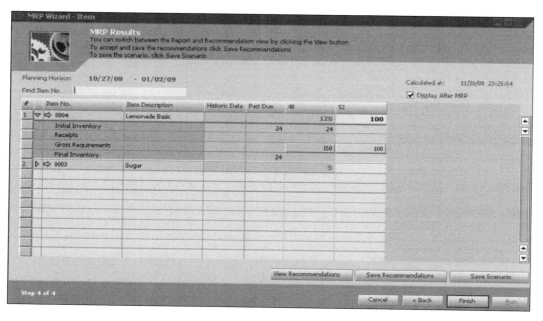

As you can see in the example, I have forecasted 50 units per week for **Lemonade Basic,** and the MRP wizard suggests the adequate quantities for the selected timeframe. Therefore, this system works if you have an inventory that you can manually oversee and where you would benefit from manually entering forecasts per item. The wizard allows the results to be saved as **recommendations**. In addition, the completed wizard can be saved as a **scenario**. You can then plan based on different scenarios that you play out. The **recommendations** are essentially **purchase orders** to achieve the required stocking levels.

Problems with the SAP Standard MRP planning method

As outlined in the rock-and-water example, we reviewed in the beginning of this chapter that it is crucial to plan inventory according to the requirements. The min/max planning method has the following shortcomings:

- Does not address seasonal fluctuations
- Leads to overstocking
- Inventory shortages may occur

Since our inventory binds capital, it must be looked at as an investment that can produce positive or negative interest. Seasonal demand is not addressed by the min/max levels. In addition, if we establish a larger inventory, with multiple item groups, each with individual brand names and customer groups, we may run out of control with the manual min/max concept. Therefore, I am introducing an advanced inventory optimization add-on available for SAP Business ONE.

Advanced inventory optimization

The inventory optimization in SAP Business ONE only includes optimization against the **min/max** values on a per-item basis. In addition, the MRP wizard only includes recommendations against the main warehouse. This could potentially cause problems in a multi-warehouse environment. Therefore, I recommend evaluating the Valogix inventory optimization add-on.

This add-on provides the following crucial features:

- Inventory optimization for multiple warehouses
- Forecasting based on statistical trend analysis versus the min/max values

Inventory optimization—establishing stocking value

The Valogix inventory optimization solution goes beyond min/max forecasting. The solution employs statistical trend analysis to forecast inventory levels for items. This is done across multiple warehouses. If you open the **Item Master Data** screen, there will be an added tab page called **History & Forecast**. The screenshot below reveals that the selected item shows all of the historic amounts. This is in the upper section called **History**. Please note that we can select the **Location**. This allows historic performance of an item to be reviewed on a location (warehouse) basis. In addition, in the lower pane, the **Forecast** is shown. The forecast can be shown per **Location** if required:

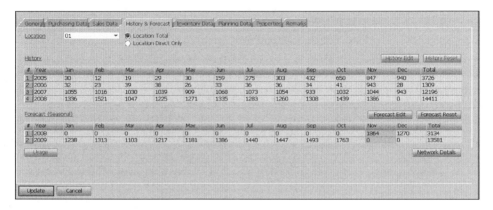

If you click on **Network Details** in the lower right section of the form, you get another view of the selected item. You can see a forecast in a list format for all locations:

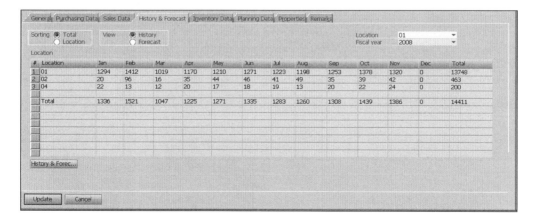

A further investigation of the **Inventory Data** tab shows that we can set a hierarchy for warehouse forecasting. For example, we can set the central warehouse location as Warehouse **01**. Then, all of the requirements of warehouse **02** and **04** will lead to additional forecasts in warehouse **01**. You can see this in the **VLGX: Roll History to Whse** and **VLGX: Network Primary Supplier** column:

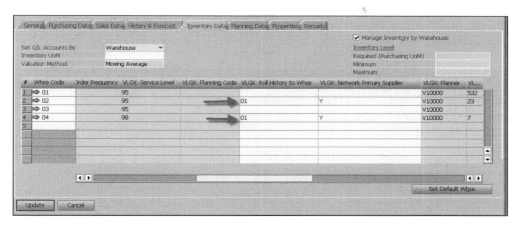

The **investment analysis** form uses all of the settings for items included in the Valogix planning solution to provide a real-time inventory investment analysis. Based on the example database I am using here, you can see that **Ideal Value** is suggested as **361,371.66** (in $), while the **Actual Value** is set as **1,052,575.0** (in $). This shows the Valogix solution attempts to significantly reduce inventory levels.

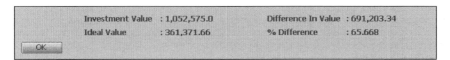

Purchase order cycle and warehouse management

As we have inventory management and planning functionality covered, it is a good time to look at purchasing, which is the remaining aspect of the logistics chain. We will look at purchasing, which is triggered by the inventory demand forecasting system. In addition, the deliveries that are incoming and those outgoing to customers are a main subject for related warehouse management functionality.

We will now continue with the process of creating a PO and the relevant deliveries processing.

The PO (purchase order) process starts with the creation of a PO. As part of the PO, there should be a negotiation process. In SAP Business ONE, this negotiation is easily supported with all of the integrated information, such as purchase history from various vendors. For example, we can use the purchase analysis report, available via the **Purchasing A/P – Purchasing Reports** menu, to get information about prices we secured in the past. In addition, we can use the overall amount we placed per year as a basis to negotiate future discounts. Once a PO is placed, the process moves to receiving the delivery, including payment. Payment can be made by clicking on the **Payment Means** icon in the main menu. See the following screenshot if you can't find the right icon:

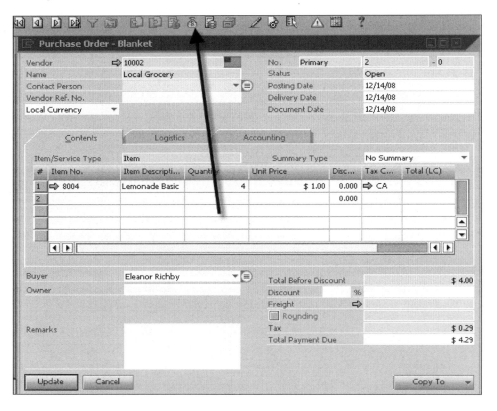

Once you click on the **Payment Means** icon while a PO is open, the available **payment options** are displayed. You can use **Check**, **Bank Transfer**, **Credit Card**, and **Cash**. A partial or full amount can be issued.

The payment is completed and all of the relevant transactions take place in the background. Note that payment is also possible via an invoice:

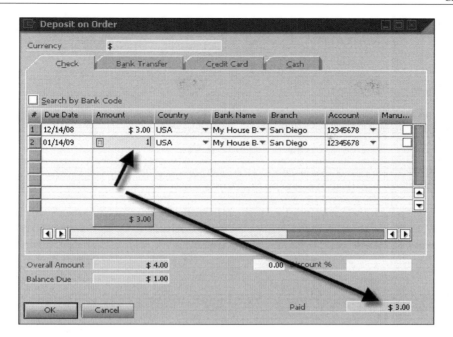

Inventory valuation and General Ledger postings

What exactly do we mean when we say **all of the transactions in the background**? This deserves a bit of attention at this point. As we receive inventory and deliver products, the inventory value in our warehouses goes up and down. In order to account for this, SAP uses valuation methods to determine the monetary values for transactions that go against the CoA.

The valuation methods are **Moving Average**, **Standard**, or **FIFO**. It is worth noting that the relevant setting is often well thought through and based on a recommendation discussed with your CPA, who may explain the preferred accounting method.

Moving Average

With this setting, items are valued based on the average price. This is calculated while transactions are booked. The calculation uses the quantity multiplied by the average price.

Standard

All of the transactions use a specified standard price that never changes.

FIFO

For this valuation method, it is assumed that products which were purchased first will also be sold first. Think of it as always selling the oldest item first.

You can see that the financial system tracks all of the business documents and the underlying financial transactions. These transactions use calculation methods, which we define in the admin section (for example, the valuation methods explained above). If your numbers are not showing the right values in your reports, it is wise to check the valuation settings in **Administration | System Initialization | Company Details | Basic Initialization**. In addition, you may verify the settings for each **Item Group via Administration | Setup | Inventory | Item Group**. Therefore, you can set the system wide default for the **Item Group Valuation Method**. However, you must verify the **Default Valuation Method** on a per-item-group basis. All of the underlying GL Accounts are driven by the stock updates we create via incoming and outgoing deliveries.

Therefore, it can be summarized that the stock updates increase the GL values if a goods receipt per PO is processed. A decrease takes place when a SO (sales order) is delivered. Note that a return can be processed by posting a credit memo. This allows values for already processed transactions to be adjusted.

Goods receipt processing in SAP

To showcase two situations that affect the inventory value, I will now provide an example for receiving goods, as well as for delivering goods. The goods receipt process is very straightforward. We enter information about the vendor and the products we received. Note that SAP always has a **base document** for payments. In this case, the invoice for the PO would refer to the PO base document. The invoice would be the target document in this scenario:

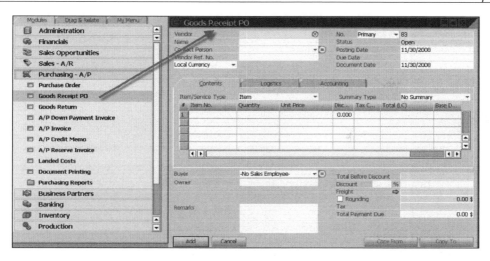

Delivery processing in SAP

In order to explain the delivery process, I would like to assume a more challenging situation utilizing **packaging**. First, let's configure the packages we need for our example. In the lemonade example, packages of 12 and 24 bottles are a good start.

Package definition

You can reach the **package definition** form via **Administration | Setup | Inventory | Package Types**. It is similar to the **Sales Stages** setup. You simply enter the type of packages you want to use:

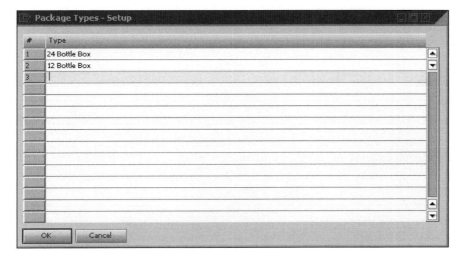

Processing a delivery using packages

We can now use the defined packages. In order to accomplish this, please open a delivery or create a new one. Next, with the delivery document open, move the cursor to the main menu and select **Goto | Packaging**. I outlined this process in the following screenshot:

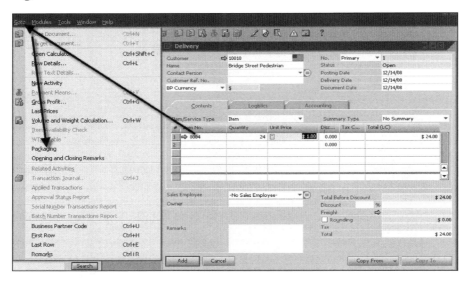

You will now see the **Packages - Setup** screen that allows the items in the delivery to be assigned to a predefined package. Note that the only items available are the ones present in the deliveries document:

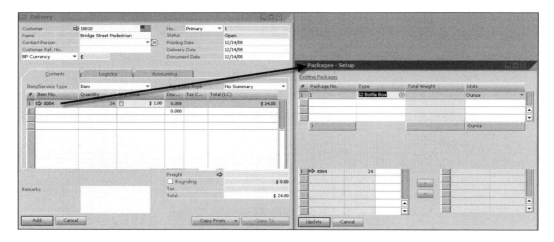

This concludes the showcase of the SAP Business ONE standard delivery processes.

Integrating barcode and warehouse management

In order to complete our goal of designing a modern distribution center, we now need to implement barcode and warehouse management. Please note that barcode management is not a part of the SAP Business ONE standard package. In addition, the warehouse management capabilities in SAP focus on a single, main warehouse. The additional warehouses that can be defined cannot be independently managed using Zoning or advanced Bin Management, and so on. In order to compensate for those potential issues, a qualified add-on is recommended.

Advanced warehouse management

The N'ware LISA add-on is a **WMS (Warehouse Management Solution)** that plugs into SAP Business ONE. It provides barcode functionality, and also RFID support. In addition, a warehouse can be **zoned** alongside a detailed bin management. Let's look at the possible features.

Warehouse mobile scanner solution

The add-on provides the following core features:

- The correct items are automatically verified on incoming and outgoing deliveries via mobile scanners
- Multiple warehouses are managed and introduces **zoning** is introduced. Zoning allows **zones** to be established in a warehouse to optimize required routes to **pick** items for orders.

Distribution platform

The N'ware product is called LISA, which stands for **Logistics Integration System Automation**. As the name suggests, LISA can help you manage all aspects related to warehouse management. The key to understanding this solution is that it builds on SAP Business ONE data. Everything done manually within SAP Business ONE can be automated with LISA by means of a wireless device that employs a barcode reader. In addition, the shortcomings in SAP Business ONE with regards to warehouse management are addressed.

The following screenshot shows how a sample wireless device may look:

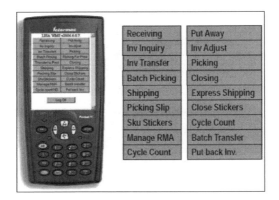

You can see a sample mobile device above based on the Intermec product line. A mobile device basically a small hand-held computer that can efficiently perform dedicated tasks. The tasks that this device can perform with LISA are listed on the right side of the screenshot. Based on the list, which is a representation of the menu on the actual device, you can see that the following can be done with this device:

- Receiving – With the Intermec device, you can manage the receiving process. This means, you can receive items based on a PO using the barcode scanner functionality. By doing this, you can automatically verify that what you are receiving matches the items in the order. Since most of the errors in a warehouse happen while receiving, this would be a great help to make sure that we are indeed receiving the right products.

- Inventory transfer – With this functionality, we can transfer inventory to another warehouse.

- Shipping – The **incoming** logistics functionality is a mirror image of the **outgoing** shipments of finished goods. The LISA warehouse management solution can manage this by using the same barcode automation features that are used for receiving.

- Inventory adjustment – Inventory values can easily be counted via the barcode system. For example, you can scan a pallet and retrieve all of the barcode numbers. If the actual number of items does not match what is accounted for in SAP, you can perform an inventory adjustment.

- Picking – This is a key functionality in a warehouse management system. In a smaller warehouse, this is a simple feature—(you just go and pick up the items). However, in a larger warehouse, you may want to pick up items which will be shipped without walking back and forth in the warehouse. Therefore, the picking process must provide an optimized picking path. A simple approach is useful to sort items by product number, and then have the product numbers increase as you walk through the warehouse. If you need to pick ten sales orders, a report can be created that lists all items and sorts them by product number. Then, you only need to enter the warehouse once and pick all items in one go. However, how do you assign the items back to each sales order? Well, that's where LISA can help you. It will automatically **pick & pack** while assigning each item to a sales order using barcode verification.

You now understand a bit more about what a warehouse management system can do. It automates and integrates barcode verification. These simple features allow us to improve the way we manage our **logistics** functionalities and reduce the level of errors encountered.

How does the logistics integration system work

In case you are a bit intimidated by the unknown wireless device, I would like to explain a bit more about the underlying technology. If you open up an Internet browser and look at the homepage of the LISA system, you can see that the entire program is actually nothing more than an Internet Explorer compatible web application that allows the listed tasks to be performed. However, the wireless device adds a crucial value of having a **digital scanner** that allows barcode labels to be read and the information to be used for further processing.

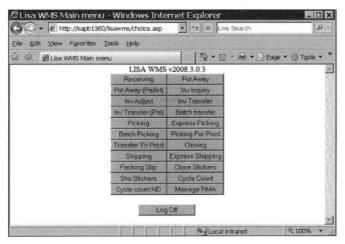

Summary

In this chapter, you learned about the logistics value chain. The basic success factors from inventory optimization to warehouse management were outlined by example. In addition, you learned about guidelines for selecting possible add-on solutions that can improve the SAP standard features for logistics.

Before reading this chapter, you may have been a bit curious as to how SAP matches up with today's challenging requirements for logistics. It is becoming evident that SAP Business ONE is a **business engine**. The available SDK functionality has led to industry-specific add-on solutions that can be seamlessly integrated with the standard system. With that in mind, you learned that multiple add-ons can work together to enhance the standard functionality. During our example tour of advanced warehouse features, we explored the Valogix add-on for inventory optimization, and the N'ware LISA warehouse management solution. Both add-ons are a proven combination as part of the 360 order to cash industry solution.

During the course of this chapter, we reviewed the following additional aspects:

- Summary of logistics trends – Understanding the key drivers in today's logistics businesses is important. You are now ready to size your system and select the right add-ons with a proven track record.

- Project status – We evaluated the project plan to identify the tasks at hand for our implementation. You learned the required tasks involved for your own project.

- Based on the project plan, we implemented a full-scale distribution center solution framework.

8
Competitive Service and Contract Management

In the previous chapter, you learned about the importance of putting the 360-degree information available in SAP Business ONE into action. In this chapter, we will take a closer look at the service module to evaluate potential actions that are triggered, based on service-related information. You may say you don't need the service module. However, the concept introduced in the following pages will utilize the service module features to establish a guaranteed response time for customers. You will see that there are various angles to look at **service**. In addition to its more traditional view, service can be used to establish a **service-level-type** management for customers and the related sales opportunities. Basically, the service module can be used as a sophisticated alert system.

What we will learn in this chapter

In this chapter, we will cover the service module and highlight how it fits in with the sales and opportunities management functionality. The key features, from taking a service call to contracting management, will be explained. In order to establish a practical platform for this, a case study will be expanded to utilize the service module. As a part of this section, a complete workflow will be configured from setting the right parameters in the admin section to connecting the information for service personnel. Finally, the chapter will conclude with a critical analysis of the functionality and some suggestions for potential enhancements.

Therefore, this chapter will cover the following topics:

- Key terms - The common terminology related to **service** management will be covered. There is nothing major waiting for you here. We will simply learn what the terms entail with regards to the SAP system.

- Service module core functions – In this section, the available functions and features will be put into perspective—what is available and how much we can expect from it. For example, you will learn what **service operations** mean.

- Case study and your own project – The available features of the service module will then be implemented for the case study. By doing so, knowledge will be provided to implement the service module in your own business. We will review some guidelines which will enable you to translate the case study implementation into a set of activities for your own project.

- Service workflow (from setup to operation) – In this section, we will configure the service module in a step-by-step manner.

- Limitations of the SAP service module – Based on the available features, we will discuss potential limitations of the service module.

- Evaluate potential add-ons for service – Add-ons which are proven to enhance the service module features, are available to overcome the limitations.

Key terms

Let's start with the key terms related to service and contract management in SAP Business ONE. By looking at the key terms, you will get an understanding of what can be accomplished with this module.

Service contract templates

In the admin section, we can define the service contract templates that can later be used as a basis for actual contracts. Please note the template character. All of the parameters we define here will automatically populate the relevant details in the contract once a template is selected. The following screenshot shows that a contract template can be created not only on a per-customer basis, but also for item groups, and a specific item based on serial numbers. In addition, please note the **Reminder** setting. You can set a reminder which will provide an alert prior to the expiry of the contract. This way, you can be sure that you contact all customers and allow them to renew their contracts.

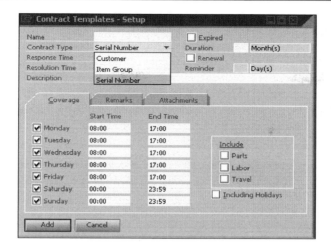

Serial number contract

The most common usage may be the **Serial Number** contract type. Each product will have a specific contractual service eligibility based on the **serial number**. Consequently, if a customer purchases an item that is managed by a serial number, a warranty contract template can be associated. This will create a **customer equipment card**.

Customer contract

However, please note that this concept does not need to be used only for items and serial numbers. As you can see in the previous screenshot, we can create contract templates for customers and whole item groups. For the case study, I will use this concept to create a **service contract** for key customers. We can then use the service functionality in SAP to make sure these customers get priority treatment. You see, we can use the service functionality in this **creative** way to improve our service quality.

Item group contract

Just as we may decide to use the service module to guarantee a specific response time to customers, we can make sure that a specific product line is managed. For example, if you have a new specific product line that requires technical expertise for implementation, then a service contract may be offered to customers. Therefore, all customers who purchase an item that belongs to this group will be eligible to purchase a contract and receive the relevant expert support.

Customer equipment card

The customer equipment card applies to the contracts that are managed by a **serial number**. Since the **serial number contract** applies a unique contract situation for each item, you will need to have the relevant information to be able to categorize a service call. For example, you need to know the serial number to identify the customer and the relevant warranty that remains for the specific serial number. In addition, if a customer calls you, you"ll want to be able to look up all of the serial numbers for this customer. This can be done using the **customer equipment card**. Please note that a customer equipment card is automatically created if a customer purchases an item that is managed by a serial number. You can assign a service contract when this happens on the level of sales order.

Service calls

Service calls are incoming service requests from business partners. The following screenshot shows that service calls can have many sources. For example, service calls may come via emails, phone calls, web requests, or any other defined **Origin**. I am highlighting this because, in essence, you can use the service module for any activity where you want to apply a specific response time management.

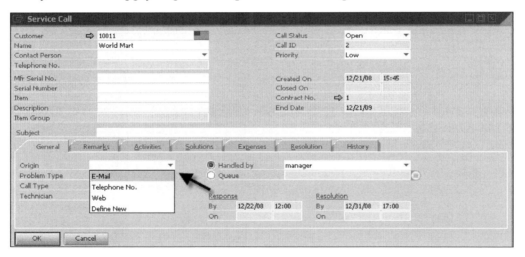

Queues

As mentioned above, the service module can be used to manage any kind of service-related activity. Queues allow your personnel to be associated with named groups. In the following screenshot, I have created two queues. The first queue is for **1st Level** and the second queue for **Resolution and Sales**. Consequently, I assign personnel who can best accomplish the relevant tasks to each queue as follows:

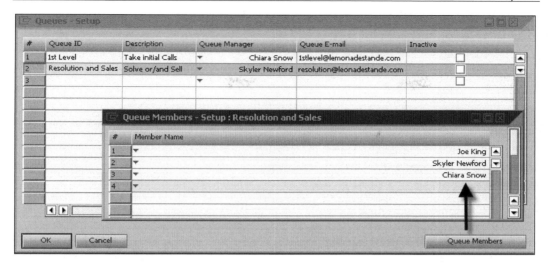

Knowledge base

As you work on service calls, you can build a **knowledge base** that documents how problems were resolved. For example, if the problem resolution department resolved a problem, it will be documented as a part of the service call. If the service call is for a serialized item, then this knowledge is available to the first-level support the next time a problem is reported for the same item type. Therefore, this can take the workload off of the specialized personnel as they can avoid repetitive tasks. In addition, new employees can benefit from the knowledge already acquired for resolved service calls.

Core features

Based on the key terminology, you now have a better understanding of how to set up the service module. The core functionality that the service module can be used for comprises the following features:

- Service operations – Create skill-based queues to work on service calls.

- Service contract management – Apply contracts to customers, item groups, or items with serial numbers based on templates. Set reminders to get information about contract expirations.

- Service planning – Allows contractual information to be utilized and queues or specific employees to be assigned. It tracks activities and documents solutions.

- Track customer interactions – This documents all customer interactions, from call initiation to problem resolution. It also allows service calls to be escalated based on contractual resolution time and actual status by using the integrated **Service Monitor**.

- Customer support – This establishes an integrated platform for support using purchase history and contracts for customers or serial numbers.

- Sales opportunity management – This aspect uses service call management to create new opportunities. In addition, it makes decisions about call priority based on open opportunities and customer account balance.

You can see that the main added value is not only to have a service module, but rather to have a service module that is fully integrated with the workflow of all your customer interactions. Therefore, the full potential of your customer interactions and product management can be improved.

Project plan status

In the project plan section called **Phase 2 – Analysis and Design**, we are currently working on the features as a part of the analysis phase. In the **Service** section, under the task group called **Divide into subjects**, we will evaluate the available features and implement a core workflow to verify the relevance of the service module for our project.

Your project

Before I proceed with the implementation of the service module for our case study, I would like to provide you with some recommendations for your own project. You can then better utilize the information provided in the case study.

- How do you want to organize your service? Categorize your service requirements into serial-number-based management, product categories, and customers. Then, create the relevant contract templates for each category.

- Design the contract templates and keep in mind that these are the only templates which will later be assigned for each serialized item, product group, or customer.

- Define queues and the people responsible to take care of service call issues. Make sure that you have a hierarchy. For example, have first-level support take the basic calls. Then, allow assigning a queue, such as second-level support, to resolve the issue. You may also have a queue called **escalation queue**. It would resolve issues that were not resolved within the resolution time defined in the contract.

- Note that the service module can be used to establish customer response times. Therefore, you may create a customer-specific contract for key accounts and then establish an alert based on a query to find qualifying customers. For example, you may want to provide customers with extra service based on their previous purchases. In this case, each customer who has purchased more than $5,000 within the last three months can receive special treatment and would be placed on the **key accounts contract** type. You may also establish surveys for lost opportunities. Using the service module, a contract template **survey** can be created and applied to the lost opportunities.

I will touch all of the aspects above in the case study. You can translate the way I am implementing it here to your own project requirements.

Case study—step-by-step implementation

We will now implement the service module for the Lemonade Stand enterprise. This will allow us to establish a guaranteed response time for all customers who have reached a specific number of orders within the last twelve months of operation. This way, we can ensure that an experienced account manager will be assigned to all customer interactions. In addition, I can document all of the interactions and monitor the status. By using the service module for this task, it can be guaranteed that the response time based on the contract type is met.

You start in the Admin Section and open the contract template setup via **Administration | Setup | Service | Contract Templates**. As you can see in the following screenshot, the **Key Customer Care** contract template was created. This contract will be assigned to every customer who has placed at least one sales order with us. You may define more detailed criteria for your own business. The criteria you use can easily be implemented via a query and then assigned to an alert.

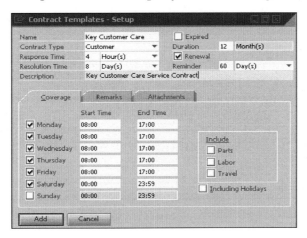

[The contract template is valid everyday except Sundays.]

As seen below, the response time is defined as **4 Hours**, and the resolution time is set as **8 Days**. An important thing to note is that the **Contract Type** is **Customer**. This means we will need to assign this contract to selected customers. I will now manually assign this contract to the customer **World Mart**. This is done by opening the service contract management form via **Service | Service Contract**. Then, I will click on **New** in the task bar. Note that the contract can be adjusted at this level. However, initially, the parameters default to the values that were set in the contract template. In addition, an owner is assigned. This means all service calls related to this customer will now go to the owner. How does the owner know that? For each new service call that is entered for this contract, an alert will automatically be sent to the owner.

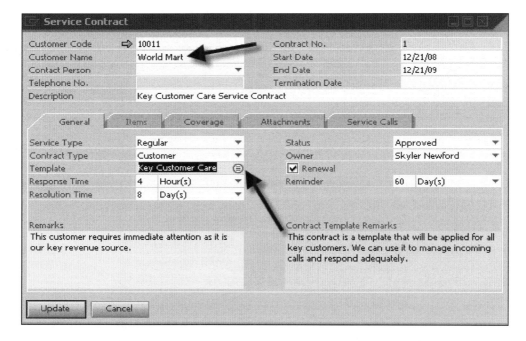

Let's see how this works. The service call form can be opened via **Service | Service Call**. In the following screenshot, you can see that the **World Mart** customer was selected. This is the customer with the **key customer contract**. The contract is automatically selected and the **Resolution and Sales** queue is assigned. Note that the resolution deadline for this call is automatically calculated based on the resolution time that was set in the contract.

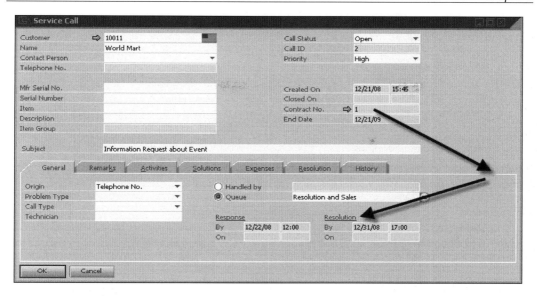

On confirming the form by clicking on **OK**, you can log in as the user who was selected to be the **owner**. If you refer to the screenshot showing the **queue** configuration with the queue members, you will see that the user **Joe King** is a member of the **Resolution and Sales** queue. Basically, this user will now get an alert that a customer has a new service call. Indeed, there is an alert when you login. The following screenshot shows the **Service call 2 has been assigned to you** alert. The details are available in the lower pane of the **Messages/Alert Overview** window. If the user clicks on the golden arrow that points to the **Service Call No.**, the service call opens up.

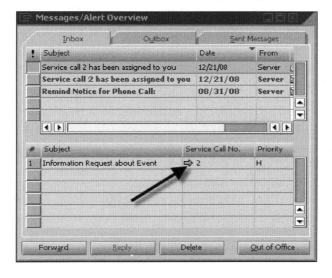

As users work on service calls, **expenses** and **activities** can be tracked. I added an invoice and a related return. You can see that these transactions are clearly visible in the **Expenses** tab page (seen below). By using this method, you can track expenses and profits made with customers. In the **Expenses Details** section, you can track deliveries, returns, invoices, and credit memos. You can also track items that were transferred to technicians for on-site repair. This is categorized as **Transferred to Technician**. In case the technician brings the item back, it is called **Returned from Technician**.

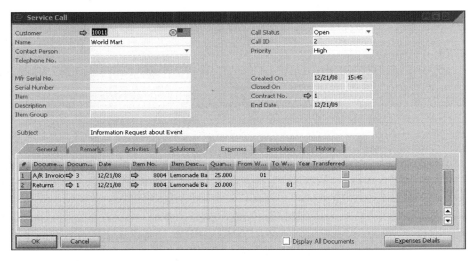

Activities can also be tracked on a per-service call basis. The benefit of tracking activities in the service call area is the advanced service-level integration we get. The activities will be measured against the **response time** and **resolution time** that were set in the contract:

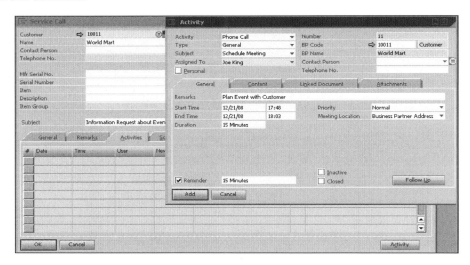

The **history** of everything related to the service call is automatically included in the **History** tab. Take a look at the history we created by adding the service call and then assigning it to the queue. As you can see, it is also documented that the expense document was added:

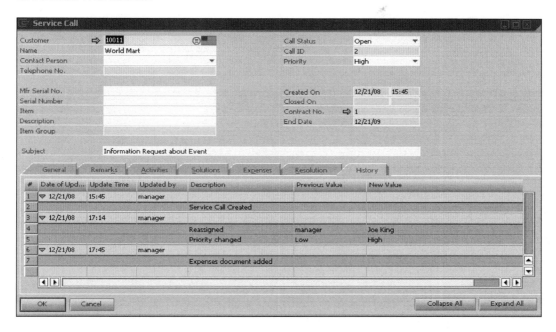

All of the information is tied together in the service call for this customer. By clicking on the **E-Mail** icon in the top task bar (seen below), an email can be generated that would send the service call details to selected recipients.

In this example, two SAP users were chosen to receive the service call details. This will result in an alert in the **Message/Alert Overview** box for those users:

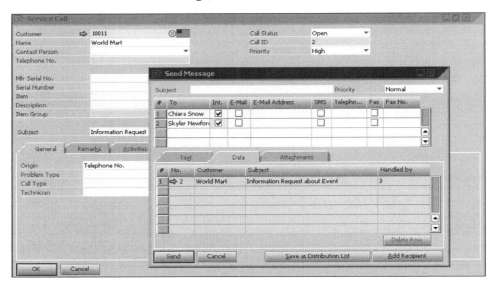

A crucial part of this workflow is the **Service Monitor** (shown in the following screenshot). A manager can use this tool to check how the service call resolution time measures up against the contract resolution time. It is here that escalation procedures can be initiated. You can see **Open Service Calls** and **Overdue Service Calls**. If you click on the **Details** button, the relevant calls open up. From the detail record, we immediately have all of the history available.

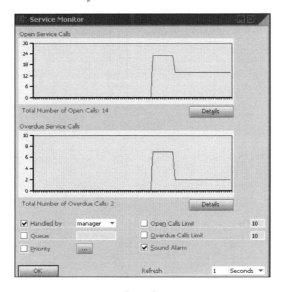

For our case study, we will ensure that every customer who has at least one purchase order will be placed on the **key customer** contract. The consequence is that the response times can be measured using **Service Monitor**. In order to accomplish this, the following steps need to be completed:

- Create a query that identifies customers who have placed at least one purchase order and are not assigned a contract yet.

- An alert needs to be created for the manager to allow assigning customers to the **key customer contract**.

The query by the name **New_Key_Customer** is shown in the following screenshot:

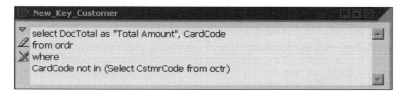

This query will show customers who have placed a sales order and who are not assigned any contracts.

The next step is to create an alert called **New_Key_Customer** (shown in the following screenshot). This alert uses the query as a basis and alerts any users who are selected in the list. In our example, only **manager** was selected:

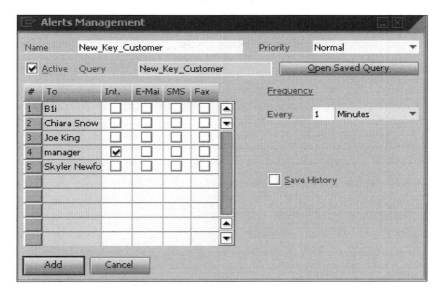

In order to showcase this scenario, another customer called Orange County Distributor was added via **Sales Opportunities**. This was accomplished by clicking on the **Business Partner Name** drop-down and then creating a new business partner master record. Then, a sales order was added for this new customer. Within a minute, an alert was received by the user called **manager** that a new customer complies with the key account eligibility:

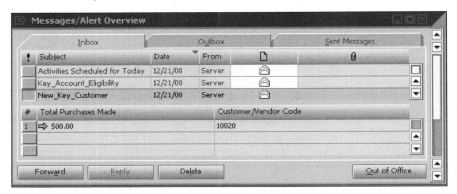

As a final step, the contract management section was opened via **Service | Service Contract** and **Key Customer Care Service Contract** was assigned to **Orange County Distributor**. Two things will happen now. If this customer calls, we can assign him to the queue, and qualified salespeople will guarantee that the response time and resolution time is met every time. Any issues, can easily be monitored via the Service Monitor. In addition, the **New_key_Customer** alert will be emptied out as there are no more records qualifying for the criteria:

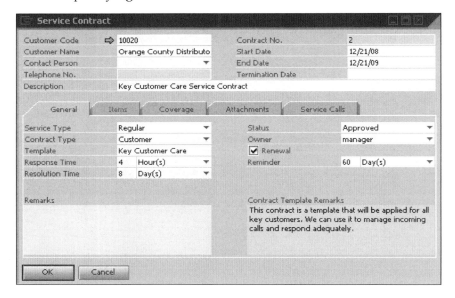

Summary of the service workflow

The workflow comprises of settings in the admin and user section in the service module.

In the admin section, the following tasks were completed:

- Define contract templates
- Select coverage for each contract based on serial, product group, or customer
- Define the response time and resolution time
- Define queues and assign members

The users then used the service module as follows:

- Call entry, tracking, and management via the service module forms
- Track types of calls and their origin
- Monitor remarks, activities, expenses, resolution, and history

The continuous usage will automatically create a knowledge base. The knowledge base can be used for solution information via keyword searches.

The concept of queues allowed specialized groups of technicians to be set up as queues. Essentially, this provided a platform for **skill-based routing**.

Via the **Service Monitor**, a supervisor is able to get a real-time view of the overall service call situation. For example, open calls and overdue calls can easily be evaluated.

During our case study, we also realized that the service module could be used to establish a guaranteed response time for selected customers based on the criteria we defined.

Service reports

The crucial element of each module is the information that can easily be extracted for reporting purposes. SAP provides a series of canned reports for the service module.

The **Service Calls** report provides information about service call activities based on the selected criteria. You can filter this report by timeframe of service call creation and also by resolution time. Additional filter ranges are available for **Customer Code, Handled By, Item, and also Queue ID**. In addition, the report allows filtering by **Problem Type, Priority, Call Type, Origin, Call Status, and Overdue Calls**. You can see that there is a wide range of options to obtain information. It is important to note that reporting can utilize the information only if all of the data is properly collected using the SAP forms. In case no options are selected for filtering, the report defaults to select all of the available information. The following additional service reports are available and have almost identical filtering capabilities as the **service calls** report: **Service Calls by Queue, Response Time by Assigned to, Average Closure Time**. The **Service Contracts** report (seen below) helps you manage the status of all maintenance contracts. If you've ever had to manage maintenance contracts with customers, you will appreciate the ease of obtaining the information here. You can filter this report by **Customer Code, Start Date Range, End Date Range and Termination Date Range**. In addition, this report can be further filtered by **Contract Type, Contract Status, and Service Type**.

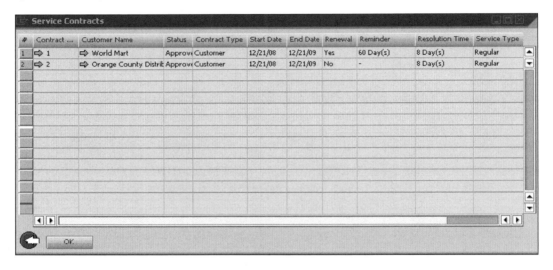

The customer equipment card report allows information to be obtained about items sold to customers based on serial number tracking. Each serial number has its own contract with expiration which is usually based on the purchase date. This report is able to be filtered by customer and item code. In addition, a more global filter can be used such as item group. The Service Monitor report provides a more real-time view of the service pipeline. We already covered this report in the previous section. Finally, **My Reports** includes **My Service Calls, My Open Service Calls, and My Overdue Service Calls**. Those reports conveniently filter the information based on the current login name. Therefore, if you run the report, you will only see information that is relevant for you based on the login.

Limitations

I have already mentioned that you can look at SAP Business ONE as the **operating system** for your business. You can use industry add-ons to seamlessly transform the standard features into an industry solution that is specific to your requirements. Therefore, let's evaluate some add-ons I've worked with that are related to the service module—specifically, the Enprise Job Costing module and the solution from Navigator called ServiceONE.

By looking at these add-ons, we can also learn the limitations of the standard service module. For example, since the Navigator promises to have all of the information available in one view, we realize that in SAP, we sometimes need to jump to different forms to get where we wanted to be initially. Let's further evaluate the features of these add-ons. The Enprise Job Costing solution introduces a web-based timesheet. This is an obvious feature that is not directly available in the SAP standard configuration. First, I will look at the Navigator solution and will then follow the Enprise offering. Often, there is more than one add-on providing industry-specific features. You then need to evaluate both solutions and decide which one best fits your requirements. Please note that I am presenting the add-on features to better define the limitations of the SAP Standard Business ONE features.

Job Costing add-on by Enprise

The Enprise Job Costing add-on is one of the first industry-specific solutions that gained widespread adoption as a standard for companies that required a detailed **job costing** solution. The advantage of this solution is that it is based on true expertise in the job costing area as it relates to the SAP service module. Let's look at a scenario that is very common for companies that work in the service industry and require what is known as **job costing**. However, I would first like to take the opportunity to explain job costing a bit. Job costing allows the profit and loss for specific services provided to be calculated. For example, if you have a company that sends out technicians to customer sites for performing equipment repairs, you need to make sure that the invoiced amount exceeds the cost you incur. The following workflow may be common in this environment:

- Serialized items are delivered to customers with each having a warranty contract that may or may not include services, parts, and replacements.
- Services may be performed on serialized items delivered by you or by another company.
- A service call may lead to a proposal (job) which will then be ordered. Technicians may use a timesheet to report the status and time. Timesheet entries must be possible via a mobile device or the Web. Furthermore, time entered needs to be **approved** before it is relevant for invoicing.

- A job may lead to subjobs that require unique management of related costs.

- As the number of jobs increase, you will require "work in progress" reporting.

- Estimating a job is crucial. Therefore, technicians need to be able to create estimates. It must then be possible to translate those estimates into orders and contracts.

- As services may require replacement parts, a feature is required that allows optimized picking of relevant items for a specific job.

- Complex jobs require milestone payments. This needs to be implemented in the contracts.

- The invoicing system needs to be integrated with the way services are completed. For example, milestone payments, fixed priced billing, and partial invoicing are common requirements in the service industry.

The Enprise Job Costing add-on resides in its own menu item called **Job Costing**. As you can see below, the menu items are well defined and provide a quick overview of the available features. In addition, it is important to note that the features seamlessly appear within the SAP interface:

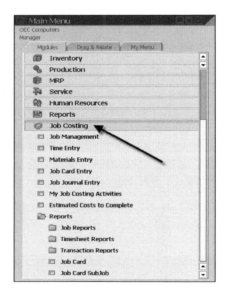

By selecting the Job Entry form, the powerful features come to light. As you can see in the following screenshot, the form allows searching **jobs** based on **Status**, **Type**, **Properties**, **Category**, and **Entered By**. The resulting list is shown in the lower pane. We can use this interface to search for specific jobs, and then click on the **Bulk Invoice** button as highlighted in the screenshot. This automates the invoicing process based on a clear, uncluttered form. Please note that we do not need to jump between multiple forms.

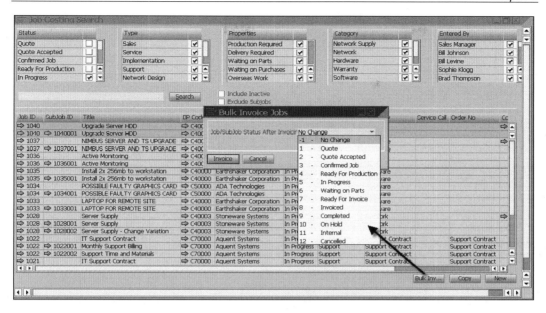

The **Direct Time Entry** form (seen below) is basically a timesheet. Therefore, technicians can use this to enter the time they spend on projects. Please note the buttons in the lower right that allow importing from the Web and also from an Excel clipboard. Enprise provides a web-based timesheet from which we can import data. However, it is important to note that we can also import from an Excel clipboard. This way, we can use the date that technicians entered in their laptops.

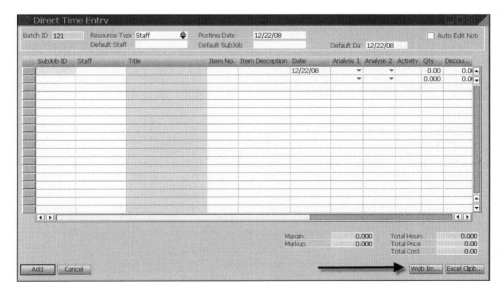

The contract list provides a link where the Enprise-enhanced contract management surfaces:

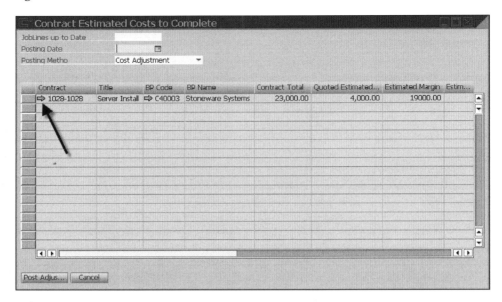

The contract management allows milestones for a contract. Each milestone to be established could lead to a milestone payment. In addition, we can directly jump to the related invoices by using the **Show Invoices** button:

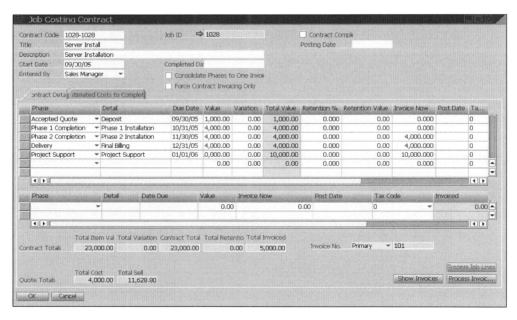

Enprise has adopted the concept of master data. For this purpose, the "Job Master Data" form was established. This is consistent with the SAP concept. Each job is defined and configured with specific parameters, which later **drive** the transactions that are based on this master data. For example, we can define the job parameters alongside a list of **subjobs**. In addition, documents can be attached as attachments:

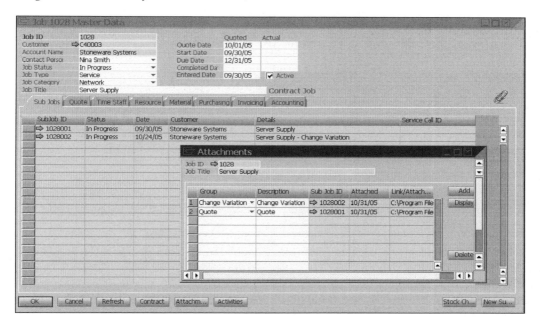

Advanced service functionality using ServiceONE by Navigator

Navigator provides a wide range of valuable add-ons. Each add-on is valuable. However, the key advantage of Navigator is the comprehensive portfolio of add-ons the cover almost all aspects of SAP Business ONE. In particular, the fact that Navigator also provides a mobile solution, which connects handheld computers with SAP Business ONE, extends the reach of the available functionality beyond the boundaries of the SAP client interface. Therefore, a mobile field service does not need to use a web-based timesheet, but could directly interact using mobile devices. However, you may need to purchase another add-on to accomplish this.

Optimized SAP form views

ServiceONE established a service window that shows all customer information in one convenient screen. Service calls have a direct link for **returns**, or allow **scheduling a resource**. The heart of this add-on is the integrated view of all service-related information via **Service Window**:

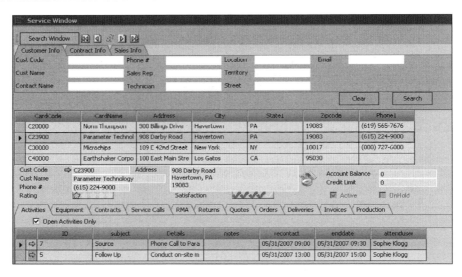

The **Dispatch Window** (shown in the following screenshot) shows a calendar-style resource planner that allows resources to be selected from a list to start the dispatching and planning process:

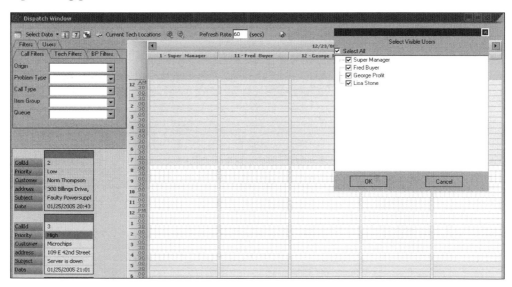

Using this interface, you can view technician availability, and schedule the technicians to complete service tasks at customer sites. You may also check the current location of a technician. This can be done via a link from the calendar to **Google Maps**, which reveals the technicians' location based on the customers' service address where the technicians are currently working.

Field service

As I mentioned earlier, field service technicians may use mobile devices to complete tasks and record the cost of labor, material, and expenses.

Billing and revenue recognition

Service calls are directly linked to business partners. This fact is accounted for in the ServiceONE add-on via a direct link on the business partner master data level to **service calls**. Therefore, you can easily obtain service-related information from the BP master record:

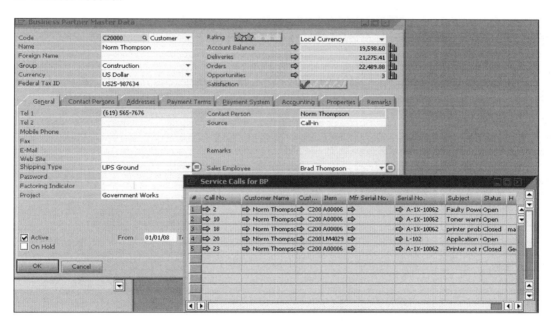

SAP service module functionality available via add-ons

By evaluating two add-ons for service management, we identified the potential additional features that we could use which are based on our strategic direction in this area. The Enprise Job Costing module was very focused on job costing features. This solution provided a great level of detail to handle job-costing-specific requirements. This add-on was embedded within SAP, but added the features within its own menu section. The Navigator ServiceONE solution was centered around the service view, which could be best operated within a second monitor. You would then have SAP on one monitor and the service view on the other monitor. Furthermore, the Navigator ServiceONE add-on is a member of a well-integrated set of add-ons provided by this vendor. We evaluated these two solutions to make sure that the activity of evaluating add-ons becomes a common activity for you.

In addition, by evaluating the added functionality, we understand what the Standard SAP service module may not provide out of the box.

The following functionality must be obtained via an add-on:

- Email case management
- Field service integration via mobile devices
- Planning of service activities via a calendar with dispatching
- Contracts with milestones and invoicing
- Timesheet entry via the Web
- Bulk invoice generation for multiple jobs
- Job master data management

Summary

In this chapter, we covered the SAP service module. We started by introducing the common terms. Alongside this discussion, the core functionality related to the service module was explained. We then continued to apply the knowledge by implementing a service feature set for the case study. Based on the case study, we implemented a service and contract system that established a defined response time for important customers.

The result was a clear workflow for the service module that you can use in your own project. Finally, we evaluated two powerful add-ons. You saw that the SAP Business ONE platform can be modified via add-ons to resemble industry-specific requirements. At this point, you have a good understanding of all of the core modules in SAP Business ONE. In the next chapter, we will focus on **data migration**.

9

Data Migration Scenarios: What to Migrate and How

Just recently, I found myself in a data migration project that served as an eye-opener. Our team had to migrate a customer system that utilized Act! and Peachtree. Both systems are not very famous for having good accessibility to their data. In fact, Peachtree is a non-SQL database that does not enforce data consistency. Act! also uses a proprietary table system that is based on a non-SQL database.

The general migration logic was rather straightforward. However, our team found that the migration and consolidation of data into the new system posed multiple challenges, not only on the technical front, but also for the customer when it came to verifying the data. We used the on-the-edge tool xFusion Studio for data migration. This tool allows migrating and synchronizing data by using simple and advanced SQL data **messaging** techniques. The xFusion Studio tool has a graphical representation of how the data flows from the source to the target. When I looked at one section of this graphical representation, I started humming the song **Welcome to the Jungle**.

Take a look at the following screenshot and find out why Guns and Roses may have provided the soundtrack for this data migration project:

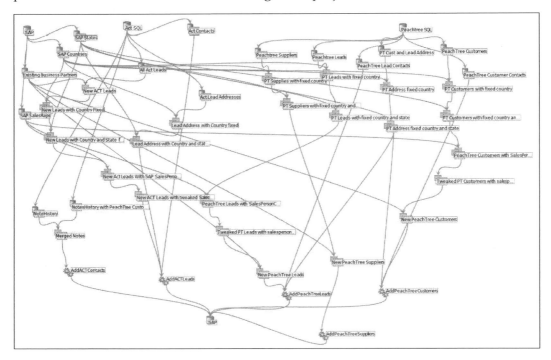

What we learned from the above screenshot is quite obvious and I have dedicated this chapter to helping you overcome these potential issues. **Keep it simple** and focus on information rather than data. You know that just by having more data does not always mean you've added more information. Sometimes, it just means a data jungle has been created. Making the right decisions at key milestones during the migration can keep the project simple and guarantee the success. Your goal should be to consolidate the **islands of data** into a more efficient and consistent database that provides real-time information.

What you will learn about data migration

In this chapter, I will introduce the tools and methods to help you migrate data from different sources into the SAP Business ONE application. In order to accomplish this task, a strategy must be designed that addresses the individual needs of the project at hand. The data migration strategy uses proven processes and templates. The data migration itself can be managed as a **mini project** depending on the complexity. During the course of this chapter, the following key topics will be covered. The goal is to help you make crucial decisions, which will keep a project simple and manageable:

- Position the data migration tasks in the project plan – We will start by positioning the **data migration** tasks in the project plan. I will further define the required tasks that you need to complete as a part of the data migration.

- Data types and scenarios – With the general project plan structure in place, it is time to cover the common terms related to data migration. I will introduce you to the main aspects, such as master data and transactional data, as well as the impact they have on the complexity of data migration.

- SAP tools available for migration – During the course of our case study, I will introduce you to the data migration tools that come with SAP. However, there are also more advanced tools for complex migrations. You will learn about the main player in this area and how to use it.

- Process of migration – To avoid problems and guarantee success, the data migration project must follow a proven procedure. We will update the project plan to include the procedure and will also use the process during our case study.

- Making decisions about what data to bring – I mentioned that it is important to focus on **information** versus **data**. With the knowledge of the right tools and procedures, it is a good time to summarize the primary known issues and explain how to tackle them.

- Apply your new knowledge - We use the case study to showcase SAP import, Data Transfer Workbench, and xFusion packs. The key concepts will be revisited during the case study and will be applied to put our skills to the test.

The project plan

We are still progressing in **Phase 2 – Analysis and Design**. The data migration is positioned in the **Solution Architecture** section and is called **Review Data Conversion Needs (Amount and Type of Data)**. A thorough evaluation of the data conversion needs will also cover the next task in the project plan called **Review Integration Points with any 3rd Party Solution**.

As you can see, the data migration task stands as a small task in the project plan. But as mentioned earlier, it can wind up being a large project depending on the number and size of data sources that need to be migrated. To honor this, we will add some more details to this task.

As the task name suggests, we must **review data conversion needs** and identify the amount and type of data. This simple task must be structured in phases, just like the entire project that is structured in phases. Therefore, data migration needs to go through the following phases to be successful:

1. Design - Identify all of the Data Sources
2. Extraction of data into Excel or SQL for review and consistency
3. Review of Data and Verification(Via Customer Feedback)
4. Load into SAP System and Verification

Note that the validation process and the consequential load could be iterative processes. For example, if the validated data has many issues, it only makes sense to perform a load into SAP if an additional verification takes place before the load. You only want to load data into an SAP system for testing if you know the quality of the records going to be loaded is good. Therefore, new phases were added in the project plan (seen below). Please do this in your project too based on the actual complexity and the number of data sources you have.

A thorough look at the tasks above will be provided when we talk about the process of migration. Before we do that, the basic terms related to data migration will be covered.

⊟ **Review Data Conversion Needs (Amount and Type of Data)**
Design - Identify all the Data Sources
Extraction of data into Excel or SQL for review and consistency
Review of Data and Verification (Via Customer Feedback)
Load into SAP System and Verification

Data sources—where is my data

There is a great variety in the potential types data sources. We will now identify the most common sources and explain their key characteristics. However, if there is a source that is not mentioned here, you can still migrate the data easily by transitioning it into one of the following formats.

Microsoft Excel and text data migration

The most common format for data migration is Excel, or text-based files. Text-based files are formatted using commas or tabs as field separators. When a comma is used as a field separator, the file format is referred to as Comma Separated Values (CSV).

Most of the migration templates and strategies are based on Excel files that have specific columns where you can manually enter data, or copy and paste larger chunks. Therefore, if there is any way for you to extract data from your current system and present it in Excel, you have already done a great deal of data migration work.

Microsoft Access

An Access database is essentially an Excel sheet on a larger scale with added data consistency capability. It is a good idea to consider extracting Access tables to Excel in order to prepare for data migration.

SQL

If you have very large sets of data, then instead of using Excel, we usually employ an SQL database. The database then has a set of tables instead of Excel sheets. Using SQL tables, we can create SQL statements that can verify data and analyze results sets. Please note that you can use any SQL database, such as Microsoft SQL Server, Oracle, IBM DB, and so on.

SaaS (Netsuite, Salesforce)

SaaS stands for Software as a Service. Essentially, it means you can use software functionality based on a subscription. However, you don't own the solution. All of the hardware and software is installed at the service center, so you don't need to worry about hardware and software maintenance. However, keep in mind that these services don't allow you to manage the service packs according to your requirements. You need to adjust your business to the schedule of the SaaS company. If you are migrating from a modern SaaS solution, such as Salesforce or Netsuite, you will probably know that the data is not at your site, but rather stored at your solution hosting provider. Getting the data out to migrate to another solution may be done by obtaining reports, which could then be saved in an Excel format.

Other legacy data

The term **legacy data** is often mentioned when evaluating larger old systems. **Legacy data** basically comprises a large set of data that a company is using on mostly obsolete systems.

AS/400 or Mainframe

The IBM AS/400 is a good example of a legacy data source. Experts who are capable of extracting data from these systems are highly sought after, and so the budget must be on a higher scale. AS/400 data can often be extracted into a text or an Excel format. However, the data may come without headings. The headings are usually documented in a file that **describes** the data. You need to make sure that you get the **file definitions**, without which the pure text files may be meaningless. In addition, the media format is worth considering. An older AS/400 system may utilize a backup tape format which is not available on your Intel server.

Peachtree, QuickBooks, and Act!

Another potential source for data migration may be a smaller PC-based system, such as Peachtree, QuickBooks, or Act!. These systems have a different data format, and are based on non-SQL databases. This means the data cannot be accessed via SQL. In order to extract data from those systems, the proprietary API must be used. For example, if Peachtree displays data in the applications forms, it uses the program logic to put the pieces together from different text files. Getting data out from these types of systems is difficult and sometimes impossible. It is recommended to employ the relevant API to access the data in a structured way.

[You may want to run reports and export the results to text or Excel.]

Data classification in SAP Business ONE

There are two main groups of data that we will migrate to the SAP Business ONE application: **master data** and **transaction data**.

Master data

Master data is the basic information that SAP Business ONE uses to **record** transactions (for example, business partner information). In addition, information about your products, such as items, finished goods, and raw materials are considered **master data**. Master data should always be migrated if possible. It can easily be verified and structured in an Excel or SQL format. For example, the data could be displayed using Excel sheets. You can then quickly verify that the data is showing up in the correct columns. In addition, you can see if the data is broken down into its required components. For example, each Excel column should represent a target field in SAP Business ONE. You should avoid having a single column in Excel that provides data for more than one target in SAP Business ONE.

Transaction data

Transaction data are proposals, orders, invoices, deliveries, and other similar information that comprise a combination of master data to create a unique business document. Customers often will want to migrate historical transactions from older systems. However, the consequences of doing this may have a landslide effect. For example, inventory is valuated based on specific settings in the finance section of a system. If these settings are not identical in the new system, transactions may look different in the old and the new system. This makes the migration very risky as the data verification becomes difficult on the customer side.

I recommend making historical transactions available via a reporting database. For example, often, **sales history** must be available when migrating data. You can create a reporting database that provides sales history information. The user can use this data via reports within the SAP Business ONE application. Therefore, **closed transactions** should be migrated via a reporting database. Closed transactions are all of the business-related activities that were fully completed in the old system. **Open transactions**, on the other hand, are all of the business-related activities that are currently not completed. It makes sense that the open transactions be migrated directly to SAP, and not to a history database because they will be completed within the new SAP system. As a result of the data migration, you would be able to access sales history information from within SAP by accessing a reporting database. Open transactions will be completed within SAP, and then consequently lead to new transactions in SAP.

 Create a history database for sales history and manually enter open transactions.

SAP DI-API

Now that we know the main data types for an SAP migration, and the most common sources, we can take a brief look at the way the data is inserted into the SAP system. Based on the SAP guidelines, you are not allowed to insert data directly in the underlying SQL tables. The reason for that is that it can cause inconsistencies. When SAP works with the database, multiple tables are often updated. If you manually update a table to insert data, there is a good chance that another table has a link that also requires updating. Therefore, unless you know the exact table structure for the data you are trying to update, don't mess with the SAP SQL tables. If you carefully read this and understand the table structure, you will now know that there may be situations where you decide to access the tables directly. If you decide to insert data directly into the SAP database tables, you run the risk of losing your warranty.

Migration scenarios and key decisions

Data migration not only takes place as a part of a new SAP implementation, but also if you have a running system and you want to import leads or a list of new items. Therefore, it is a good idea to learn about the scenarios that you may come across and be able to select the right migration and integration tools. As outlined before, data can be divided into two groups: master data and transaction data. It is important that you separate the two, and structure each data migration accordingly. Master data is an essential component for manifesting transactions. Therefore, even if you need to bring over transactional data, the master data must already be in place. Always start with the master data alongside a verification procedure, and then continue with the relevant transaction data. Let's now briefly look at the most common situations where you may require the evaluation of potential data migration options.

New company (start-up)

In this setup, you may not have extensive amounts of existing data to migrate. However, you may want to bring over lead lists or lists of items. During the course of this chapter, we will import a list of leads into SAP using the Excel Import functionality. Many new companies require the capability to easily import data into SAP. As you already know by now, the import of leads and item information will be considered as importing master data. Working with this master data by entering sales orders and so forth, would constitute transaction data. Transaction data is considered **closed** if all of the relevant actions are performed. For example, a sales order is considered **closed** if the items are delivered, invoiced, and paid for. If the **chain of events** is not complete, the transaction is **open**.

Islands of data scenario

This is the classic situation for an SAP implementation. You will first need to identify the available data sources and their formats. Then, you select the master data you want to bring over. With multiple islands of data, an SAP master record may result from more than one source. A business partner record may come, in part, from an existing accounting system, such as QuickBooks or Peachtree. Whereas other parts may come from a CRM system, such as Act!. For example, the billing information may be retrieved from the finance system and the relevant lead and sales information, such as specific contacts and notes, may come from the CRM system. In such a case, you need to merge this information into a new consistent master record in SAP. For this situation, first manually put the pieces together. Once the manual process works, you can attempt to automate the process. Don't try to directly import all of the data. You should always establish an intermediary level that allows for data verification. Only then import the data into SAP. For example, if you have QuickBooks and Act!, first merge the information into Excel for verification, and then import it into SAP. If the amount of data is large, you can also establish an SQL database. In that case, the Excel sheets would be replaced by SQL tables.

IBM legacy data migration

The migration of IBM legacy data is potentially the most challenging because the IBM systems are not directly compatible with Windows-based systems. Therefore, almost naturally, you will establish a text-based, or an Excel-formatted, representation of the IBM data. You can then proceed with verifying the information.

SQL migration

The easiest migration type is obviously the one where all of the data is already structured and consistent. However, you will not always have documentation of the table structure where the data resides. In this case, you need to create queries against the SQL tables to verify the data. The queries can then be saved as **views**. The views you create should always represent a consistent set of information that you can migrate.

For example, if you have one table with address information, and another table with customer ID fields, you can create a view that consolidates this information into a single consistent set.

Process of migration for your project

I briefly touched upon the most common data migration scenarios so you can get a feel for the process. As you can see, whatever the source of data is, we always attempt to create an intermediary platform that allows the data to be verified. This intermediary platform is most commonly Excel or an SQL database. The process of data migration has the following subtasks:

1. Identify available data sources
2. Structure data into master data and transaction data
3. Establish an intermediary platform with Excel or SQL
4. Verify data
5. Match data columns with Excel templates
6. Run migration based on templates and verify data

Based on this procedure, I have added more detail to the project plan. As you can see in this example, based on the required level of detail, we can make adjustments to the project plan to address the requirements:

⊟ **Review Data Conversion Needs (Amount and Type of Data)**
Design - Identify all the Data Sources
Structure Data into Master Data and Transaction Data
Extraction of data into Excel or SQL for review and consistency
Review of Data and Verification (Via Customer Feedback)
Match Data Columns with Excel Migration Templates
Load into SAP System and Verification

SAP standard import features

Let's take a look at the available data exchange features in SAP. SAP provides two main tools for data migration. The first option is to use the available menu in the SAP Business ONE client interface to exchange data. The other option is to use the Data Transfer Workbench (DTW).

Standard import/export features— walk-through

You can reach the **Import from Excel** form via **Administration | Data Import/ Export**. As you can see in the following screenshot on the right top section of the form, the type of import is a drop-down selection. The options are **BP** and **Items**. In the screenshot, we have selected **BP**, which allows business partner information to be imported. There are drop-down fields that you can select based on the data you want to import. However, keep in mind that certain fields are mandatory, such as the **BP Code** field, whereas others are optional. The fields you select are associated with a column as you can see here:

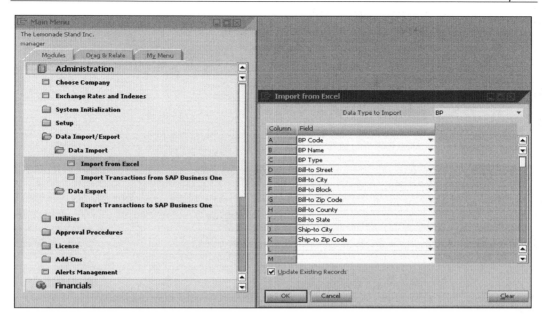

If you want to find out if a field is mandatory or not, simply open SAP and attempt to enter the data directly in the relevant SAP form. For example, if you are trying to import business partner information, enter the fields you want to import and see if the record can be saved. If you are missing any mandatory fields, SAP will provide an error message. You can modify the data that you are planning to import based on that.

When you click on the **OK** button in the **Import from Excel** form (seen above), the Excel sheet with all of the data needs to be selected. In the following screenshot, you can see how the Excel sheet in our example looks. For example, column **A** has all of the BP Codes. This is in line with the mapping of columns to fields that we can see on the **Import from Excel** form.

A	B	C	D	E	F	G	H	I	J	K	L
10040	LA County Distributor	L	Ventura Blvd.	San Diego	Block A	92121	US	CA	San Diego	92121	
10050	Las Vegas Distributor	L	Main Str.	Las Vegas	Block B	89166	US	NV	Las Vegas	89166	

Please note that the file we select must be in a `.txt` format. For this example, I used the **Save As** feature in Excel (seen in the following screenshot) to save the file in the **Text MS-DOS (*.txt)** format. I was then able to select the `BP Migration.txt` file. This is actually a good thing because it points to the fact that you can use any application that can save data in the `.txt` format as the data source.

The following screenshot shows the **Save As** screen:

I imported the file and a success message confirms that the records were imported into SAP:

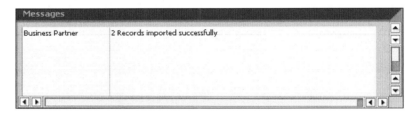

A subsequent check in SAP confirms that the BP records that I had in the text file are now available in SAP:

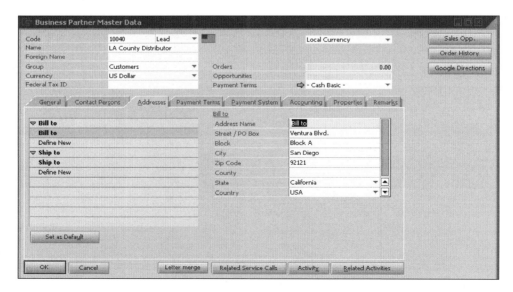

In the example, we only used two records. It is recommended to start out with a limited number of records to verify that the import is working. Therefore, you may start by reducing your import file to five records. This has the advantage of the import not taking a long time and you can immediately verify the result. See the following screenshot:

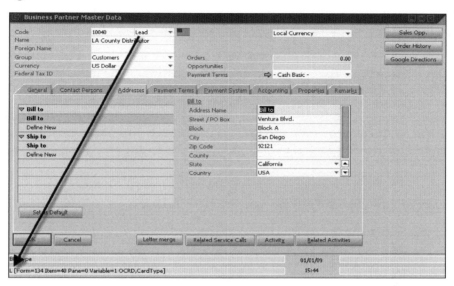

Sometimes, it is not clear what kind of information SAP expects when importing. For example, at first **Lead**, **Customer**, **Vendor** were used in Column C to indicate the type of BP that was to be imported. However, this resulted in an error message upon completion of the import. Therefore, system information was activated to check what information SAP requires for the **BP Type** representation. As you can see in the screenshot of the Excel sheet you get when you click on the **OK** button in the **Import from Excel** form, the **BP Type** information is indicated by only one letter using **L**, **C**, or **V**. In the example screenshot above, you can clearly see **L** in the lower left section. The same thing is done for **Country** in the **Addresses** section. You can try that by navigating to **Administration | Sales | Countries**, and then hovering over the country you will be importing. In my example, USA was internally represented by SAP as **US**. It is a minor issue. However, when importing data, all of these issues need to be addressed.

Please note that the file you are trying to import should not be open in Excel at the same time, as this may trigger an error.

 The Excel or text file does not have a **header** with a description of the data.

Standard import/export features for your own project

SAP's standard import functionality for business partners and items is very straightforward. For your own project, you can prepare an Excel sheet for business partners and items. If you need to import BP or item information from another system, you can get this done quickly.

If you get an error during the import process, try to manually enter the data in SAP. In addition, you can use the **System Information** feature to identify how SAP stores information in the database.

I recommend you first create an Excel sheet with a maximum of two records to see if the basic information and data format is correct. Once you have this running, you can add all of the data you want to import.

Overall, this functionality is a quick way to get your own data into the system.

This feature can also be used in case you regularly receive address information. For example, if you have salespeople visiting trade fairs, you can provide them with the Excel sheet that you may have prepared for BP import. The salespeople can directly add their information there. Once they return from the trade fair with the Excel files, you can easily import the information into SAP and schedule follow-up activities using the Opportunity Management System.

The item import is useful if you work with a vendor who updates his or her price lists and item information on a monthly basis. You can prepare an Excel template where the item information will regularly be entered and you can easily import the updates into SAP.

Data Migration Workbench—DTW

The SAP standard import/export features are straightforward, but may not address the full complexity of the data that you need to import. For this situation, you may want to evaluate the SAP **Data Migration Workbench (DTW)**. The functionality of this tool provides a greater level of detail to address the potential data structures that you want to import. To understand the basic concept of the DTW, it is a good idea to look at the different master data sections in SAP as **business objects**. A business object groups related information together. For example, BP information can have much more detail than what was previously shown in the standard import.

The DTW templates and business objects

To better understand the **business object** metaphor, you need to navigate to the DTW directory and evaluate the `Templates` folder. The templates are organized by business objects. The `oBusinessPartners` business object is represented by the folder with the same name (seen below). In this folder, you can find Excel template files that can be used to provide information for this type of business object. The following objects are available as Excel templates:

- BPAccountReceivables
- BPAddresses
- BPBankAccounts
- BPPaymentDates
- BPPaymentMethods
- BPWithholdingTax
- BusinessPartners
- ContactEmployees

 Please notice that these templates are Excel `.xlt` files, which is the Excel template extension.

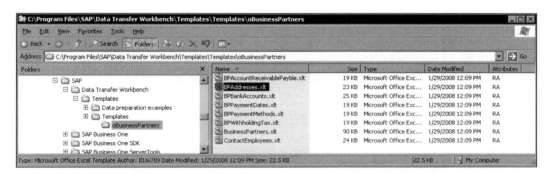

It is a good idea to browse through the list of templates and see the relevant templates. In a nutshell, you essentially add your own data to the templates and use DTW to import the data.

Connecting to DTW

In order to work with DTW, you need to connect to your SAP system using the DTW interface. The following screenshot shows the parameters I used to connect to the Lemonade Stand database:

Once you are connected, a wizard-type interface walks you through the required steps to get started. Look at the next screenshot:

The DTW examples and templates

There is also an example folder in the DTW installation location on your system. This example folder has information about how to add information to your Excel templates. The following screenshot shows an example for business partner migration.

You can see that the Excel template does have a header line on top that explains the content in the particular column. The actual template files also have comments in the header file, which provide information about the data format expected, such as String, Date, and so on. See the example in this screenshot:

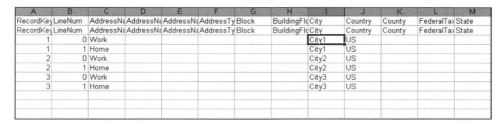

A	B	C	D	E	F	G	H	I	J	K	L	M
RecordKey	LineNum	AddressNa	AddressNa	AddressNa	AddressTy	Block	BuildingFlo	City	Country	County	FederalTax	State
RecordKey	LineNum	AddressNa	AddressNa	AddressNa	AddressTy	Block	BuildingFlo	City	Country	County	FederalTax	State
1	0	Work						City1	US			
1	1	Home						City1	US			
2	0	Work						City2	US			
2	1	Home						City2	US			
3	0	Work						City3	US			
3	1	Home						City3	US			

The actual template is empty and you need to add your information as shown here:

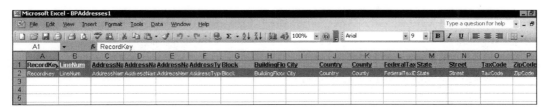

DTW for your own project

If you realize that the basic import features in SAP are not sufficient, and your requirements are more challenging, evaluate DTW. Think of the data you want to import as business objects where information is logically grouped. If you are able to group your data together, you can modify the Excel templates with your own information. The DTW example folder provides working examples that you can use to get started. Please note that you should establish a test database before you start importing data this way. This is because once new data arrives in SAP, you need to verify the results based on the procedure discussed earlier. In addition, be prepared to fine-tune the import. Often, an import and data verification process takes four attempts of data importing and verification.

Advanced data migration tools—xFusion Studio

For our own projects, we have adopted a tool called **xFusion**. Using this tool, you gain flexibility and are able to reuse migration settings for specific project environments. The tool provides connectivity to directly extract data from applications (including QuickBooks and Peachtree). In addition, it also supports building rules for data profiling, validation, and conversions. For example, our project team participated in the development of the template for the Peachtree interface. We configured the mappings from Peachtree, and connected the data with the right fields in SAP. This was then saved as a migration **template**. Therefore, it would be easy and straightforward to migrate data from Peachtree to SAP in any future projects.

xFusion packs save migration knowledge

Based on the concept of establishing templates for migrations, xFusion provides preconfigured templates for the SAP Business ONE application. In xFusion, templates are called **xFusion packs**. Please note that these preconfigured **packs** may include master data packs, and also **xFusion packs** for transaction data. The following xFusion packs are provided for an SAP Business ONE migration:

- Administration
- Banking
- Business partner
- Finance
- HR
- Inventory and production
- Marketing documents and receipts
- MRP
- UDFs
- Services

You can see that the packs are also grouped by **business object**. For example, you have a group of xFusion packs for inventory and production. You can open the pack and find a group of xFusion files that contain the configuration information. If you open the inventory and production pack, a list of folders will be revealed. Each folder has a set of Excel templates and xFusion files (seen in the following screenshot). An xFusion pack essentially incorporates the configuration and data manipulation procedures required to bring data from a source into SAP. The source settings can be saved in xFusion packs so that you can reuse the knowledge with regards to data manipulation and formatting.

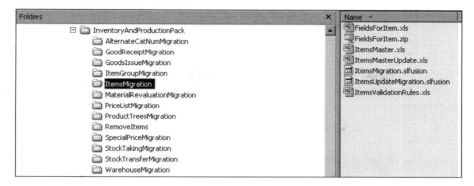

Data "massaging" using SQL

The key for the migration procedure is the capability to do **data massaging** in order to adjust formats and columns, in a step-by-step manner, based on requirements. Data manipulation is not done programmatically, but rather via a step-by-step process, where each step uses SQL statements to verify and format data. The entire process is represented visually, and thereby documents the steps required. This makes it easy to adjust settings and fine-tune them.

The following applications are supported and can, therefore, be used as a source for an SAP migration: (They are existing xFusion packs)

- SAP Business ONE
- Sage ACT!
- SAP
- SAP BW
- Peachtree
- QuickBooks
- Microsoft Dynamics CRM

The following is a list of supported databases:

- Oracle
- ODBC
- MySQL
- OLE DB
- SQL Server
- PostgrSQL

The following examples are ISAM/files:

- Text
- BTrieve
- Microsoft Access
- Microsoft Excel
- XML

Working with xFusion

The workflow in xFusion starts when you open an existing xFusion pack, or create a new one. In this example, an xFusion pack for business partner migration was opened. You can see the graphical representation of the migration process in the main window (in the following screenshot). Each icon in the graphic representation represents a data manipulation and formatting step. If you click on an icon, the complete path from the data source to the icon is highlighted. Therefore, you can select the previous steps to adjust the data. The core concept is that you do not directly change the input data, but define rules to convert data from the source format to the target format. If you open an xFusion pack for the SAP Business ONE application, the target is obviously SAP Business ONE. Therefore, you need to enter the privileges and database name so that the pack knows how to access the SAP system. In addition, the source parameters need to be provided. xFusion packs come with example Excel files. You need to select the Excel files as the relevant source. However, it is important to note that you don't need to use the Excel files. You can use any database, or other source, as long as you adjust the data format using the step-by-step process to represent the same format as provided in Excel.

In xFusion. you can use the sample files that come in Excel format.

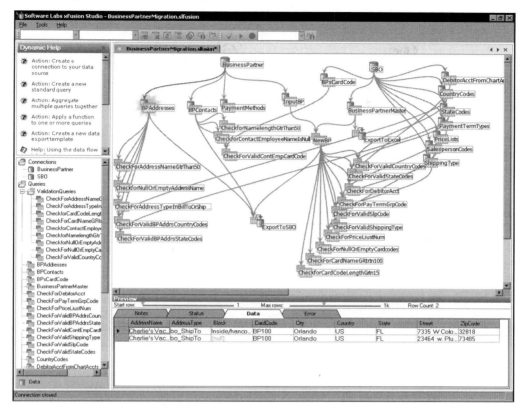

The connection parameters are presented once you double-click on any of the connections listed in the **Connections** section as follows:

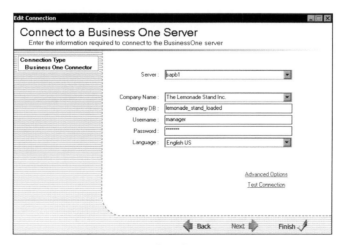

It is recommended to click on **Test Connection** to verify the proper parameters.

If all of the connections are right, you can run a migration from the source to the target by right-clicking on an icon and selecting **Run Export** as shown here:

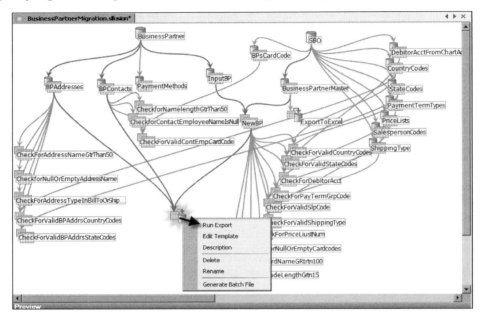

The progress and export is visually documented. This way, you can verify the success. There is also a log file in the directory where the currently utilized xFusion pack resides, as shown in the following screenshot:

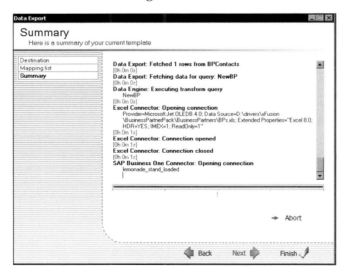

Tips and recommendations for your own project

Now you know all of the main migration tools and methods. If you want to select the right tool and method for your specific situation, you will see that even though there may be many templates and preconfigured packs out there, your own project potentially comes with some individual aspects. When organizing the data migration project, use the project task skeleton I provided. It is important to subdivide the required migration steps into a group of easy-to-understand steps, where data can be verified at each level. If it gets complicated, it is probably not the right way to move forward, and you need to re-think the methods and tools you are using.

Common issues

The most common issue I found in similar projects is that the data to be migrated is not entirely **clean** and **consistent**. Therefore, be sure to use a data verification procedure at each step. Don't just import data, only to find out later that the database is overloaded with data that is not right.

Recommendation

Separate the master data and the transaction data. If you don't want to lose valuable transaction data, you can establish a reporting database which will save all of the historic transactions. For example, sales history can easily be migrated to an SQL database. You can then provide access to this information from the required SAP forms using queries or Crystal Reports.

Case study

During the course of evaluating the data import features available in the SAP Business ONE application, we have already learned how to import business partner information and item data. This can easily be done using the standard SAP data import features based on the Excel or text files.

Using this method allows the lead, customer, and vendor data to be imported. Let's say that the Lemonade Stand enterprise has salespeople who travel to trade fairs and collect contact information. We can import the address information using the proven BP import method. But after this data is imported, what would the next step be? It would be a good idea to create and manage **opportunities** based on the address material. Basically, you already know how to use Excel to bring over address information. Let's enhance this concept to bring over **opportunity information**. We will use xFusion to import opportunity data into the SAP Business ONE application. The basis will be the xFusion pack for opportunities.

Importing sales opportunities for the Lemonade Stand

The xFusion pack is open, and you can see that it is a nice and clean example without major complexity. That's how it should be, as you see here:

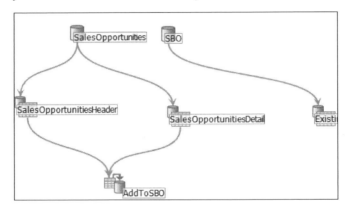

Specifying source and target

The dataflow in the previous example is top down, and that's the case for most xFusion packs. There, you can see that the data source is on the top, while the data destination is at the bottom. In this case, the source is an Excel file. I opened the Excel file to investigate the data structure and columns. You can see that the Excel document has two sheets. One is called **SalesOpportunities** and the other is called **SalesOpportunitiesLines**:

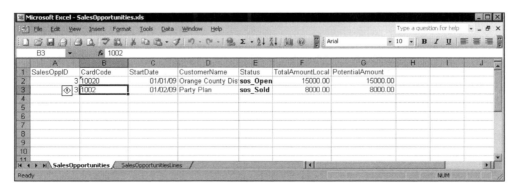

Please review the **SalesOpportunitiesLines** tab sheet here:

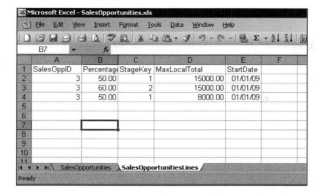

The first sheet essentially has the required information to establish a new opportunity with the salesperson ID, the customer CardCode, and the potential amount. The second sheet has information about the sales stages.

Remember that in xFusion, we need to adjust the source and target information:

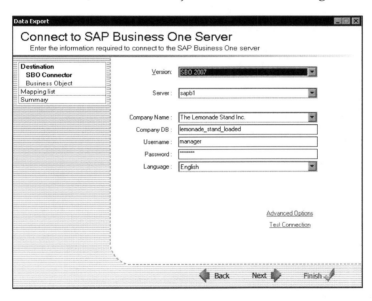

Clicking on the **Test Connection** link confirms that we are connected.

Selecting the target "business object"

By clicking on **Next**, you will see a drop-down box that allows specifying the business object that we will be transferring the data to. In this example, **Sales Opportunities** was selected in the **Insert** mode.

If you closely investigate this example, you can see that the migration can also run in the **Update** or **Delete** mode. Furthermore, you can also do a **Test Run** first. This is often used if your data migration is complex, and you need to potentially wait many hours only to find out that there were errors. Using this mode, you can save time and test the data first:

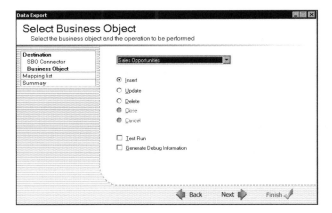

Data mapping

The crucial part during migration is the correct mapping of fields. Since we selected the Excel file with its two sheets, we can now map the columns in those sheets to the target fields provided by the **Sales Opportunities** business object. Check out this screenshot:

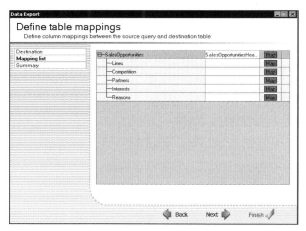

When you click on the **Map** button, a field-mapping tool opens up. As you click on the columns, you can drag a line from the source to the target. This would map the fields, which means that the source column called **CardCode** will be mapped to the actual SAP column **CardCode**. The mapping process is often not so obvious when the names are not identical and many columns with similar content exist.

As shown in the following screenshot, I am mapping two Excel sheets: **Sales Opportunities Header Sales Opportunities Detail**:

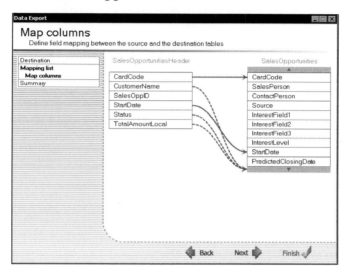

When this is complete, all of the source data fields will have a proper destination in the target SAP database:

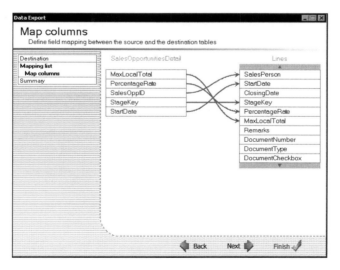

When you click on **Next**, a new form opens (seen below) which allows you to start the export via the **Run Export** button. The data is now transferred from the Excel sheets to SAP. A status window and a log file will document the successful transactions or any errors that have occurred. This is helpful if you have large data sources because often, 99% of the data comes through while a set of records does not. You can make notes of the problem records and use this information to manually enter the right information.

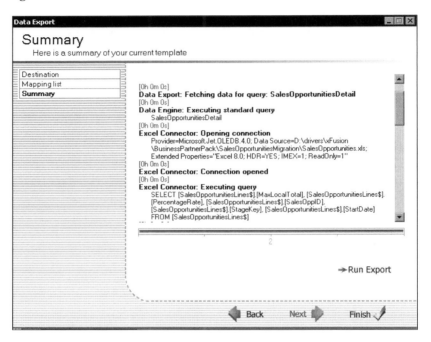

Review the data transfer in SAP

The final step for data migration is the verification of the data in SAP. We now have a new opportunity, which corresponds to the data that previously only existed in Excel. The **Potential** tab page shows the potential amount. The **Stages** tab page shows the stages as specified in the second Excel sheet:

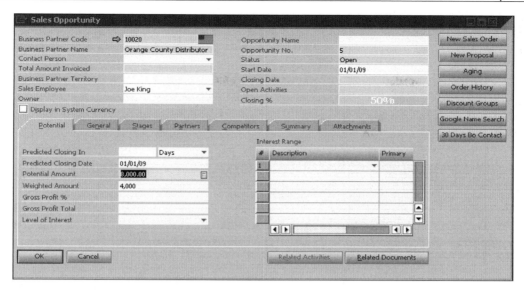

We can conclude that the data migration was successful. The migration templates can be used to easily bring in the lead data. In addition, we can migrate opportunities and continue managing our sales according to the established sales stages.

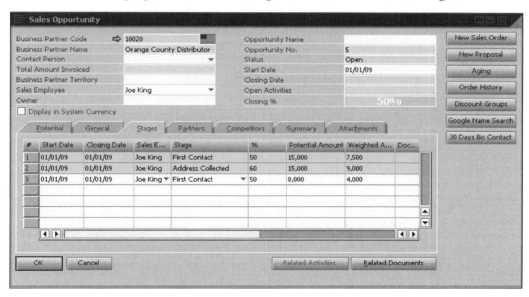

Essentially, you can see that even if your field salespeople don't have access to the SAP Business One application, they can collect data using the Excel templates. These templates can then be used to easily import data into SAP.

Summary

In this chapter, we covered the tasks related to data migration. This also included some practical examples for simple data imports related to business partner information and items. In addition, more advanced topics were covered by introducing the SAP DTW (Data Transfer Workbench) and the related aspects to get you started. The advanced tool, xFusion, was used to further expand on the examples and introduce preconfigured migration projects called **xFusion packs**.

During the course of this chapter, we positioned the data migration task in the project plan. The project plan was then fine-tuned with more detail to give some justice to the potential complexity of a data migration project. The data migration tasks established a process, from design to data mapping and verification of the data. Notably, the establishment of an intermediary data platform was recommended for your projects. This will help you verify data at each step of the migration. The key message of keeping it simple will be the basis for every migration project. The data verification task ensures simplicity and the quality of your data.

With the knowledge of the right tools and process, we performed a data migration to add opportunities for our case study.

Overall, the tools and methodologies provided in this chapter will help you manage your own project, and also make the right decisions to keep the data migration simple and successful. In addition, you can get started quickly by using the SAP import tools, or plan a project if your requirements are more challenging. In the following chapter about reporting, we will be looking at ways to make the best use of the data that is available in SAP.

10
Consolidated Reporting and Dashboard Design

During a large SAP implementation, I worked as the project manager to coordinate the progress of the implementation for the customer teams and implementation teams.

The team leader on the customer project side had made it a habit to measure the SAP functionality against Excel. Therefore, it became the logo of the project and project members would say "I can do this in Excel faster." Basically, the obvious value of an integrated SAP solution was challenged. Even though the claim was ridiculous to some extent, it also had some truth to it. It is essentially true that if you look at each form in SAP, you can quickly recreate it in Excel and enter data. However, with SAP, you take an integrated approach that goes beyond a series of Excel sheets. In fact, the true value is the real-time integrated view that eliminates all of the Excel islands. Furthermore, SAP allows collecting the data required for reporting as users work with the system by using the right form fields as data is entered.

This data collection framework has two main purposes. First, the legal financial reporting requirements need to be addressed. This is done via the CoA (Chart of Accounts) configuration. Second, another data collection takes place which will provide the information that is required to support adequate business decisions. This is the controlling framework. **What cannot be measured cannot be improved** is the key philosophy behind this. Therefore, the SAP system must be looked at as a data collection framework that stores data for financial and reporting purposes.

Consequently, it is true that almost any report can be run in Excel. However, how it is being run must be considered. Is the report manually created each time, or are the Excel reports driven in real time and automatically distributed to recipients?

With the available SAP tools today, what you can do in Excel can also be done in real time with SAP data, and there is no faster way than **real time**.

What you will learn about reporting in this chapter

The SAP Business ONE application is based on an SQL database. This means most of the business-related data is available for reporting. You can design custom reports and also use the **canned** reports that come with SAP. As reports are the foundation of the decisions made by owners, sales personnel, and so on, it is a crucial element of the SAP system. In fact, I will go as far as to say that reporting is the most important element of the system. Therefore, in this chapter, we will reserve some time to pay close attention to all of the key success factors related to reporting within the SAP Business ONE application.

The following topics will be covered during the course of this chapter:

- Update the project plan – We will first position the **reporting-related** tasks within the project plan. I will connect our previous efforts made as a part of the **process analysis** with reference to reporting.

- Introduce the most common terms related to reporting – When talking about reports in SAP, there are common terms and areas in the SAP Business ONE application that are often touched upon. We will look at them and enable you to join the conversation about reporting.

- Showcase the reporting tools in the SAP Business ONE application – We will continue the discovery of SAP reporting tools. This will in part build on the previous efforts made in the first section of this book.

- Designing a report – When designing a report, there is a specific workflow that you can follow to be sure the report will be structured, and the information will be presented in the right way.

- Focus on the Crystal add-on – I will stress the new Crystal Reports add-on from SAP. With the takeover of the French company **Business Objects**, SAP now owns Crystal Reports. Crystal Reports is considered as an industry-standard reporting tool.

- A brief look at SAP XL reporter – Even though Crystal Reports is important, there is also the SAP tool called XL reporter. I will introduce you to the architecture of this tool, and the sophisticated sample Excel reports.

- The limitations of the SAP Crystal add-on – The Crystal add-on has some limitations. We will uncover these current limitations and investigate another reporting tool that overcomes these limits.

- Design a dashboard for the case study – Applying the gathered knowledge to our case study is the final step of this chapter. I will design a simple Excel dashboard for our Lemonade enterprise.

The project plan

Reporting takes a key position during the implementation. Therefore, it is a good idea to revisit the business process analysis we completed earlier. For your own project, you may use the process analysis to additionally clarify the strategic direction of your own business. A strategic direction directly impacts the reporting requirements you will have as a business owner. The strategic goals set the terms which will determine how you will measure progress and accomplishment. These factors indicate **progress** and must be defined. They will be the data points we will report about.

In addition to the strategic reporting requirements, more operative reports are directly derived. For example, sales stage analysis are reports that must be available for salespeople. Therefore, you can see that the information we extract using reports must include the data points we plan to measure according to our strategic direction. In addition to the strategic aspect, reports also need to provide information about data points related to our operative goals.

Take a look at the project plan tasks (seen below) and see how the reporting strategy is implemented. First, we put the information requirements into perspective by relating our information needs to the overall strategic direction of the business. Then, we establish departmental reports which will support the departments in reaching the operative goals. Once the information requirements are clear, we evaluate the available standard reports and see if they cover the needs. If additional data points are needed, we implement UDFs in the appropriate SAP forms to collect the data. If a report is not available, we use Queries, XL Reporter, or Crystal Reports to extract the data.

⊟ **Reporting**
⊟ **Identify Information Needs based on Strategic Direction (Process Analysis)**
List Datapoints
⊟ **Identify operative reporting needs per Department**
List data points
Evalute Standard Reports
Reports per Department and UDFs
Evalute Queries and Drill Down
Group Reports by Department
Group Reports by Frequency
Decide for Presentation Methodology (List, Summary, Graphics)
Define Report Delivery Method
Assign Recipients for Reports

Reporting strategy for your own project

For your own project, it is a good idea to revisit the process analysis paper you created. Look at the strategic direction you defined for your business. What information do you need to collect in order to make progress in the direction of your goal? Let's quickly look at the **Lemonade Stand** example. It is our goal to establish a world-class distribution center and outsource production. Therefore, we do not need to collect too much information related to production. However, we need to make sure that everything related to inventory management and optimization, as well as optimizing the warehouse receiving and sending, is measured so that we can improve over time. It is a good idea to place additional data points for progress measurement in areas that can be improved. For example, it is a known fact that most errors in a warehouse occur during **shipping** and **receiving**. We need to collect data to make sure we understand exactly what happens here. You can only report on data that was entered into the system. Therefore, make sure that everything you want reports on is entered using standard fields in the available forms, or via the custom UDF fields that you added.

Standard terms related to reporting

Before we continue defining the aspects of a reporting strategy, I would like to summarize the most important terms related to reporting.

SQL, query, and stored procedure

When reports are discussed, SQL, queries, and stored procedures are frequently mentioned. SQL stands for Structured Query Language. It is a method to extract information from relational tables in the form of a machine-type language called a query. In SAP, you can see the names of tables by switching on the **System Information** in the menu. If you move the mouse over the **cardcode** column while the business partner screen is open, you can see the table is called **OCRD**. You can see this in the footer section of the SAP application. A query to get all of the customer information will look like this: `Select * from OCRD`. A stored procedure in this environment is a query, which uses parameters to calculate the results.

Crystal Reports

Crystal Reports, formerly owned by Business Objects, is now an SAP product since SAP acquired Business Objects. Crystal Reports is also considered an industry standard for reporting against SQL databases. SAP published a Crystal add-on that allows Crystal Reports to be run within the SAP Business ONE application. We will evaluate this add-on in this chapter.

Data warehousing

Data warehousing is a sophisticated information analysis framework that comprises reports, queries, and more, to extract business information from multiple data sources. As you already know, having more data does not mean that you have more information. Using a data warehousing concept, data is collected from different sources and then stored in a single reporting database which is the data warehouse. Tools are used to summarize and analyze this data to obtain actual information.

SAP reporting components

Within the SAP Business ONE application, we use a specific set of terms when talking about reporting. Here are the most important terms.

Reports in SAP Business ONE

SAP Business ONE has a **Reporting** button per menu section. Basically, there is a specific set of reports for each departmental function. However, you also have all of the reports available in the reporting section. I guess you can look at it as having reports that support each department. In addition, there is an entire department that only does reporting. It makes sense if you think about it. A salesperson may only be interested in sales-related reports. However, an owner wants to see all of the reports without having to browse through each department.

Drag and Relate

This is the most basic form of reporting, and is also a very nice one. I explained this method in the first section of this book. You can refer back to that section for details. Basically, you can drag any form field to a target reporting object and get an immediate result set. For example, if you have the business partner master data open, you can drag the cardcode to **Deliveries** and see all of the deliveries for this cardcode. Therefore, you don't need to design a report for everything. Sometimes, you just drag the form field and create your report on the fly.

Queries

A query in SAP has a special functions because you can utilize the drill-down option. This is available via the red arrows that show up on the query results. If you remember, the drill-down arrows allow you to click on them and see related detail information per record.

Formatted Search

A **Formatted Search** is a form field that you can add to any SAP form and fill it with related information based on the current data in the form. This is how it works: If you open the form and select data, the selected data will be taken as input for a query to search the database for related data. This data then shows up in the form field that is connected to the **Formatted Search**. I think an example can clarify this a bit better.

Let's say you have the Business Partner Master open. However, you want to allow the user to write down extensive notes for a customer. You will add a user-defined field and link it to a formatted search, which would query the notes related to a customer each time a new customer is selected.

XL Reporter

XL Reporter is an SAP reporting tool that allows query results to be obtained within Microsoft Excel. In fact, SAP has a large set of sample XL reports that include sophisticated dashboards that are all based on SAP business information. I actually believe that the usage of this tool will challenge the most experienced Excel user when it comes to design. However, the samples can guide you when you attempt to use XL Reporter. You can also run simple queries in XL Reporter. I will introduce you to the architecture of XL Reporter in this chapter, and we will also design some reports using this tool. Please note that XL Reporter's integration with Excel is standard since SAP 2007. In SAP 2005, this tool had to be installed separately.

Crystal Reports

In this chapter, we will install the Crystal Reports add-on, prepare a report, and make the report available in the SAP Business ONE application for selected users. Crystal Reports has a design component and a runtime component that requires Microsoft .NET. The design component allows the report to be designed. The runtime component runs the report for the users. The add-on integrates those functionalities with the SAP Business ONE application.

Report design from information requirement to query and report

How can we create the right report? In this section, I will introduce you to a workflow that you can use to derive a reporting strategy based on your actual information requirements.

As explained before, reporting has a strategic and an operational component. The strategic component is derived from your mid-term goals. The operations component needs to satisfy the daily information needs on a per-department basis. Since SAP has a multitude of reporting technologies, such as canned reports, queries, Crystal Reports, and XL Reporter, the question is which tool to use for what reporting need.

Canned reports in SAP

First, evaluate the available reports per section. As you know, each menu section has a category called Reports. You can evaluate the available reports and see if they cover your needs. Note that most of the canned reports cannot be manipulated. Therefore, if a canned report isn't a perfect fit, continue evaluating the other reporting options. You can spend some time with all of the available reports and evaluate their potential value for your business. However, as these reports are pretty much available without further setup, I will not focus on them here.

Queries

Queries allow you to extract specific information based on your requirements, and then show the results in a list format. The advantage of queries within SAP is that you can use the drill-down feature. This means the reporting data is fully integrated with the functionality in the SAP Business ONE application. For example, if you look at the query we had implemented earlier called **30 Days No Contact**, you can see that the returned list has an orange arrow in front of each result record. This means you can drill down to each record from here. In this example, the Business Partner master record will show up once you click on the orange arrow. Look at the following screenshot:

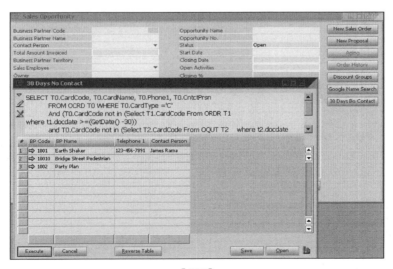

Excel or Crystal

Some reporting requirements are a bit more complex than just a simple list. In addition, you sometimes want to save the reporting results and distribute them to a list of recipients. If you want to add some graphical representation, such as pie charts, you must choose between Excel and Crystal. This depends a bit on your company's preference. However, there are also some technical aspects that may impact your decision. For example, if you don't want to allow further processing of the reporting data, Crystal Reports can be configured to make sure that you can only print a report. In addition, Crystal allows a report to be deployed via the Web. Therefore, reports are accessible without a specific application. XL Reporter requires Excel on the computer, which needs to run the reports. You can take advantage of all of the features and functionalities available in Excel.

In summary, the decision of what reporting tool to use is based on the level of integration with SAP and also the desired platform.

Information requirement (list, summary, monthly, real-time, and presentation)

Now that you know about the available reporting technologies, you can focus on the actual requirements for your information needs. The following steps summarize the process you can follow to prepare reports:

- Define the information you need and organize it into columns in a list format. Now, decide if you want to evaluate the data in a summarized form to get a better overview. If the presentation benefits from the use of graphics, decide on the appropriate presentation, such as pie charts or graphs.

- Evaluate the frequency of the report. For example, you need to define if you want to look at the report daily, weekly, monthly, etc.

- Once you have decided how you want to present the data, and the frequency of the report, you can assign the relevant recipients. You can distribute reports as an alert. In this case, each recipient gets an alert once it's time to look at the new report.

At this point, I recommend that you evaluate your own project and prepare a list of reports that you want to have in SAP. Please use the strategy paper we prepared in Chapter 5 - Business Process Analysis and SMBs as a guideline. After you complete the list, organize it into sections that correspond with the SAP modules. You can then evaluate the canned reports per section and continue with the above workflow to create your own reports.

Budget activation and budget reporting for your own business—the center of every reporting strategy

Let's focus on a reporting area that applies to pretty much every business. At the same time, it is an often-overlooked aspect. I am talking about the **budget**. For your own business, you should always balance your actual business performance with the intended budget. In the SAP Business ONE application, there is an integrated budget system that you can use.

Here are some important types of reports you should be looking for:

- Create a budget report that compares your estimated income, on a per-month basis, with the expected cost to maintain your business per month.

- Run a 12-month-based budget scenario that allows you to compare the expected income with the costs.

In order to get started with the budget system, you first need to **initialize** it in **System Initialization | General Settings**. Here, you open the **Budget** tab page and check **Budget Initialization** as shown in the following screenshot:

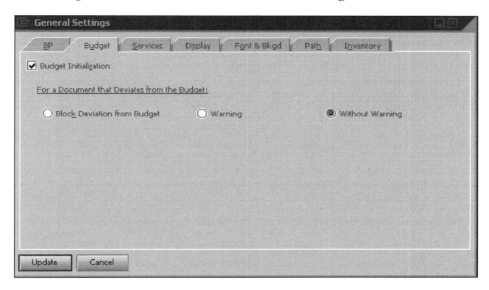

As you can see, the system can be configured to provide a **Warning, Block Deviation from Budget**, or continue **Without Warning**.

In order to define the budget, you can define the budget scenarios against your CoA. This way, the transactions you are completing in SAP as you work with the system can be evaluated against the budgetary limits that you set in the scenario.

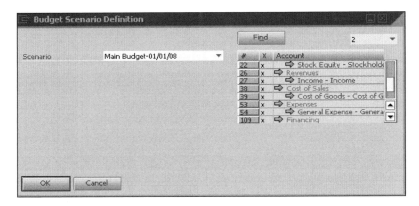

In the previous screenshot, you can see that I have selected level **2** in the top right corner. This indicates that I want to set my budget against a level-two account in the CoA. I am introducing the budget settings at this point because with all of the reports available, you should know that the budget is the most important aspect. However, it is yet an often-disregarded aspect. Therefore, I encourage you to make use of the budget system in SAP and plan your business based on budget scenarios. Additionally, keep reporting on the performance against this budget continuously. In SAP, you can activate an alert that is available by default to notify the selected users if there is any deviation from planned budget values:

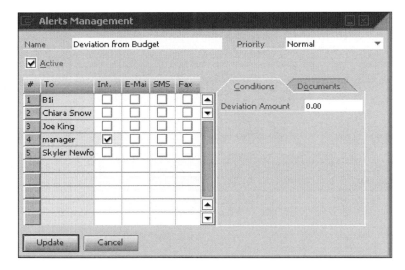

SAP Crystal Reports add-on

Crystal Reports is the future of all forms and layouts in the SAP Business ONE application. That's at least the most logical prediction based on the fact that SAP now owns Crystal Reports. Therefore, any investment into Crystal Reports may be a good decision compared to another third-party tool. Therefore, let's look at Crystal Reports for the SAP Business ONE application.

The Crystal Reports add-on

In order to install the Crystal Reports add-on, you need the following:

- Microsoft .NET framework (the version currently required by the Crystal Reports add-on is 5.5)
- Crystal Runtime Environment
- Crystal add-on for SAP Business ONE
- Crystal Designer to design reports
- Microsoft native SQL Client depending on the platform

Most of these components are on the Crystal add-on CD. Consequently, there is no need to search places and find the right components. Please note that the actual Crystal add-on from SAP comes with a source code. This means you can take it as a starting point to develop a more customized Crystal add-on solution.

However, if you think about it, the requirements of the SAP Crystal add-on are pretty steep considering that they need to be installed on each workstation. It would have been a more efficient approach if SAP had implemented the add-on to be server-based so clients could take advantage of the reports without additional installation requirements.

The installation requires you to either install the Crystal Designer or the Crystal Runtime on the client machine. The Crystal Designer is required if you are planning to design and create reports. The runtime is free and is sufficient if you want to only run reports. Once this basic requirement is met, you can design and run crystal reports. The add-on gets installed like most other add-ons without special setup requirements. With the SAP Crystal add-on installed, you can integrate reports with the SAP Business ONE menu system.

Crystal add-on installation

Installing the Crystal add-on requires you to open the **Administration** | **Add-ONs** | **Administration** menu. The installation procedure uses the standard add-on installer file that ends with `*.ard`. The installer will be generated in the `C:\Program Files\SAP\SAP Business One\AddOns\SAP_CR` directory once you execute the `SAPCrystalSetup.exe` file on the installation CD like this:

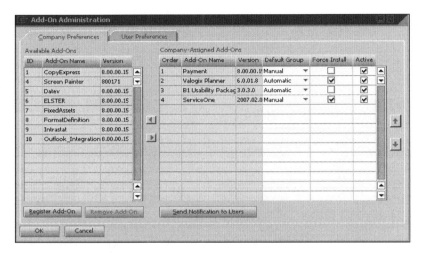

I am walking you through the steps to install the Crystal add-on because it requires a bit of planning. First, you need the .NET components and the Crystal Designer or Runtime. You then need to install the add-on in the SAP Business ONE application.

The add-on installation starts with the selection of the **Register Add-On** button. A file browser will open up, allowing you to select the `*.ard` file. A `*.ard` file is a packaged installer that can be called from the add-on installer interface.

You will need to select the **SAP_CR.ard** add-on installer file. Once you have completed this step, the installer procedure will guide you through the remaining steps to install the add-on. Take a look at this screenshot:

Make sure the add-on is set to **Automatic** for the startup type, and also check the **active** checkbox. In the following screenshot, the checkbox in the top right corner is the active checkbox:

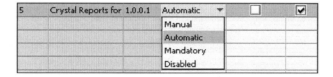

The Crystal add-on is now almost installed in the add-on manager. It will be available in the **Pending Add-Ons** tab page. Select the Crystal add-on and click on **Install** again:

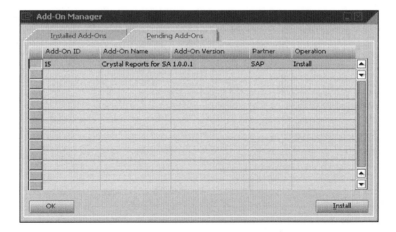

The Crystal add-on is now installed and will appear in the SAP Business ONE menu system. Check the menu path via **Administration | Crystal Reports Administration**. You can now configure the parameters for Crystal Reports. For example, Crystal needs to know how to access the database. For administrator access, the username and password must be specified in **SAP Business One: Crystal Reports Account Setup,** as shown in the following screenshot:

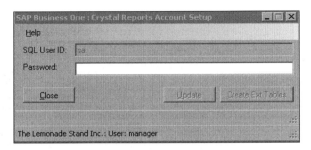

The default password for the admin user is **sa**, which is represented by **sa** in the SQL database. However, this may be different on your system if you have a more secure setup. In that case, you need to get the superuser and password information for the SQL database. After you enter this, you need to generate the tables that Crystal will use to manage the configuration information. This is done with the help of the **Create Ext Tables** button.

You are now set to add Crystal Reports to the SAP menu, and then users can run them. The following example shows the **30 Days No Contact** report based on the query having the same name. The report was created using the Crystal wizard. The **Permitted Groups** checkbox is set to **Public**. This means everybody has access to this report. This also points to the fact that you can configure security groups which will have selected access to specific reports. In this example, the report was copied to a common directory in the SAP Business ONE installation folder. With the selection of this report, and the security set to **Public**, every user has access to this report from within the SAP Business ONE application.

I recommend you copy Crystal Reports to a shared directory that every SAP client has access to. Otherwise, you would need to copy the report to each client computer.

This concludes the discussion about the level of integration for Crystal Reports with SAP Business ONE. You can see that this add-on is very basic, but has the essential features nicely assembled so that you can use the advanced crystal reports functionality. One final note about the reports is that you can only run one report at a time. This sometimes becomes an issue if you intend to run multiple reports and then compare the data side-by-side. This is a limitation of the SAP Crystal Reports add-on.

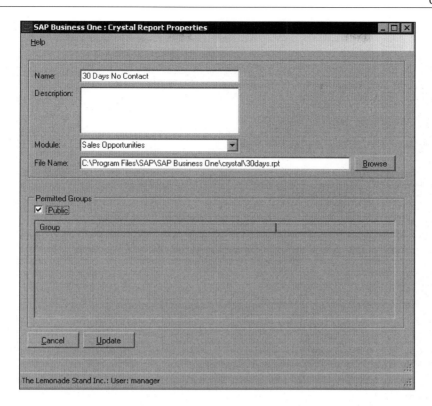

SAP XL Reporter

XL Reporter is a reporting add-on that does not require any specific installation. The only requirement is that Microsoft Excel must be installed on your computer. This tool is very advanced and mature. There is a huge list of predesigned reports available from SAP. The reports are a good learning experience as their features and graphics will give an understanding of what to look for. Let's investigate some examples in this section to help better understand how the XL Reporter tool works. With the advent of SAP 2007, the XL Reporter add-on is an integral part of the SAP client installation. No specific action is required as XL Reporter will automatically get installed. I will now show you the process you can follow to create your own reports and start experimenting with this sophisticated tool.

XL Reporter design process

Getting started with the XL Reporter tool is straightforward. If you go to the **Menu | Tools | XL Reporter** menu section, **Report Organizer** will open up. XL Reporter has two main parts: **Report Organizer** and **Report Composer**.

Open the Report Organizer

The arrow in the following the screenshot points to the Report Composer. Therefore, the two main parts of XL Reporter are linked together and can easily be reached through a button click. You can see that the left side of the Report Composer is organized into sections just like the SAP menu. On the right side, the actual reports show up. This way, you can create reports and then integrate their functionality into the SAP menu. I will later show you the **Update Business ONE Main Menu** feature, which allows you to update the SAP menu. A link will appear in the menu that allows calling the XL Reporter report.

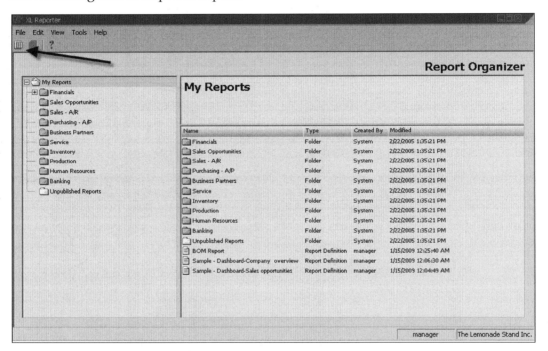

Open the Report Composer

The power of this tool is represented by the Report Composer. Here, you will find a list of the SAP information objects organized by tab pages. In the following example, these items were selected: **Sales Opportunity, Sales Stage, and Sales Employee**. With this selection, we can click on the arrow icons on the form and retrieve the preview data. This way, we can quickly decide if our report works in a specific system environment.

You can see that the preview functionality may also be a good feature when it comes to developing your own complex report. Please note that it is a good idea to keep reports as simple as possible. That way, users will be more comfortable when running the reports. In the following screenshot, the single arrow in the main menu represents points to the **Preview** icon. The arrow coming from the left side of the screenshot is pointing towards the **Preview** icon. The other dual arrow to the right side of the **Preview** icon is the **Refresh** functionality.

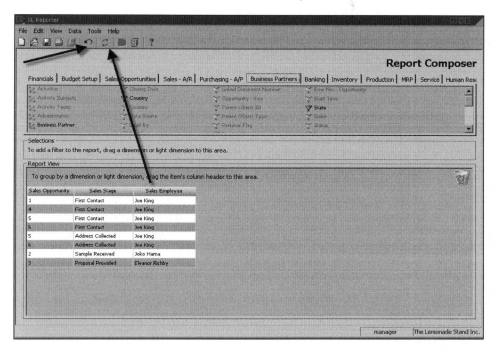

Once the preview data is complete, we can move on and save the report.

Drag report dimensions into lower pane

As shown in the previous screenshot, the top section in the Report Composer shows the tab pages with relevant columns available for the business objects. You can drag a selected column to the lower section, which will indicate that the report will show information represented by the selected columns. Please preview the result.

Create a report using Report Generator

The report will be generated using the selected columns. The result will be an Excel template file that can be used by any user. Please note that the generated reports can be edited to reflect your specific design and layout.

Save the report

In the following screenshot, the **BP Lemonade Stand** report was saved in the source directory of the XL Reporter reports. You can decide if you want to use an Excel template. For example, you may have an Excel template with your company logo or other preformatted data.

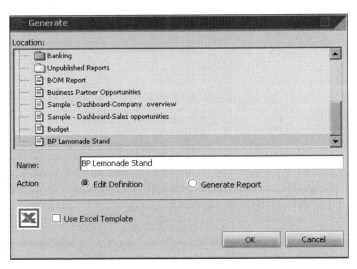

Import into Report Manager

If you get your hands on the large XL reporting repository that SAP provides to partners, you can import an XL Reporter report using the import function. You should then test the imported report to make sure the data is picked up correctly.

Update the SAP menu

If you are happy with a particular report, you can update the SAP navigation menu. After you do this, the XL Reporter functionality will be available to every user with the right privileges to access the XL Reporter report.

Evaluate sample reports

Please note that SAP provides a repository with a large list of available predesigned reports for SAP Business ONE. For example purposes, we will look at several reports. The first report from the repository is the **Bill of Material Report**. This shows all of the products that are made up of a list of other items. Directly retrieving the results in Excel can be a true relief if you are planning to analyze your BOM master data:

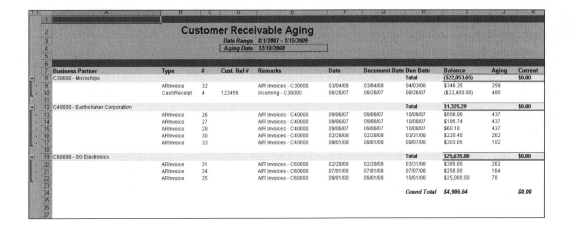

Bill Of Material Report

Selected Warehouse: 01

Parent	BOM Type	Component Code	Component Name	BOM Price	Quantity	Unit Cost	Total
C87879 - Basic package with a low processo	Production				Total Cost		$6,659.00
		H104501	IC, 5V Flash Memory SOIC	$0.00	1	$1.00	$1.00
		B20349	Tape Backup 1920	$0.00	1	$150.00	$150.00
		S10002	Server Point 6600	$0.00	1	$6,500.00	$6,500.00
		A1146SS	Packing Nut	$0.00	8	$1.00	$8.00
CR-1125-4-200 - REEL,LP,L/H,HAND RWD	Production				Total Cost		$0.00
		CR-880	PAINT,POWDER,BLUE ST	$1.00	0.6	$0.00	$0.00
		CR-7455-12	FRAME,MANUAL,1125 SE	$1.00	1	$0.00	$0.00
		CR-7415	DISC,17-1/2" (PAINTED)	$1.00	1	$0.00	$0.00
		CR-7416	DISC,17-1/2" (PAINTED)	$1.00	1	$0.00	$0.00
		CR-7414-12	DRUM,CENTER,1125 (PAI	$1.00	1	$0.00	$0.00
		CR-7408-12	AXLE,PLUMBING,1/2",112	$1.00	1	$0.00	$0.00
		CR-439	SWIVEL,1/2"NPT,NITRILE	$1.00	1	$0.00	$0.00
		CR-20064-T	HOUSING,BEARING,TOP	$1.00	2	$0.00	$0.00
		CR-20064-B	HOUSING,BEARING,BOTT	$1.00	2	$0.00	$0.00
		CR-20649	BEARING,SPHERICAL,1/2	$1.00	2	$0.00	$0.00
		CR-153	RETAINING RING (5100-81	$1.00	4	$0.00	$0.00
		CR-20843	LOCKING PIN (ASSY.)	$1.00	1	$0.00	$0.00
		CR-7419-1	HAND CRANK,1/2",1125 (A	$1.00	1	$0.00	$0.00
		CR-312	BOLT,HEX,5/16-18X3/4",GF	$1.00	10	$0.00	$0.00
		CR-111	NUT,LOCK,5/16-18	$1.00	2	$0.00	$0.00
		CR-7460-9.75	TRIM,DRUM EDGE (10.25"	$1.00	1	$0.00	$0.00
		CR-112	WASHER,LOCK,5/16"	$1.00	8	$0.00	$0.00
		CR-20171	WASHER,FLAT,5/16"	$1.00	2	$0.00	$0.00
		CR-157	WASHER,FLAT,3/8" (ID.42	$1.00	4	$0.00	$0.00
		CR-20016	BOLT,HEX,3/8-16 X 1",GR !	$1.00	4	$0.00	$0.00
		CR-435	NUT,LOCK,3/8-16, .437"W	$1.00	4	$0.00	$0.00
		CR-7429-4	DRAG BRAKE,1/2" (ASSY	$1.00	1	$0.00	$0.00
		CR-PKG-047	KIT,PACKAGE/LABELING	$1.00	1	$0.00	$0.00
CR-15454-12 - RAIL,SPACER,12"W. 1125/12	Production				Total Cost		$0.00
CR-7408-12 - AXLE,PLUMBING,1/2",1125 (P	Production				Total Cost		$0.00

Sheet1

Another good example is **Customer Receivable Aging**. This shows all of the customer sales that were generated in the example database. Also, it shows a list of all of the customers who actually made a purchase within the timeframe. The timeframe is a parameter that can be provided when the report is run:

Customer Receivable Aging

Date Range 8/1/2007 - 1/15/2009
Aging Date 12/18/2008

Business Partner	Type	#	Cust. Ref #	Remarks	Date	Document Date	Due Date	Balance	Aging	Current
C30000 - Microchips							Total	($22,053.65)		$0.00
	ARInvoice	32		A/R Invoices - C30000	03/04/08	03/04/08	04/03/08	$346.35	259	
	CashReceipt	4	123456	Incoming - C30000	08/26/07	08/26/07	08/26/07	($22,400.00)	480	
C40000 - Earthshaker Corporation							Total	$1,325.29		$0.00
	ARInvoice	26		A/R Invoices - C40000	09/06/07	09/06/07	10/08/07	$556.00	437	
	ARInvoice	27		A/R Invoices - C40000	09/06/07	09/06/07	10/08/07	$185.74	437	
	ARInvoice	28		A/R Invoices - C40000	09/06/07	09/06/07	10/08/07	$60.10	437	
	ARInvoice	30		A/R Invoices - C40000	02/28/08	02/28/08	03/31/08	$220.40	262	
	ARInvoice	33		A/R Invoices - C40000	09/01/08	09/01/08	09/07/08	$303.05	102	
C60000 - SG Electronics							Total	$25,635.00		$0.00
	ARInvoice	31		A/R Invoices - C60000	02/28/08	02/28/08	03/31/08	$385.00	262	
	ARInvoice	34		A/R Invoices - C60000	07/01/08	07/01/08	07/07/08	$250.00	164	
	ARInvoice	35		A/R Invoices - C60000	09/01/08	09/01/08	10/01/08	$25,000.00	78	
							Grand Total	$4,906.64		$0.00

Your own project

Make sure that Excel is installed on the same computer where you are running the SAP Business ONE client. In addition, since XL Reporter makes heavy use of the Visual Basic integration, it is recommended that you allow VBA scripts in the Excel security settings. Next, you can follow this procedure:

1. Open the Report Organizer
2. Open the Report Composer
3. Drag report dimensions into lower pane
4. Create a report using the Report Generator
5. Save the report
6. If you have existing reports, import them into the Report Manager
7. Update the menu

Once you have completed this, preview the data to make sure that all of the right information was brought over.

CrystalWave reporting

At this point, you have a solid understanding of the various reporting functionalities provided by SAP. In order to define the limitations of the reporting tools that come with SAP Business ONE, you will now be introduced to another reporting add-on. The CrystalWave add-on has a high level of integration with SAP Business ONE, and exceeds the available functionality as compared to the SAP Crystal Reports add-on. In the sections that follow, you will learn about these features which you can utilize with the Crystal Wave add-on:

- Automatic report distribution to lists in SAP Business ONE.
- Obtaining reports from a legacy system other than SAP Business ONE
- Compare legacy data with live SAP transactions within the SAP Business ONE context.
- Utilize the letter merge functionality, combined with Crystal's PDF formatting option, to send emails and attach business documents in PDF format.

The add-on is configured via the **Report Maintenance** form, which also reveals its most essential features. In the top section, you can see a list of SAP Business ONE forms. In the lower section, there are three tab pages that group the general settings, delivery options, and printing options.

General settings

In this example, the **Business Partners** report was selected. In the **General** tab, which is active by default, the report location was specified. Please note the **Select Database** option. Here, we can select the database that the report uses to present data. Basically, this allows the seamless integration of third-party database information within SAP Business ONE. A good usage example would be the integration of sales history within SAP. For example, if you start a new implementation of SAP Business ONE, you often need to migrate historic data into SAP Business ONE. However, you can make historic information available via reports. It is completely transparent for the user. The high level of integration with SAP Business ONE is shown via the **Create Activity on Print** option that automatically creates an activity in SAP.

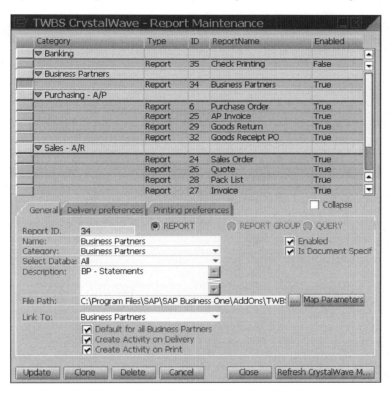

Delivery options

Here, we can specify that the report will be attached as a PDF attachment for the selected email provider. Note that you can add a default email recipient for the Cc list:

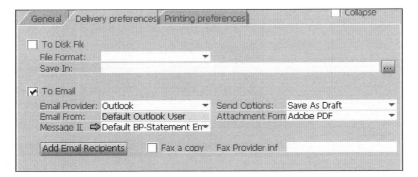

Printing preferences

The printing options add a good level of automation. You can specify a list of printers where copies are automaticallly printed. This is often a common requirement as you may want to print backup copies automatically:

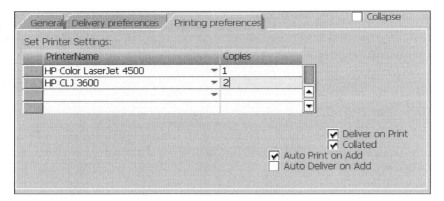

Example email creation

From a user's perspective, the creation of an email with an attachment is easy. The following screenshot shows an open sales order. A simple click on the **E-Mail** icon in the top menu section will open the specified email program, such as Outlook, and prepare an email with the email address that is specified for the business partner in the open sales order:

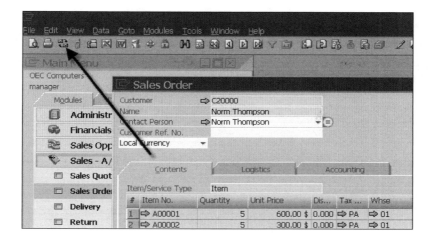

You can see the result. The first name is used in the email with the default text. If you think about it, this can be used as a customer newsletter tool:

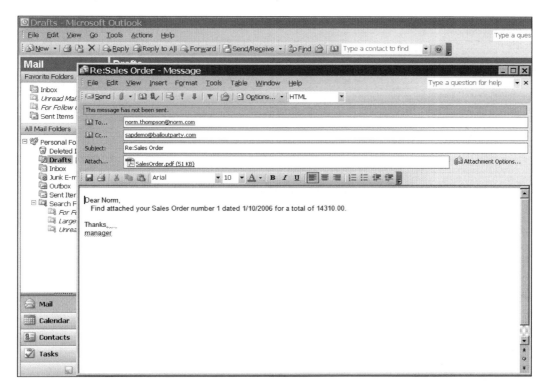

Crystal Wave summary

The Crystal Wave add-on shows that the SAP Business ONE functionality is not limited to what you see in the standard features. The true power of SAP Business ONE is in the SDK and programming environment that allows the features to be seamlessly enhanced. By doing so, Crystal Wave adds the following core features:

- Multicompany reporting
- Mail any form
- Print delivery options

Case study (the XL Reporter dashboard)

What's a dashboard? Even if you don't know, just get the XL Reporter sample reports from SAP and check out the list of available dashboards for Excel. The dashboard report called **Operating cash flow** will serve as a good example. The report was copied to a directory on the server and imported using the Report Organizer. The SAP menu was updated, and the fully functional dashboard report was installed on the system.

With that said, you can now see what a dashboard is. The **Operating cash flow** dashboard presents cash flow related data within six sections of the screen. On the left side, there is a traditional list and summary representation of the data. Consequently, a dashboard is a combination of different presentation methods that allow for a quick visual analysis of data.

Designing a dashboard starts with the definition of the information requirements and the design of queries. Then, the retrieved information is presented as a list and grouped together. Finally, visual-gadget-type representations allow for of the information to immediately be understood:

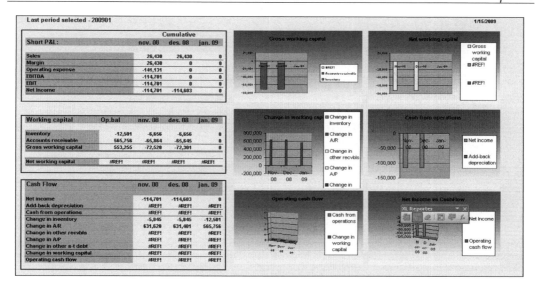

The second dashboard we will look at is called **Sales Overview**. If you ever wondered what Excel is capable of, then investigating the XL Reporter reports may be a good idea:

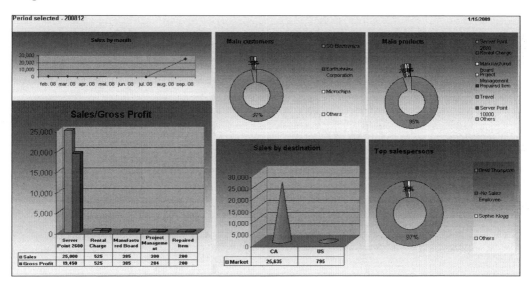

Summary

In this chapter, we visited all of the main reporting tools available within SAP Business ONE. Among queries, we also focused on XL Reporter and Crystal Reports. In addition, a powerful add-on that enhances the standard SAP reporting functionality was reviewed.

During the course of this chapter, we analyzed how your information requirements can be structured, managed, and accomplished using the project plan. With the knowledge of the common terms related to reporting, you understood the language that specialists use when talking about reports. With this background, we learned about the workflow that you can follow when designing reports.

Crystal Reports is available as an add-on for SAP Business ONE. We focused on how to install the required components to get Crystal Reports activated within SAP Business ONE. Another major reporting tool is available for Excel, and is called XL Reporter. You learned how to prepare your own XL Reporter reports.

During the case study, we quickly implemented a dashboard based on sample reports available from SAP.

In summary, you can see that reports are the most important aspect of your ERP system.

In the next chapter, we will connect SAP Business ONE to the Web. You will generate an e-commerce store that integrates both sales orders and newsletters in real time.

11
E-commerce and Web Sales

The latest hype in the IT market is **SaaS**. It stands for **Software as a Service** and means that the customer does not install his software on a server located in his office, but rather uses just a pre-installed version of the software on a server hosted on the Internet. Usage is most commonly charged based on a service contract on a monthly or yearly basis.

This concept works for a selected market with specific requirements. The benefit is that you don't need to worry about server issues anymore. However, the downside is that you have no control over your data, which is the most important asset of your company. This does not sound like a good combination. There are also local government regulations related to data auditing and control that are problematic for this concept.

However, there are new technologies on the horizon which may lead to a new SaaS evolution (for example, the Amazon AWS services). By using this service, you can host Windows-based servers in a virtual environment at the Amazon data center. Basically, this technology allows you to install **your own server** using a hosted environment. This is **True SaaS** because now you have control over your own data. Based on this new technology, the SAP Business ONE solution may get an unexpected boost. As we will see in this chapter, the DI-API allows the creation of web-based forms and functionality that interface with SAP in real time. In this chapter, we will be extending SAP Business ONE with real-time web technologies.

What you will learn in this chapter about SAP web technologies

During the course of this book, we have frequently talked about **islands of data.** Now that you understand the value of an integrated system, you may wonder: Why would anybody establish separate systems instead of a single, integrated system? Well, e-commerce is a good example. Traditional software solutions run on servers in your office. E-commerce solutions are most commonly hosted on the Internet. Therefore, when companies decide to start an e-commerce business, it most often leads to (you guessed it) a new island of data. Therefore, a new island is established when new technologies are used to gain a competitive advantage. Given the dynamic nature of web-related technologies, along with their inherent complexity, it is a good idea to outsource this part of your business.

The more disparate the systems are, the more gaps your workflow must overcome. Therefore, integrating new technologies with the existing SAP workflows is key.

In this chapter, we will define a workflow that helps you evaluate the available web tools for e-commerce and CRM. The complete lifecycle from evaluation to integration with SAP is covered here. At the same time, we will evaluate existing web-related solutions and explain their architecture. As we cover these aspects, we will cover the following topics:

- Project plan – The key challenges related to an e-commerce implementation will be explained. In addition, a project plan workflow will be established. This will help you manage an SAP project that includes web technologies.

- Using web sales technologies in your own project – You will learn how to apply the knowledge to your own project.

- Standard terms related to e-commerce – We will briefly cover the common terms related to e-commerce and web-related technologies.

- SAP-related web technologies – SAP has an e-commerce and CRM solution. Let's position this solution and relate it to other available web solutions that integrate with SAP Business ONE.

- Case study- Finally, we will add e-commerce to our Lemonade Stand case study. The lemonade stand goes online!

- Automation and self-service - Based on the case study, we will establish an extended business process using web technologies. This will help you get used to the idea of **automation** and self-service.

The project plan

When adding web technologies, such as e-commerce or mobile sales, to our business solution, we are essentially extending the existing business processes. By extending a process beyond its initial boundaries, we need to make sure that the overall end-to-end workflow is as seamless as possible. It would be easy to just add any e-commerce store. However, we would then need to manually add the products. In addition, we need to manage the pricing per customer group, and also maintain customer information. This may lead to additional manual steps that are required to keep the e-commerce data up-to-date. In order to structure the required areas, we look at the process analysis and see where web-based technologies fit in. Web technologies are most commonly used in the following areas:

- E-commerce
- Service automation
- Mobile sales automation
- Supply chain integration

For your own project, you first need to identify how you are planning to **extend** the business processes. Then, identify the **sections** in the project plan that are relevant. If you remember, the department-specific functions in SAP are organized into menu sections. Those sections helped us group the department-specific functionalities in the project plan. Let's look at the above examples and see how they fit in.

E-commerce

E-commerce represents an online store environment where customers can view items, review details, and then complete a purchase via a checkout cart. What do we need do in SAP Business ONE to accomplish this? We basically need to enter a sales order. Therefore, we can say that an e-commerce order is nothing but a web-based sales order entry presented in a web format. Therefore, the existing sales and order entry process, including shipping and so forth, must be extended. For your own project, I recommend you to think about the existing processes you have in place and extend the workflow to represent e-commerce. This should be end-to-end from order placement to replenishment. Where can you start? Use the strategy paper we prepared and investigate the processes you documented. Find the sales process and the order entry area. Then use this as a basis to see how the e-commerce functionality fits in.

Service automation

Another example of a beneficial use of web technologies is **service automation**. Essentially, with a web presence, you provide a 24x7 sales-and-service contact to your customers. You can automate the service and support personnel's repetitive tasks. For example, if you get a number of calls per day about store opening hours, you can place this information on the Web. Another good example is that customers may often call to request warranty information about products that they previously purchased. You can provide a login for customers where they can find all of the previous orders they placed with the warranty information. In addition, you can allow new orders to be placed based on the old orders. To some extent, you can automate your business. This will allow the sales and service people to focus on more efficient tasks.

For your own project, identify the service processes of your company. Then, see if there are any time-consuming tasks that can easily be automated using web technologies. It is important to weigh the benefits against the costs. Therefore, try to identify the current time and cost of the repetitive tasks in the service department. Then, compare the benefits for automating the process.

Mobile sales automation

Today, salespeople require access to customer information from any location. If you have a mobile sales organization, you should evaluate their information requirements. They may benefit from having a web-based CRM system. Your mobile sales personnel will require web access to their customer information, including their sales history. In addition, customers should be able to place orders via the Web. Based on how the mobile sales are organized, we may also need to manage sales stages and relevant opportunities.

As you can see in this example, the level of detail depends on your own requirements. Therefore, make sure you define your own specific requirements for a mobile sales organization.

Supply chain integration

Another important area of automation is called **supply chain integration**. This extends the process flow from your internal company boundaries to your suppliers. Let's say the lead time for an item you are selling is only one day. In such a case, you can think about not maintaining an item in your warehouse because you can just order it from the supplier once you get an order. This could be automated. This means every time you receive an order for this item, a replenishment order at your supplier is automatically placed.

This is a crucial aspect for your own project. Do you have any integration points with suppliers or manufacturers? Follow the same process and extend your companies' workflow. Start by documenting how the end-to-end process works from a manual processing perspective. For example, review the tasks you need to complete from receiving an order, to placing your purchase order, to obtaining inventory. Look at the data in the documents since this information will be the data points you will use to define the integration.

End-to-end integration

The goal of automation is to complete an end-to-end workflow. As you extend the processes, you will see that there are some crucial aspects to think about. The order placement process may start with an e-commerce order that requires payment processing, and may end with a delivery where tracking information for the order is provided to the customer. Define the end-to-end processes for your own project. Use analysis of the existing process and extend the workflow to the Web.

Updated project plan

Based on the established workflow, the project plan was updated. A new task group in the **Divide into Subjects** area was added. Therefore, we first identify the business processes that need to be extended. Then, each of those areas will be documented by extending the workflow with an end-to-end perspective. In this example, the most common process extensions were listed: **E-Commerce**, **Service**, **Sales**, and **Supply Chain Integration**:

⊟ **Web Business**
Identify Extended Processes
E-Commerce
Service
Sales
Supply Chain Integration

Using web sales technologies in your own project

If you review the information provided so far, you can see that it is essential to look at your business requirements before you look at any products. However, what comes next is looking at the products that come into play to perform the task. In the following section, the key differentiators for web technologies will be explained. As mentioned before, an important factor is the level of integration. There are two main integration levels:

- Real-time integration
- Synchronized integration

Real-time integration

Real-time integration essentially means that any data used and worked on, is actual live data from the SAP database. Any transaction entered via an e-commerce order immediately shows up in the system. The advantage is that we can show real inventory levels to customers, and we will also be able to send alerts to sales personnel.

There may be a disadvantage, though. You need real-time access to the SAP database. Advanced security measures must be implemented. In addition, your hosting environment must provide the right resources.

Synchronized or offline integration

In this environment, the web front end works with a copy of the live data. Any transactions that are entered will be synchronized with the live data based on a schedule. The problem here is that you may end up **synchronizing** a lot. As a matter of fact, this may wind up being an **island of data**. The advantage is that you can run an e-commerce store independently from SAP. You need to weigh the benefits against the cost and time you need to set up a separate system with synchronization.

Status

Based on the information provided so far, you know how to update your project plan. You can evaluate your workflow to extend the existing processes to the Web. You also know how to compare potential solutions based on their level of integration. We will now cover the key terms related to web technologies, and then move on to look at the products.

Standard terms related to e-commerce and web sales

Many terms that are related to e-commerce often lead to misunderstandings and can cause problems later. Therefore, we will now identify the key terms, and briefly explain their meaning in a web-related context. The following terms are often used:

- Hosting
- Shopping cart
- Amazon AWS
- Firewall
- Security and SSL certificates

Hosting

Hosting comes in various flavors. There are different forms of hosting that must be chosen based on requirements and the available budget. The most high-end hosting is a **dedicated server**. This is a server at a data center, which is managed by a professional team at the data center. Most commonly, the server is provided by the data center. You can also bring your own server and manage it via remote access. This is called **co-location**. The third option for hosting is a **shared server**. In this environment, you will share a single server with a group of customers. Management software will make sure that all participants get the server resources they pay for. Often, a shared server may look like a dedicated server. Hosting companies can do this by using so-called virtual machines that look like a dedicated server, but are really installed on another server which shares its resources with many virtual machines.

Shopping cart

The **shopping cart** allows items to be collected and a step-by-step sales process to be completed. There are many third-party shopping carts out there. For example, Yahoo! and Google have their own checkout carts. They offer to manage items and process payments. However, these providers may require you to sign up for their services, and they may take a percentage of each sale that is processed. You should calculate your expected web sales volume and make sure the percentage taken does not go beyond your expectations. These third-party shopping carts do not interface with SAP in real time. Therefore, you can compare the real-time shopping carts with their cost. Often, the credit card percentage taken by cart providers is reason enough to implement a dedicated solution that integrates with SAP Business ONE. It is recommended that you evaluate shopping carts that integrate with SAP in real time, or have a defined synchronization system with SAP.

Amazon AWS

Amazon AWS is a cloud computing service. This means your server will be hosted at the Amazon data center. You can use it as if it were a server in the office. This technology will become more dominant in the future because you can use your own software to establish a customized SaaS framework. Compared to other SaaS solutions, you have the option of bringing the server back into your own office if you like. In addition, you can extract your own data at any time.

Firewall

A **firewall** separates and integrates. It separates the in-house network from the external public Internet. The firewall also allows access to Internet resources. The configuration requires the definition of a security concept. For example, if you decide to establish real-time e-commerce functionality for your web presence, you need to allow access to the SAP system. At the same time, you don't want to run the risk of exposing crucial business data over the Web.

Security and SSL certificates

During the checkout process, data is sent back and forth between the customer's computer and the SAP system. If data streams are not secured, all of the information can be tracked. Therefore, a secure protocol must be used that connects the communication parties via unique certificates and establishes a secure channel. For example, SSL certificates are available to create a secure web site. Such web sites may start with `https://`.

SAP web tools

The web solutions offered by SAP are based on the initial developments of a company called Praxis Software. This company was taken over by SAP and the web products, including an e-commerce store solution and a CRM platform, are now SAP products called **web tools**.

The value of these solutions is the high level of integration, and the long history of alignment, with SAP Business ONE. Therefore, it is not a solution that was somehow integrated with SAP, but rather, it was meant to be integrated with SAP from the beginning.

Instead of explaining how those tools work, I recommend visiting the latest online demos.

In order to position the SAP web tools based on our criteria, it can be said that they do not provide real-time integration and require synchronization. Therefore, you have the advantage of running the web section of your processes on a completely separate server that integrates with SAP Business ONE via synchronization.

A real-time solution

Now that you know about the SAP web tools and their level of integration, it is a good time to evaluate a solution that provides real-time integration. The solution is called SAP **N2ONE** Portal, and it provides industry-specific functionality based on a web interface. The key features include:

- An e-commerce store
- Multiple e-commerce store creation and management
- A reporting portal
- A customer and vendor portal
- Service call placement
- Newsletter

Case study

For our case study, an e-commerce store for the Lemonade Stand enterprise will be published. A simple design template was prepared, and a new product category was activated for the storefront. For this purpose, a new item was created in the SAP system. It is a book (as seen in the following screenshot) that contains all of the Lemonade recipes we are using. This is basically a collection of old-fashioned lemonade recipes. We will offer this for a price of **$25**, but it can be purchased for free if you order a lemonade sample. This way, we can win potential new customers and collect their address information at the same time.

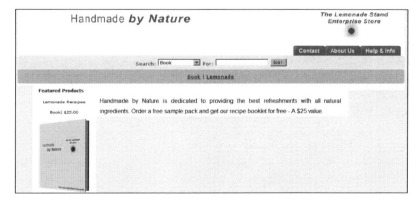

You can see that the book is highlighted as a featured product in the left section of the previous screen. In the top section, the user has the option to access his or her account information via the **My Account** button. Here, any previous orders or service calls are shown. The main menu shows **Book** and **Lemonade**. These are the store categories where the user can enter the store and add items to the shopping cart.

Navigating to the **Book** link will show the book and its details. This data comes directly from SAP. Therefore, if there are any changes in SAP, they will be immediately be reflected in the storefront shown here:

In order to confirm this information, let's open SAP and check out the item in the inventory master:

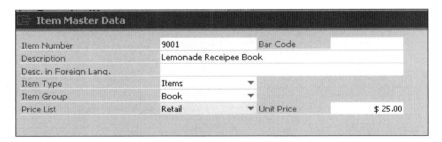

You can see that the pricing is correct based on the **Retail** price list. The retail price list is the default price list in the store. Another price list will only be used if you register and are approved as a distributor.

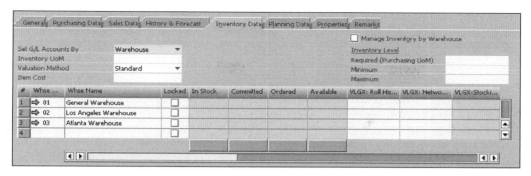

Since there is no inventory configured for the book (as seen in the previous screenshot), it shows up as **Backorder** in the e-commerce store frontend. The image in the e-commerce store is based on the image that was attached in the **Remarks** section of the item master data record:

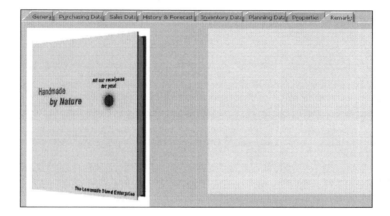

Note the spelling mistake in the e-commerce storefront for the item description. If this had not been a real-time integration, we would have had to correct this in SAP and then re-synchronize, potentially creating some downtime for our web store. But since this is a real-time solution, all we need to do is update the item once in SAP. The e-store will automatically update the change:

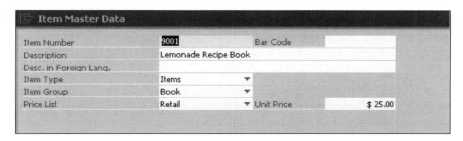

The SAP screen below shows the corrected item description. The web store screenshot proves that the information is real time as the description is instantly updated. This highlights the point that a real-time integrated system is beneficial on all levels. Basically, each time you agree on managing an island of data, your system will add clutter and repetitive tasks which may lead to errors and incorrect data. That's why evaluating the potential for integration and keeping data in one system has a significant value.

I added the book to the shopping cart and a registration is required upon checkout. Basically, the system is now gathering the required information to generate a sales order in SAP. It is a good idea to look at any web process as a web representation of the actual SAP forms. The forms are adjusted to fit the web format and are optimized to represent the relevant information. In addition, since we are now receiving orders via the Web into the SAP system, we may have customers who want to log in using their account information to place an order based on their assigned price list and payment terms.

You now understand that the web functionality really is an extension of the existing SAP processes to the Web. If we did not have the web portal solution, the customer would have had to call us, and the order would have needed to be entered manually into SAP. Furthermore, in case a new customer wanted to order, we would have had to enter his BP information by creating a new BP record.

The same will now happen in the N2ONE Portal solution. The only difference is that customers do all of the work themselves. The process starts with the online registration. This will instantly generate a new BP master record in SAP. The relevant screenshots for the registration procedure are shown next. First, the customer selects the type of business partner. The example has the following categories: **Retail**, **Wholesaler**, **Distributor**, and **Default**:

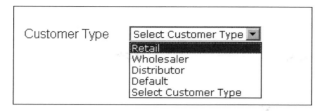

Once the customer type is selected, the relevant form opens up. In SAP, these forms are represented by the business partner master fields, or user-defined fields that were created based on your requirements. In this example, retail customer information for **James Dean** was entered. With the completion of this form, the data in SAP will be available in real time. Look at the next screenshot:

Upon checking the actual SAP system using the business partner master record, we confirm the new business partner's master record. We could extend the workflow by generating a new alert for all of the new customer registrations that come in via the Web. This would be a good time to verify contact information of customers who registered. A follow-up call would allow you to verify the contact data and also further specify their requirements. In addition, if the customer is already registered, we can immediately put a hold on any new orders if his outstanding balance exceeds a certain amount. Again, the advantage of having all of the information becomes clear. It allows workflow actions to be triggered based on your data. Therefore, a more integrated workflow can improve the way you operate your business. See the following screenshot:

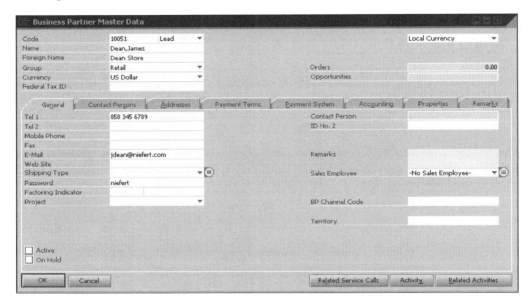

The N2ONE Portal application and its workflow

Based on the case study features, we can conclude the process flow for the most common web application scenarios. Here are the key features of web processes that are extensions of the existing SAP Business ONE processes:

- Generate an e-commerce store
- Show the retail price list by default
- Register via the Web
- Receive alerts in SAP

- Approve BP for relevant price list
- BP can log in and is assigned a price list
- Orders and service calls can be placed based on assigned pricelist
- **My Account** will show order history
- Dynamic newsletters will update the list based on buying behavior

Generate a store

The most common task related to web-based functionalities is the generation of an e-commerce store. We are using the term **generation** because the data is provided in real time by SAP, and we only need to **assign styles** so that that the presentation is in a web format. For your own project, you need to decide which products should be offered via the Web, and then group those products together. Assigning styles and formatting data is done via **CSS | Cascading Style Sheets**. Basically, the SAP master data is retrieved and formatted so that it fits in the web browser and looks good. Consequently, you should identify the products you want to present via the Web, and then decide how you want to present them.

Show the retail price list by default

Customers accessing the e-commerce store will see the retail price list by default. However, once they log in, the price list will default to the price list according to the SAP settings for each BP master record. This means that a wholesale customer should see wholesale pricing, whereas a new retail customer should view the standard retail pricing per product.

Register via the Web

New customers can register via the Web. Again, visualize the required process without a web interface. The customer must call in and get registered. Using the Web, this can be automated. Define the data that you need to collect and then decide how you want to present it (using CSS). Based on your business, you may require a very detailed registration procedure. First, you would create all of the UDFs in SAP to accommodate the required data. The N2ONE Portal solution will automatically provide form fields that can be used for registration on the Web.

Receive alerts in SAP

With every successful registration via the Web, we saved some time because we did not need to take a call to enter the customer information. However, we still need to be informed if a new customer registers. This should be done via alerts. This allows us to assign an employee to get an alert for specific web events, such as a new customer registration. The employee can then verify the information and follow it up.

Approve BP for relevant price list

Once a customer completes a registration, a price list needs to be assigned based on the customer type. The price list is assigned in SAP on a business partner master level. Once a new BP master is registered via the Web, a pricelist can be assigned in SAP. This price list will then be applied to subsequent logins of the registered BP.

BP logs in and gets assigned pricing based on price list

Once the BP information is approved, verified, and the right price list is assigned, the business partner will automatically utilize this information once they log in. As you can see, there are many steps to verify and manage customer information. It is a good thing that all of it is integrated into one system and we don't need to perform repetitive data entry.

Orders and service calls can be placed based on price list

The master data is now managed using the Web and traditional technology. However, in order to extend the process to the Web, customers should be able to enter orders or place service calls. These actions should lead to alerts in SAP so the assigned employees can handle it and verify the transactions.

"My Account" will show order history

Based on the process extensions we've discussed so far, you can see that most of the web-related process extensions are about automation. The ROI (Return on Investment) comes into play when processes and transactions are created without requiring company resources. A good example is the self-service functionality where customers can log in and review their account history, including their previous orders and service call history.

Dynamic newsletter will update a list based on buying behavior

The next step in automation is the sending of newsletter information to existing customers and new leads. This works by creating lists of target audiences, and sending grouped and formatted content to the list members. However, if you have ever used this technology, you may have noticed that you need to first create the list and then upload it to a newsletter service. Then, the recipients can either unsubscribe or respond. Based on these kind of changes, the list will be updated. In addition, new list members may be added based on transactions within SAP. In order to keep data consistent for your newsletter service and your business management solution, you have to update both systems on an ongoing basis. Basically, you are busy synchronizing and updating. Newsletter lists are a common **web island of data**. The N2ONE Portal solution allows dynamic lists to be created within SAP. A dynamic list is automatically populated based on the customer buying behaviour. For example, we can define a list of customers who were not contacted within the last 30 days. The list will be populated dynamically. The recipients will get a newsletter which will target their information requirements by offering a discount coupon. You see, there is always a new potential **island of data**. If you think ahead, you can integrate the functionality and benefit from **real-time** integration.

Summary

In this chapter, we covered web technologies and their relation to SAP Business ONE. You now understand that web technologies **extend** the existing SAP processes. The result is an automated workflow that reduces your cost and adds value.

We first expanded the project plan and included web-related tasks. As part of that process, we related those tasks to your own project. Advocating the thought that web functionalities are an extension of what is already in SAP Business ONE, you learned how to include the right tasks in the project plan for your own project.

We discussed the common terms used by experts when they talk about web solutions. This enables you to obtain assistance from external consultants and understand their offerings. In addition, you are able to integrate these services with your SAP system and avoid the creation of islands of data.

The key differentiators of available technologies are based on the two levels of integration— either realtime and synchronization. We clearly explained the benefits of a real-time solution using the N2ONE Portal.

We implemented this solution in the case study. The result was a recommendation about how you can extend your business processes using this technology to implement automation and self-service.

As a final comment about the future of SAP and web technologies, I believe that the future will further separate the user interface from the underlying data. This means the user will work with one data set. However, the interface will be generated based on the media used to access this data.

In the next chapter, we will focus on **managing growth**. You will learn what to do if you think your business will benefit from additional locations.

12
Managing Growth: Franchising Example

Just recently, the Franchise Expo was held in San Diego. This was a great opportunity to learn about this business model and its unique challenges. Upon further investigation, it appeared that a significant percentage of exhibitors seemed to have a well-defined product with a franchise-type, multilevel sales concept attached to it. An important aspect of franchising is that you have an initial franchisor who designs and establishes the franchise idea. The franchise idea usually comprises products or services and a well-defined sales strategy. In a franchise environment, this comes with the vision of having multiple locations that operate on the basis of blueprints. Blueprints are a sort of quintessential process documentation. It proves the point that a process analysis does not need to cause complicated documentations. In fact, if it is done right, simplicity is a key factor. You almost get the feeling that franchise operations are so simple that anybody can run them. Ultimately, the key aspect of successful franchise operations is a simple business concept that hits the target.

It implies that all processes be documented and simplified to the level that another entity (the franchisee) can take over and run the business using the established processes. Thinking in terms of franchising your own business is beneficial even if you don't plan to run your business as a franchise. Your process documentations will have the right information if you adopt the mindset that another person may need to understand it and run his business based on the information provided. How can you adopt this type of thinking? You can plan a virtual franchise for your own business. The core idea is to think big, but start small. Think big so that you design the business with many franchisee offices in place. Then, think small and find out how you can actually run this with one store.

In this chapter, we will evaluate your virtual franchise and practice **thinking in terms of franchising** by applying the concept to the Lemonade Stand case study. As part of this activity, we will be establishing a framework based on SAP Business ONE. Using this framework, you can employ a competitive architecture and run a **virtual enterprise** with independent business units that connect to a central head office. The key aspect of this framework is **simplicity**, not only upon startup, but also when growth requires you to look beyond the established limits and boundaries of your business.

What you will learn in this chapter about multilevel SAP Business ONE implementations

Preparing an architecture for franchise organizations is the goal of this chapter. The challenge is to establish a framework that can be implemented quickly, and allows us to start **small**. At the same time, the initial design should consider a potential rapid growth. In other words, the **think big** part of the concept should be accounted for as well.

During the course of this endeavour, the following topics will be covered:

- Project plan update – We will update the project plan and include the tasks that need to be completed in order to establish a platform for growth.

- Standard terms related to larger rollouts and integration with SAP NetWeaver – When your business grows, technology is used to integrate and automate your system. The most important technologies and terms will be covered.

- Framework for franchise organizations – Let's define the required components which will allow the franchise processes to be mapped against SAP to establish a platform for growth.

- What to do in your own project – Using the project tasks and technology explained up to that point, you will get assistance related to **franchising** your own business.

- Case study – During the case study, a multilevel sales organization using web technology will be implemented. The solution integrates with the advanced distribution center configuration based on our case study.

The project plan and managing growth

First, the project plan needs to be updated in order to include a set of tasks which will help you manage **growth**. A section called **Implementing a Framework for Growth** was added. As you can see in the following screenshot, new tasks have been added in **Phase 2 – Analysis and Design**. This new section will address the requirements of the franchise example. Therefore, the first step should always be to identify the relevant solution components for your growth plan. In our franchise example, this basically entails a multilevel sales organization that seamlessly integrates with SAP. Then, the distribution center should be able to plan and optimize an inventory based on the incoming sales orders. In addition, this requirement was added to the project plan as most franchise organizations have a storefront. Finally, the distribution center back end and the potential integration with a larger system, such as SAP Business Suite, was included.

As you can see in the project plan below, the solution components were identified, and then a task group was added per component. It would also be a good idea to align the strategic direction of the business based on this growth plan. Therefore, you should revisit the strategy paper and document the direction. Remember the A3 sheet paper we designed initially to define the strategy of the business? Now we are thinking about strategy again.

⊟ **Phase 2 - Analysis and Design**
⊞ **Process Analysis and Design**
Establish Schedule for Workshops
⊞ **Divide into subjects**
⊞ **Solution Architecture**
⊞ **Explore solution possibilities such as**
⊟ **Implementing a Framework for Growth**
⊟ **Identify Solution Components**
Sales
Distribution Center
Integration with SAP Netweaver
⊟ **Multi-Level Sales Organization**
Web Enterprise
⊟ **Templating for Satellite Offices**
Strore Front with SAP B1
⊟ **Backend Architecture**
Inter-Company Transactions
Distribution Center Backend
⊟ **Integrating with larger SAP Landscape**
SAP Business Suite
Netweaver
Update Project Binder and Review

Franchise processes

In this section, the core processes related to the franchising concept will be explained.

Organizational architecture

The basic concept is that a back-end distribution center will act on behalf of a franchisor. The distribution center will supply inventory for each order based on web orders and store orders. Each store operates as a satellite office and runs independently, but is integrated with the central distribution center. Inventory can be optimized by means of integration. The reporting data is available in real time at all locations.

Multilevel sales

Multilevel sales is often compared to a snowball concept because if you take a small snowball and roll it down a mountain where new snow has fallen, the snowball gets bigger and bigger on the way and may eventually cause an avalanche. Therefore, when establishing a multilevel sales organization, you start by creating an independent sales unit per city, for example. Then, each sales unit per city can assign sales units in each neighborhood, and so on. Therefore, you have coverage and can establish a hierarchy where each sales unit acts independently. A franchise organization may utilize the concept partially to increase sales. The difference of a snowball system, as opposed to a solid sales organization, is that the former eats up the market and leaves nothing behind, whereas the latter seeks to grow the market in the long term. For our example, we will utilize a web sales channel to establish an additional layer of sales with the goal of growing the market.

Storefronts

When growing a franchise business, storefronts will often be opened by franchisees. This requires a POS (Point of Sales) system. How can we integrate a POS with SAP on the store level, and then connect with the distribution center in the back end? Our framework will address this via middleware.

Distribution center back end

The distribution center back end runs on the basis of the established Lemonade Stand solution. In this scenario, inventory is managed and optimized using the advanced inventory forecasting solution from Valogix. Please review Chapter 7 - Logistics and Supply Chain Management of this book for more information about this add-on. Depending on the size of our warehouse today and in the near future, the N'ware solution for warehouse management can be utilized. This would allow the integration of barcode readers and mobile devices to manage inventory. The integration of the back end with the satellite office can be accomplished using the integration platform called Magic iBolt, or the Software Labs xFusion tool we used during data migration. In this chapter, the iBolt solution will briefly be covered. The xFusion tool is suited for this task just as well. However, we already learned about this solution in Chapter 9 - Data Migration Scenarios: What to Migrate and How.

Integration with the SAP Business Suite

The distribution center back end can be integrated with SAP. This may be required if a larger parent company runs an existing SAP landscape, for example. This way, we can keep the Business ONE business units active and integrate them with the parent company. Such integration may be completed using the SAP middleware called Netweaver.

Standard terms related to larger SAP Business ONE rollouts and integration with the SAP Business Suite

In this section, we will lay the groundwork for the franchise framework and explain the common terms related to the technologies involved in this architecture.

Inter-company transactions

Inter-company transactions are repetitive business documents that are regularly exchanged among established business partners. In our scenario, this comprises any transactions between the satellite offices and the distribution center back end. For example, sales orders at the satellite office level will always trigger purchase orders at the distribution center. This can be done manually. However, it can also be automated to better integrate the workflow. In order to automate this, the communication aspect of these types of transactions must be evaluated.

The basis of automation is always a well-documented manual process. You can achieve automation by collecting the documents you are exchanging in a **manual** way. Look at the information on these documents. These information components will be the basis of the automation using your preferred middleware. Examples for middleware are Software Labs xFusion, Magic iBolt, and SAP Netweaver.

Real-time and asynchronous middleware

In a real-time scenario, the originator of the communication waits for an immediate reply. With asynchronous and synchronous communication, there may be a timed delay until the response takes place. The real-time integration we investigated in the previous chapter works well if information must be immediately processed. This works for web-based orders where the user can order based on inventory l evels. However, if we have a storefront, transactions will first be collected at the storefront and later processed in batches at the month end, for example. This is called **batch processing** . Think of it as sending out a package via UPS. You prepare the package with content in an envelope and then write the address on top. Then, UPS will receive and deliver the envelope. What UPS or similar services do in the real world is called **middleware** in the software industry. The quality of such a solution is guaranteed via a layered approach. Each layer focuses on one aspect and allows for error handling. Middleware also encapsulates the underlying technology so that you don't need to write custom code to utilize data. This is done by providing **adapters** that are designed to prepare information for a specific source and target. For example, there may be an SAP Business ONE adapter that takes the connection parameters and allows for connecting against SAP Business ONE. The franchise framework will include a middleware called iBolt by Magic software and also SAP Netweaver. The previously discussed xFusion tool can be used for this purpose as well. In fact, it may be easier to understand how this works by reviewing Chapter 9 - Data Migration Scenarios: What to Migrate and How. The xFusion tool has connectors for various data sources. The graphical representation of the data flow in xFusion helps you visualize what a middleware is doing. It is the automation of workflows that comprise more than one system. Therefore, the xFusion tool is a good solution to get started on data migration, and then expand the solution to work as a middleware.

ETL (Extract-Transform-Load)

When it comes to moving data from one system to another, a common term used is ETL. **ETL** stands for **Extract – Transform – Load**. The extraction portion usually requires us to use an API (Application Programming Interface) and map data fields, which have the information you need. Other data extraction sources could be connected via ODBC or native database drivers. The transformation portion of the process requires us to map the source data columns to the destination. For example, if we transform data from a QuickBooks system to an SAP system, the relevant fields need to be mapped so data from the source is transformed into the target format. The load part of the process finally loads the data from the source to the target via the path defined by the **transformation** mappings. If you reviewed the data migration chapter, you will note that the xFusion product is an example of an ETP product for SAP Business ONE. This solution has many adapters that allow your SAP solution to be connected with various other ERP vendors.

The SAP Business Suite

In order to explain the SAP Business Suite, we will be reviewing the main SAP solution offerings. SAP initially developed R/2 as a mainframe-based solution. With the trend towards client-server technology, R/3 was established as a new evolution of R/2. The R/3 system was a single integrated solution, but was organized into modules that comprised FI, MM, SD, CO, PS, PP, and so on. This solution was developed until the release of version 4.7, and is now called R/3 Enterprise. This package was further standardized and enhanced to be called SAP ERP. The SAP Business Suite added Project Portfolio Management, Compliance, and CRM applications. SAP ERP is considered an application in the SAP Business Suite environment. The applications are using the SAP middleware called Netweaver. SAP also has a **solution manager** that allows you to manage the applications with regards to installation and license management. mySAP ERP is identical to the SAP Business Suite, with ERP added as an application. So as you can see, SAP has multiple applications in its portfolio and is integrated via the Netweaver middleware.

SAP Netweaver

Netweaver is an SAP product. It is a middleware platform that integrates multiple applications and allows their data to be connected using XML packages. The vision is that all business-related functionality is based on a service that can be provided by Netweaver. The interface for the end user is a portal-type application that presents the functionality in a single interface and consumes the required services in the background. Please note that end users will not know they are using Netweaver. In fact, the purpose of the middleware is to make use of various systems that are transparent to the user.

SAP Business ONE integration platform

The integration of SAP Business ONE satellite offices with the SAP Business Suite works via Netweaver. SAP provides a collection of interfaces that establish the XML data adapters and processes that SAP Business ONE may add to Netweaver. These processes can be connected to the SAP Business Suite via mapping of the source to the target. The interface is XML based, which allows data to be seamlessly formatted and transformed.

Framework for franchise organizations

A framework describes a defined set of tools that are grouped together to accomplish an integrated set of tasks. For our purpose, the framework consists of technologies that address the needs of franchise organizations in both the short and the long term.

The following architectural components require technological coverage:

- The distribution center back end
- The web enterprise sales organization
- The storefront POS platform
- The inter-company transaction management
- The interface with SAP Netweaver

In order to avoid a **one-shot** implementation where we gather the requirements and implement one time, the framework provides the tools and technologies which will establish an infrastructure. This infrastructure can then be used to implement changes as the business grows. Using the framework, standard procedures that can assist in improved implementation times can be established.

The core organizational architecture may look like what is shown in the following screenshot. We have a single **Main Head Office** and multiple storefronts attached. The transactions between storefronts (satellite offices) and the main office (distribution center) will be automated using the middleware called iBolt from Magic. This solution allows for inter-company transaction management among multiple SAP Business ONE installations. You may ask why we chose iBolt over SAP Netweaver. SAP Netweaver is recommended if you want to integrate your SAP Business ONE systems with an existing SAP landscape where SAP Business Suite products are used. In our franchise example, we assume that there is no pre-existing SAP system. Therefore, we can utilize a middleware that offers multiple adapters for various systems. Have a look at this figure:

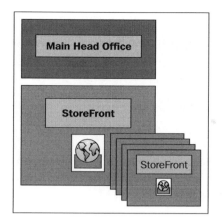

In order to apply the right technologies for our framework, a **layered** representation of the overall implementation was chosen. Each layer needs to be covered by the middleware to allow for integration like this:

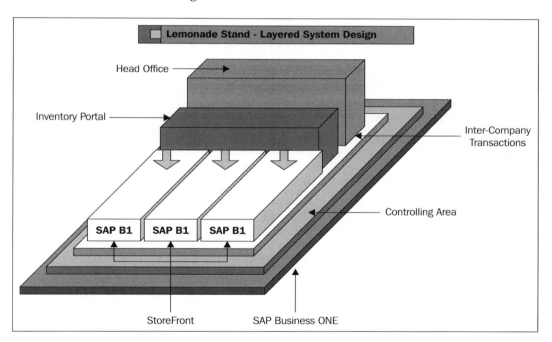

Based on the layers, the following technologies will be implemented:

- SAP Business ONE for the distribution center including Valogix inventory optimization and N'ware warehouse management
- Web enterprise with real-time access to the distribution center inventory using the N2ONE portal solution
- Storefront implementation with independent SAP Business ONE systems, which requires a POS system
- Inter-company middleware based on iBolt by Magic, or xFusion by Software Labs, to implement inter-company transactions
- SAP Netweaver and SAP Business ONE integration components for possible integration with the SAP Business Suite
- Reporting and analysis functionality using SAP Business Intelligence solutions

The main processes of the framework are outlined in the following graphical representation:

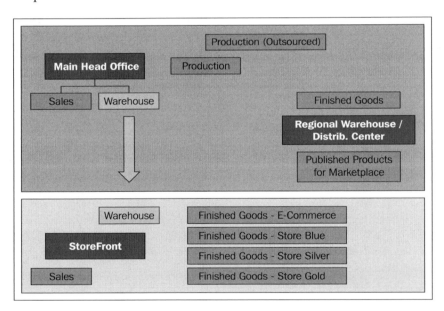

Distribution center with inventory optimization and warehouse management

The distribution center configuration resembles the solution we established for the Lemonade Enterprise in Chapter 7 - Logistics and Supply Chain Management. If you remember, we had developed a strategy with a focus on implementing a distribution center. As part of this, the inventory optimization solution from Valogix was introduced. The warehouse management using barcode scanners and mobile computers will be implemented via N'ware.

Storefront with industry settings and POS

The storefront needs to manage the transactions on the store level using a POS system. There is not a single best POS which will be recommended because the nature of the framework is flexibility, and the POS should be selected based on specific requirements. For your own project, you may identify a POS that is established for the industry that comes closest to your business. The next step would be to integrate the data sources, namely the POS of your choice, and SAP Business ONE using your preferred middleware.

Web enterprise solution based on the N2ONE portal

The web enterprise is a solution based on the N2ONE portal. It integrates with the distribution center back end in real time. This solution can be employed to publish different web sites with unique designs. Basically, a unique web site can be published for any product category defined in SAP Business ONE.

iBolt middleware by Magic

The iBolt middleware takes a central role in this framework. First, it provides established adapters and connectors to integrate SAP Business ONE systems, and implements functionality for **inter-company** transactions. Secondly, it also provides adapters and connectors for other systems that may require integration in the future.

In the following screenshot, you can see the iBolt interface. SAP Business ONE was added in the trigger area where you can connect a workflow to transform data based on a trigger. As mentioned above, each connector can be configured using the parameters that tell the connector how to connect to the source system. In the screenshot, you can see that there are other various systems that could potentially be integrated by simply dragging the icon to the trigger area and configuring the connection parameters:

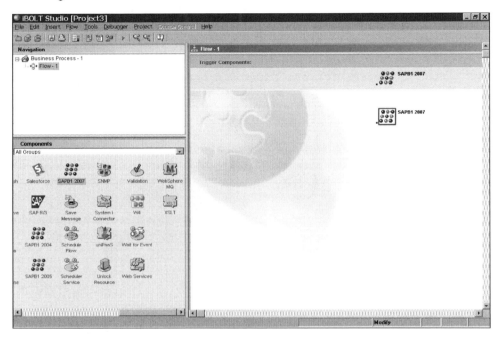

The following screenshot shows the parameters required to connect to the Lemonade Stand enterprise distribution center system:

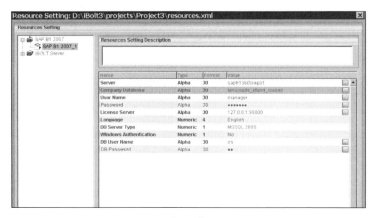

The iBolt middleware solution allows you to easily configure the connectors, and then visually document the flow of the data. Therefore, the transformation part of the data is visually documented and you can adjust it based on your requirements.

SAP Netweaver

The potential integration with the SAP Business Suite is done via the SAP middleware solution called Netweaver. As mentioned before, Netweaver is the platform for the SAP Business Suite. The functionalities of the SAP Business Suite run as **applications** in the Netweaver platform. The SAP Solution Manager allows all of the applications that you are planning to use. For example, the various patch requirements are managed via the SAP Solution Manager. Netweaver provides a **semantic** interface. This means you don't need to program anything. You provide configuration parameters that are then used by Netweaver. In order to get started, you need to integrate SAP Business ONE with Netweaver. SAP provides a free SAP Business ONE Integration Solution for the existing SAP Business ONE customers. This comes in the form of software that implements the adapters required to configure the SAP Business ONE source system, and then defines the data that you want to integrate.

Three-layered approach for your franchise framework

In our example, we have a three-layered approach to integrate all of the systems from the various storefronts to the SAP Business ONE distribution center and the SAP Business Suite headquarters. The first layer is covered via iBolt by Magic, or xFusion by Software Labs, and allows for inter-company transactions based on multiple Business ONE systems. The second layer is the integration of the distribution center with Netweaver. The third layer represents the connection of the SAP Business ONE Integration component in Netweaver with the relevant SAP Business Suite application in Netweaver:

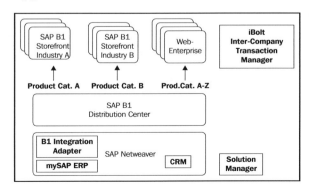

What to do in your own project

You can use this framework in various scenarios. Therefore, the following question may arise, "How can you use this in your own project?" I will first explain some important aspects that you may want to consider, and then move on to show you how this framework can be used for the Lemonade Stand enterprise, which is our case study.

First, structure your project plan and follow the suggestions provided. This will help you identify the project entities you'll need to plan with. Next, organize the entities into layers and see what technology can cover each layer. In order to get a more practical example, it is recommended that you think in terms of **franchising** your business. Basically, you're attempting to create process documentations and simplify how things are done to the level that you can easily teach another smart person how to do it.

Once you identify the main players in your process, try to list them in the project plan. Each player would be a section that you need to manage separately using tasks. Once the overall processes are in place, you need to map the workflow to actual SAP systems. You would start with a central office that has SAP implemented, and then continue with the satellite offices based on the templates you have established.

The central distribution center can be based on a standard SAP Business ONE system, or can enhanced via add-ons, depending on your requirements. The rollout of satellite offices can be simplified using preconfigured SAP Business ONE configurations, which allow each satellite office to get started quickly. In order to do this, you configure a company, and then use it as a **template** to create a new one. Consequently, for each satellite office, you make a new copy of the template and send it out to the person who is running the new location.

Regarding the **inter-company transaction**, you first collect all of the documents that are exchanged between satellite offices and the distribution center. Once you have this, you can automate the transactions using iBolt or xFusion for inter-company transaction management. The basis of automation is always the manual workflow that has a repetitive character.

The web representation can be utilized in real time using the N2ONE portal. You can establish dozens of web sites with unique designs based on the N2ONE portal solution. For you own project, you may need to identify the web-related processes prior to using any web solution.

Case study

During the final section of our case study, we will further fine-tune the idea of an automated franchise organization for the Lemonade Stand enterprise. During the previous case study, we implemented a web representation using the N2ONE portal. We can now take the next steps as follows.

Allow registration of a new store location via an online form using the N2ONE portal. Once the application process is confirmed, a new SAP company is dynamically configured using the parameters provided during the registration. Then, a new company is generated using the AWS hosting service. The store is immediately up and running. The only thing required is an Internet connection. Another option is to configure an on-site copy of the system on a small server. These options must be documented in your company-specific **AIP (Accelerated Implementation Plan)**. In order to multiply your franchise in such a way, you may want to prepare your own modified AIP using the suggested framework strategy. Therefore, you are preparing a blueprint, not only about how your business will work and operate, but also for how you will establish new locations and implement the required software to connect all of the data.

Template

Before you can multiply the operation via storefronts that integrate with the distribution center, you need to create a template configuration. The Lemonade Enterprise company was used as a template to create a new company. In SAP Business ONE, this is done via the **New** button in the **Choose Company** screen. In the following screenshot, you can see that the new company was created by selecting the **The Lemonade Stand Inc.** company, and then clicking on the **New** button. This is a simple step, but the core idea is powerful:

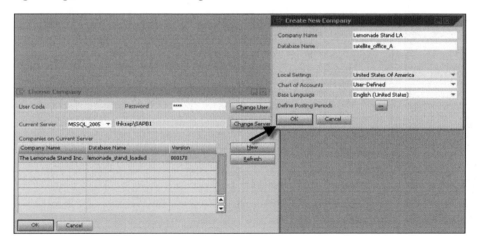

Swimlane processes

For the case study, we will briefly revisit the process analysis concept, which was already reviewed in Chapter 5 - Business Process Analysis and SMBs. The relevant processes are organized into swimlane-type charts. Each swimlane goes from the left to the right. As you can see, **Web-Enterprise** is connected to **Distribution Center (DC)** in real time. This means we are directly creating a sales order in the distribution center for each order that is coming in at the **Web-Enterprise** level. The storefronts are integrated with the DC using the iBolt or xFusion inter-company functionality. An additional layer was added for this. Look at the following figure:

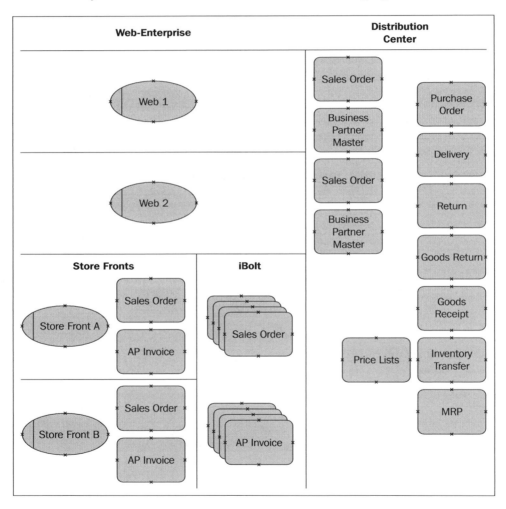

Summary

In this chapter, we covered the franchise framework based on SAP Business ONE technologies. We started out with the project plan and evaluated the required steps to plan for **growth**. The project plan needs to account for the right tasks to accomplish our goals. Based on this project plan, the basic processes that are common for the franchise business model were defined. Specifically, the unique aspects were highlighted, such as the **multilevel** sales organization and the connection to a central distribution center. We covered the most common terms related to large-scale Business ONE rollouts. As part of this, we explained the historical evolution of SAP products and their current position. Managing growth in a franchise environment means that we want to add new sales locations that are seamlessly integrated with the central headquarters. We covered this aspect by means of templates. Once the new locations are running based on the templated SAP companies, we had to plan for integration. How are the new locations communicating with the central head office? The franchise framework helped us establish a simple configuration to plan for this. The iBolt and xFusion middleware solutions provide inter-company transaction features. Netweaver is the SAP middleware solution that integrates every SAP software, and also the third-party software. The core idea is that additional software packages need to offer a value that can be offered as a service. Using the Netweaver platform, the services can be connected to provide a value based on your requirements.

Finally, the franchise framework was further expanded as a part of the case study. Templated companies were created, and we completed the case study with a high-level process flowchart for the franchise business model. We used the **swimlane** representation to show the different processes for the web enterprise that integrate with SAP Business ONE in real time. Now that you know all of the tricks and technologies about SAP Business ONE, you can leverage your investment and challenge the established markets with new ideas.

Index

merce

About Packt Publishing

Packt, pronounced 'packed', published its first book "*Mastering phpMyAdmin for Effective MySQL Management*" in April 2004 and subsequently continued to specialize in publishing highly focused books on specific technologies and solutions.

Our books and publications share the experiences of your fellow IT professionals in adapting and customizing today's systems, applications, and frameworks. Our solution based books give you the knowledge and power to customize the software and technologies you're using to get the job done. Packt books are more specific and less general than the IT books you have seen in the past. Our unique business model allows us to bring you more focused information, giving you more of what you need to know, and less of what you don't.

Packt is a modern, yet unique publishing company, which focuses on producing quality, cutting-edge books for communities of developers, administrators, and newbies alike. For more information, please visit our website: www.packtpub.com.

Writing for Packt

We welcome all inquiries from people who are interested in authoring. Book proposals should be sent to author@packtpub.com. If your book idea is still at an early stage and you would like to discuss it first before writing a formal book proposal, contact us; one of our commissioning editors will get in touch with you.

We're not just looking for published authors; if you have strong technical skills but no writing experience, our experienced editors can help you develop a writing career, or simply get some additional reward for your expertise.

Apache OFBiz Development: The Beginner's Tutorial

ISBN: 978-1-847194-00-8   Paperback: 472 pages

Using Services, Entities, and Widgets to build custom ERP and CRM systems

1. Understand how OFBiz is put together

2. Learn to create and customize business applications with OFBiz

3. Gain valuable development and performance hints

4. A fully illustrated tutorial with functional step-by-step examples

Quality Assurance for Dynamics AX-Based ERP Solutions

ISBN: 978-1-847192-91-2   Paperback: 168 pages

Verifying Dynamics AX customization to the Microsoft IBI Standards

1. Learn rapidly how to test Dynamics AX applications

2. Verify Industry Builder Initiative (IBI) compliance of your ERP software

3. Readymade testing templates

4. Code, design, and test a quality Dynamics AX-based ERP solution

Please check **www.PacktPub.com** for information on our titles

Programming Microsoft® Dynamics™ NAV

ISBN: 978-1-904811-74-9   Paperback: 480 pages

Create, modify, and maintain applications in NAV 5.0, the latest version of the ERP application formerly known as Navision

1. For experienced programmers with little or no previous knowledge of NAV development

2. Learn as quickly as possible to create, modify, and maintain NAV applications

3. Written for version 5.0 of NAV; applicable for all versions

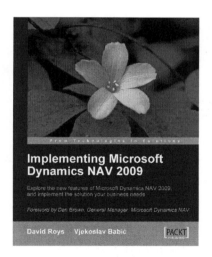

Implementing Microsoft Dynamics NAV 2009

ISBN: 978-1-847195-82-1   Paperback: 552 pages

Explore the new features of Microsoft Dynamics NAV 2009, and implement the solution your business needs

1. First book to show you how to implement Microsoft Dynamics NAV 2009 in your business

2. Meet the new features in Dynamics NAV 2009 that give your business the flexibility to adapt to new opportunities and growth

3. Easy-to-read style, packed with hard-won practical advice

3. Real-world examples with step-by-step explanations

Please check **www.PacktPub.com** for information on our titles

Printed in Great Britain by
Amazon.co.uk, Ltd.,
Marston Gate.